C000019640

Signal Failure

London to Birmingham, HS2 on Foot

Tom Jeffreys

Influx Press, London

Published by Influx Press

5a Wayland Avenue, London, E8 2HP

www.influxpress.com / @InfluxPress

All rights reserved.

© Tom Jeffreys, 2017

Copyright of the text rests with the author.

The right of Tom Jeffreys to be identified as the author of this work has been
asserted in accordance with section 77 of the Copyright, Designs and Patents Act 1988.

This book is in copyright. Subject to statutory exception and to provisions of
relevant collective licensing agreements, no reproduction of any part may take place
without the written permission of Influx Press.

First published 2017. Printed and bound in the UK by Clays Ltd., St Ives plc.

ISBN: 978-1-910312-14-8

Editor: Gary Budden

Copy-editor/Proofreader: Dan Coxon, Momus Editorial

Cover art: Maxim Griffin Design: Austin Burke

This book is sold subject to the condition that it shall not, by way of trade or
otherwise, be lent, re-sold, hired out, or otherwise circulated without the publisher's
prior consent in any form of binding or cover other than that in which it is published
and without a similar condition including this condition being imposed on the
subsequent purchaser.

Contents

'Between words is silence, around ink whiteness, behind every map's information is what's left out, the unmapped and unmappable.'

– Rebecca Solnit, *A Field Guide to Getting Lost*

'I see, so your statistics are facts, and my facts are merely statistics?'

– Paul Eddington as Prime Minister Jim Hacker in *Yes, Prime Minister*

'At our backs, surrounding the picture,
Is the whole world.'

– Ronald Johnson, *The Book of the Green Man*

Introduction

The world goes by at several speeds. Events move loud and fast, as the trackside trees rush by the window in an autumnal blur. But distance can transcribe noise, make it legible. Dark against the horizon, a black scribble of a treeline arcs to the gusting rhythms of a different wind.

Times have changed since I set out to walk from London to Birmingham along the proposed route of HS2. Britain voted to leave the European Union. America elected Donald Trump. 'The far right rises,' I wrote with a certain self-conscious portentousness in the final chapter of *Signal Failure*. Since then, it has already risen, and in so doing it has shown how wrong I was. For the far right is not an 'it', not a thing that could 'rise' like a golden tower or a monstrous kraken from the deep. It cannot be identified, located, or addressed like a person or an object. Maybe instead we should be thinking of tides or viruses, spectres or electromagnetic fields or sudden tempests. Maybe we should be thinking of 'does' instead of 'is'. How important now are definitions?

Times have changed too between the walk and the writing, between the writing and the publishing. In the time between the first drafts and the final manuscript, Osborne and Cameron have both left the Cabinet. Philip Hammond – whose 2011 appearance before the parliamentary transport committee forms a focal point for the final chapter – went from Transport Secretary to Defence Secretary to Chancellor of the Exchequer. Now what? Jeremy Corbyn, the entire Labour Cabinet, Nigel Farage, Boris Johnson, Zac Goldsmith: all took a turn on the political merry-go-round. One inexplicable constant: Jeremy Hunt. One more: HS2.

By the time you read this, more politicians will have come and gone. There will be more news, another crisis. Politics has adapted to fit the medium of the day – Twitter, Facebook, the live blog, rolling 24-hour news coverage – and always there is somebody talking.

Amid this atmosphere of apparently constant upheaval, infrastructure projects like Hinkley Point, Heathrow's third runway and HS2 have been subject to much speculation. Philip Hammond championed HS2 as Transport Secretary, but might he change course as Chancellor? Might Theresa May abandon the project in order to draw a line between her and her predecessors? In September 2016, chief executive Simon Kirby announced that he was leaving HS2 to join Rolls Royce. Two months later, the *Yorkshire Post* quoted a local businessman declaring that HS2 would be obsolete by the time it was built. Could the same be said for this book?

Some of the observations, analysis, and ideas contained in these pages are probably already redundant. Others may now be seen in a different light. Many I met between London and Birmingham warned me about the rise of UKIP in the 2015 General Election. Once the UK's first-past-the-post system failed to translate their irritation into parliamentary seats it was hardly surprising that many subsequently chose Brexit as the means to express their ire. I have little doubt that most of those I met along the route voted to leave the EU.

*

In July 2016, I paid a visit to Arup, one of the engineering companies closely involved with HS2. In the basement of the firm's Fitzrovia headquarters, I sat on a stool before SoundLab, an audiovisual simulation of the entire route of HS2. The camera flies over the land, surveying it from above. The resulting image combines helicopter footage with Google maps, 3D animations and digital renderings. I am surrounded by the team of people who worked together to produce this view of the route – this smooth, magical glide above the complex tangle of people and places that lie below. There are no people present in the SoundLab simulation.

In a larger room next door, I sit between Colin Stewart (Arup's head of global rail) and a press officer, the three of us together at one end of a long, wooden meeting table. Its surface is glossy and blond – the kind you could slide a drink down, if you were so inclined. Nobody is. Stewart is dressed in a dark pin-striped suit and practical, round-toed, rubber-soled shoes. The engineer is now the executive. He talks fast, looks frequently at his watch. I get the impression he doesn't really want to be here. *But it's you who wanted to meet with me*, I think.

Like Hammond before the select committee, Stewart's language is that of carefully considered neutrality. He speaks eloquently of 'efficiency', of 'solutions'. Many an answer is a non-answer:

'At the end of the day, any project you do will affect people – some negatively, some positively.'

'People don't like change very often.'

'It's important to look at the whole lifespan of the project.'

One of Stewart's most intriguing arguments – to me at least – concerns the lessons learnt from HS1 – the £6 billion rail connection between London and the Channel Tunnel, of which Stewart, incidentally, was technical director. 'There are benefits that are not quantifiable,' he tells me, citing regeneration projects at King's Cross, Ashford and Ebbsfleet that have come in the wake of HS1's opening in 2007. 'You don't know what would happen if you hadn't built it.'

This is undoubtedly true. But this is also coming from the mouth of a man who, lest we forget, works for a company paid huge sums of public money to produce feasibility studies, detailed statistical predictions, environmental impact assessments, cost-benefit analyses ... Arup's global rail business has a turnover of approximately £180 million. Its job, in short, is to quantify. And yet here is Stewart resorting to the counter-factual, arguing that it is the *unquantifiable* which really ought to persuade us of the benefits of HS2.

What niggles is the strange similarity between Stewart's argument and that which underpinned my own walk from London to Birmingham. The walk, and this book, constitute an attempt to acknowledge, to take account of, to render visible the people, places, histories, animals and ecosystems that not only evade the drone's-eye view from the London boardroom, but also the entire logic upon which such projects are conceived, assessed and implemented; the logic of taking account, of quantifiability, of cost-benefit analysis. What Green Party politician Natalie Bennett, quoted in Chapter III, described as value beyond valuation. Somebody once wrote that as the mayor he would like to see his local country lanes neat and tidy and easily passable. But as a poet he would prefer them artfully overgrown. The values of the walker are not those of the engineer or the politician, the bureaucrat or the economist. Nor should they be.

Doubtless, Stewart is speaking in good faith. He means what he says, I'm sure. Nonetheless, it feels to me like a sleight of hand: the co-option of an argument conceived to resist power, suddenly re-appropriated in the service of that power.

This kind of strange inversion has been happening in politics too. I can't help but think of Michael Gove's famous outburst: 'people in this country have had enough of experts'. As with Stewart, it is not only the truth of the statement that matters, but the ends to which the truth is put. After all, in many ways Gove was right: a poll in December 2016 showed that fewer people trust politicians, bankers, lawyers and economists than trust their hairdressers. Then again, 51% don't trust the pollsters who tell them they don't trust pollsters. How quickly contemporary politics ends up in a hall of mirrors.

In February 2016, James Meek wrote an article for the *London Review of Books* about the myth of Robin Hood. Robin Hood, as we all know, lives in the woods with his merry men. Together they steal from the rich to give to the poor. In the old version of the story, Robin Hood is the champion of 'a great mass of heavily taxed poor people who work terribly hard for little reward'. His enemy is, of course, the sheriff of Nottingham, who in this version of the myth represents, for Meek, 'the ruthless figure of a bureaucrat-aristocrat, personification of the careerist-capitalist elite'. Robin Hood is redistributionist. 'Robin Hood is Jeremy Corbyn.'

But gradually in recent years the myth has been flipped. In this new version, the sheriff of Nottingham is part of the liberal elite, taking from honest, hard-working, tax-paying families to finance what Meek terms 'the conceptual rich' – the unemployed, disabled, refugees, working-class single mothers:

In this version of the myth, Robin Hood is a tax-cutter and a handout-denouncer. He's Jeremy Clarkson. He's Nigel Farage. He's Margaret Thatcher and Ronald Reagan. He's by your elbow in the pub, telling you he knows an immigrant who just waltzed into the social security office and walked out with a cheque for £1000. He's in the pages of the *Daily Mail*, fingering a workshy good-for-nothing with eleven children, living in a luxury house on the public purse. He's sabotaging the sheriff of Nottingham's wicked tax-gathering devices – speed cameras and parking meters. He's on talk radio, denouncing inheritance tax. He's winning elections.

What strikes me as especially strange is that in both versions of the myth, a vast, difficult-to-justify infrastructure project like HS2 is held up as the epitome of everything that is wrong with the world. And yet somehow, despite opposition from both sides, it rushed on regardless. Why? This is the question I attempt to address in this book's final chapter.

To return to the Robin Hood myth, it is worth pointing out the absurdity of thinking that the big beasts of the right can somehow liberate us from the strictures of state bureaucracy. Free trade does not equal free people. Besides, state bureaucracy and big businesses are not in opposition; they are mutually conditioning, mutually reinforcing. The revolving door between high-ranking civil servants and the private sector is only the most recent manifestation. As David Graeber points out in *Utopia of Rules*, it is the state that functions as the guarantor of the free market, through its bureaucratic structures and, where necessary, through the police and the military. It is in the era of neo-liberalism that the state has swelled larger than ever. That is the absurdity of Brexit: the belief that bureaucrats – accountants, politicians, lawyers, civil servants – could somehow be set to work to liberate us from bureaucracy. Management can only breed management. Graeber again, this time following German philosopher Max Weber: 'The only real way to rid oneself of an established bureaucracy ... is to simply kill them all.' (Please note, alt-right types: he is not espousing that we do this.)

An inversion has taken place. Today the son of a billionaire businessman positions himself as a radical alternative to the political mainstream. An ex-banker funded by offshore fortunes claims to represent the voice of the disenfranchised. In the early ballads, Robin Hood was a yeoman; it was not until the sixteenth century onwards that he came to be depicted as a noble aristocrat dispossessed of his family lands. Today, a Conservative Prime Minister addresses poor people, black people, the working class, those with mental health problems, as Theresa May did upon taking office, as follows: 'When we take the big calls, we'll think not of the powerful, but you. When we pass new laws, we'll listen not to the mighty, but to you.' That May can acknowledge the hardships facing society's least privileged without recognising the role that her party has played during two terms in power, and as far back as Thatcher, and indeed long before, is the conjuring trick of the contemporary politician. So many sentences that sound like sense. So many arguments that sound almost plausible until you re-focus on who is making them, and why.

'We will make Britain a country that works not for a privileged few,' says May, 'but for every one of us.' Note the slippage here: from 'we' the Conservative Party to 'us', the audience, the taxpayer, the hard-working British people (whoever they are; we are; you are). 'We'; 'you'; 'we'; 'us': the sleight of hand is complete. In a memorable scene in that great film, *Gladiator*, Derek Jacobi, in the role of Senator Gracchus, responds with the poise of the orator to criticism of his cultured tastes: 'I don't pretend to be a man of the people, senator. But I do try to be a man for the people.' Corbyn tries to be a man for the people. Farage poses as a man of the people. May, however, is staking her claim to be both.

We've heard this before of course. 'We're all in this together,' chortled David Cameron, once upon a time. If Cameron and Osborne represented a certain conception of the establishment, then May is one of us. But what she might seek to represent is nothing compared to what she will do.

What has dawned on me since writing this book is that an argument is not just about its premises and its internal logic. Who is making the argument? And to what end? When Natalie Bennet underscores the importance of the unquantifiable it is not the same as when Colin Stewart does it. Bennet does so in order to oppose a project like HS2; Stewart in order to endorse it. When controversial biologist Rupert Sheldrake criticises scientific dogmatism (in order to improve the way science can understand the world) it is very different from when oil lobbyists do it, or Jeremy Clarkson. And when Michael Gove says that 'people in this country have had enough of experts' what matters is not only the truth (or otherwise) of the statement but what he is seeking to do by proclaiming it; namely to discredit those who oppose his position. He is not encouraging a healthy scepticism but championing the pick-and-choose approach of the politician towards expert research: cite forever if it fits the argument; ignore or suppress if it does not. That is 'post-truth' politics: not the dissemination of lies per se, but the realisation that facts no longer matter once the truth is merely a tool.

During the Brexit debate, there was a meme doing the rounds online. It was an image of an advertising hoarding by artist Robert Montgomery. On it the following words:

England is the first lie. England is a lie invading kings told you to take your actual land from you. This land is your land, from the flat Norfolk night to the blue Cornish morning. Just a wild pagan land with no name and no flag. Just this cold beach that nourishes you. Just the wind on this grassland that nourishes you. Just the rain on your face in the morning in this blank springtime that nourishes you.

What it meant to show, in part at least, is that the world is a wild place and our structures of meaning and knowledge lie uneasily upon it. 'The map is not the territory,' as Alfred Korzybski famously proclaimed – especially when you're as bad at map-reading as I am.

More specifically, Montgomery is trying to show that nation states are not a natural reality. They are real now and have real power but they are also products of history. They have a beginning and therefore, one day, an end. Nationalism's lie is its tie to nature – blood to soil. But perhaps Montgomery's text here could be expanded upon. Perhaps there was a more fundamental lie. Perhaps the first lie was not 'England' but a pronoun: 'we'. Underpinning this little word is the idea of a coherent community based on similarity that could be opposed, along clearly definable lines, to a near or distant, but always different, 'they'. Nothing would change – once all the maps were in place, no border could be breached nor lines crossed.

But a lie can have a life. A lie can found a truth. As May's speech shows, 'we' is always open to slippage, however much we reinforce the borders and purge the enemies within. Montgomery's text knows this too. Look how 'you' gets used, in English the exact same word in the singular and the plural. No wonder advertisers love it so. No wonder May addresses us (you, me, them) as 'you' directly. Here Montgomery adopts the same language: but who does he mean? May pits 'you' against 'the mighty'; Montgomery against 'invading kings'. But where are they invading from? Across what border? How can the land be my land (our land) if it has no name and no flag? Ownership has its limits. Property requires borders. Borders can always – at least in principle – be crossed, for example by a train line. 'Thinking takes place in the relationship of territory and the earth,' wrote Deleuze and Guattari. The very place I hope this walk traverses too.

Montgomery's text decries a lie but it contains within it the seeds of another. Or maybe it's the same lie growing again – each time a little different. It is not just nation states or political parties or pronouns. Everywhere there is the urge to simplify: two-party politics, yes/no referenda, males and females, right and wrong. Everywhere the logic of the yes or no, the either/or. Every act, every word is a simplification. But nothing is simple now. It never was.

Every word trembles at its own complexity.

Difficulty is hard, by definition, and thought can be exhausting.

When reason retreats it is time for action.

Today there are repeated calls to make a stand, to pick a side, to do something. But maybe we also need to cling to complexity, to embrace difficulty and diversity, to resist the appeal of simplicity in the name of right or wrong, them or us.

Then again ... There are times when words are actions in themselves. But there are times too that call for actions more than words. Maybe that's what this walk was about after all, even without knowing it at the time – a desire to do something when, honestly, I don't know what to do.

– Tom Jeffreys, December 2016

I

London:
Leaving the City

*Euston Station – Camden – Hampstead –
Queen's Park – Kensal Green Cemetery –
Wormwood Scrubs*

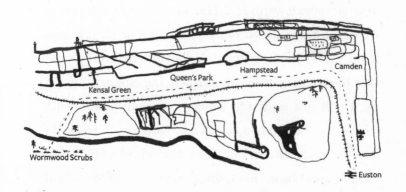

In November 2014 I set out to walk the route of HS2: 119 miles from London Euston to Birmingham Curzon Street. I marked it out in orange highlighter across a succession of nine Ordnance Survey maps. My intention was never to follow it absolutely – through hedges and streams, across gardens or under lakes. I'm not a performance artist, or a ghost. Instead I planned to stick mostly to footpaths and minor roads, staying as close to the route as possible, while meandering off from time to time to meet local residents or investigate sites of potential interest, or find a pub. I was careful to allow as much room as possible for stopping, thinking, taking detours and having conversations. I wanted the journey to lead itself. I thought it would take ten days.

Along the way, I wanted to find out as much as I could about attitudes towards HS2. HS2 affects every single person in the UK; those closest to the route most of all. If it goes ahead, this will be the country's largest infrastructure project since the building of the motorways. The official estimates say it will cost some £50 billion; the unofficial estimates are closer to £200 billion. It will take between six and eight years to build. That is only after Parliament's HS2 select committee has heard the 1,925 petitions against the hybrid bill, which could take several years to process. For some, the proposed high-speed rail network will cause untold disruption; for others, it offers the solution to this country's transport problems, and may even solve the economic divisions between north and south, between London and everywhere else. For everybody, it is a powerful symbol of what a possible future might bring. Whether it is a future to be feared or heralded remains to be seen.

But the aim of this walk was not so much to compile arguments for and against the project itself – that has been done thoroughly enough already – but to think about what these attitudes might say about the state of the country today. I started the walk five months before the 2015 general election and the subject of politics was never far away. The route takes me from London's bustling commuter centre, through interminable suburbs and out into the Chiltern Hills. Along the way are housing estates, battlefields, motorways and farms. The country is littered with what once was: disused railways, closed-down pubs and boarded-up hospitals. It is also full of life: foxes and foxgloves, dogs, sparrowhawks, old oak trees and red kites.

*

Monday morning in November. Euston. 8 a.m. I'm standing outside the station, feeling distinctly peculiar. In my hand my gnarled old walking stick, on my back an enormous rucksack. I can barely carry it. Commuters squint at me as they hustle by in the November glare. I must look odd. Too strangely dressed to be a fellow commuter; too clean to be a tramp. In a city I've lived in and called home for the past eight years, suddenly I stick out like a stranger, or worse, a tourist. It's exciting.

I walk perhaps a hundred yards, and stop – almost before I've begun. On the corner of Melton Street and Drummond Street is a disused station, a past version of Euston, its tiles glowing a rich maroon. I hear the growling hum of a leaf-blower. A man in a yellow high-vis jacket is blowing into piles the brown leaves that have fallen disobediently on to the bright green lawn. St James' Gardens was originally a burial ground when it first opened in 1788. Today it is kept neat and tidy by Camden Council, and only a few headstones remain. What does it say about our society that men are employed by the local council to move leaves from one place to another? I stop to make a note and take a photo. As I do so, the man turns and catches sight of me. He looks confused. What does it say about our society, I imagine him thinking, that men get dressed up for a walk in the country in order to take some photos next to Euston station? His question might be more perceptive than mine. I should try and answer it.

The seeds for this walk were sown back in 2008. It was then that I attended a drift around east London organised by artist Laura Oldfield Ford. This was my first experience of the approach to walking known as psychogeography and, in retrospect, I think, it turned out to be formative. It sparked an interest in the currents that whirl and eddy under the mainstream urban narratives of consumerism, progress and cleanliness.

The purpose of that particular walk was to explore and analyse the area from Bethnal Green to Stratford that was in the process of being transformed ahead of the 2012 Olympics. It was memorable chiefly for a performance by artist Robin Bale. We all stood in a loose circle on a bridge over the busy A12 in east London. With beard and fraying overcoat, Bale walked to the centre, anger or mischief in his narrowed eyes. 'They never had us in mind,' he growled. 'They never had us in mind.' As the cars rushed by beneath us, we had to strain to hear what he was saying. The circle began to tighten. Three times he poured Special Brew on to the ground, in an invocation, he told us, to Papa Legba, the Voodoo intermediary between the mortal and immortal worlds. There was something solemn and intimidating about Bale's performance, and also faintly ridiculous. Everyone was captivated.

It was not until more recently, however, that I felt the need to undertake this kind of thing myself. On Christmas Eve 2013, I set off for an afternoon walk with my wife.

The apparently straightforward aim was to walk from my parents' house in Chesham Bois, Buckinghamshire, in which they have lived since before I was born, to the nearby village of Great Missenden and back. It's a walk my father has done every Saturday for as long as I can remember, and one I must have done a hundred times. And yet, within minutes of leaving the house I'd missed the turning for the right footpath. We got very lost and ended up, hours later, walking back along a narrow road in the pitch black, cars glaring by only inches away from us.

Until moving to London, I'd lived in Buckinghamshire my entire life. I called it home, yet I hardly knew it at all. I began to realise that I could say the same about London, and the UK more generally: places I felt I knew, but was increasingly aware that I did not.

A long section of this country is set to be altered irrevocably by HS2. This walk and this book are my attempts to get to know it while I still can. Here in London, I specifically wanted to think about how a large-scale infrastructure project like HS2 – and the opposition to it – might shine a light on the larger story of the capital: specifically, the rapid developments that are changing parts of this city beyond recognition. So much is being swept away that we're at risk from a form of cultural amnesia. Some of this walk will be about clinging on to the past; some about navigating the future.

Why walking? Plenty of other writers have sought to engage with place or landscape through different modes of movement. Philosopher Mark Rowlands has written a book about running. 'Running,' he wrote, 'is a place where I remember.' Poet Helen Mort has written extensively about climbing. Elizabeth-Jane Burnett has produced poetry from swimming. Then there are the great travel writers: Paul Theroux on trains from Massachusetts to Patagonia; Jack Kerouac in cars and buses across America. But there is something, I think, unique about walking. Firstly, it's the pace – or lack of it – which gives you the chance to take detours and observe details. To walk is to be in a place, to experience it, not merely to pass through it – although I will be doing that too. I also simply like walking.

Walking as a form of thinking has a long and rich tradition, one which is currently at risk of drifting towards cliché. Philosophers such as Kierkegaard and Thoreau were champions of walking. Kant took his afternoon walks as a matter of monotonous routine. Nietzsche climbed mountains obsessively. Wordsworth and Coleridge popularised the Lake District. Richard Long trod lines in the landscape outside Bristol. More recently, walking-related literature has proliferated – more or less self-consciously – in the wake of W. G. Sebald and Iain Sinclair. In 2012 alone we saw the publication of Robert Macfarlane's *The Old Ways*, Merlin Coverley's *The Art of Wandering* and Simon Armitage's *Walking Home*.

Ten years earlier saw the publication of Sinclair's *London Orbital*, which documented various walks that the author undertook around the M25. It is a well-known recent example of psychogeography, a tool that, for some, is of increasing relevance again. It was Oldfield Ford's walk that led me to find out more about the history of this approach to walking, which was originally developed in the 1950s by artist group the Letterist International. In the words of co-founder Guy Debord, psychogeography is 'the study of the precise laws and specific effects of the geographical environment, consciously organised or not, on the emotions and behaviour of individuals'. Those same relationships – between individuals and the environment, between law and behaviour, geography and emotion – are at the heart of my walk too. In London, psychogeography is undergoing a renaissance.

Our pre-Olympics walk was part of what is called a 'dérive' in Situationist parlance. In an email exchange, Oldfield Ford described the process like this: 'Sometimes I go out on walks with people using obsolete maps to show how much public space has been enclosed, eroded or gated off. I think it is important to coax out the hidden histories in an area, to allow the repressed voices of the city to reverberate and to say that this is not the only way.'

I too am looking to explore the diverse layers of narrative that underpin our cities, to question them, and see how they overlap or contradict each other. I too will encounter a rich cast of characters between Euston and Birmingham and will experience a disconnect between map and place. I also think there may be an element of performance about the walk I'm doing – a self-conscious act geared towards a subsequent creation (writing, in this instance, rather than art). I may not be pouring beer on the ground and invoking ancient deities, but a sense of my own ridiculousness is never far away.

But if there is one thing psychogeographers and their ilk like to critique more than the city, it is each other. Stewart Home – one of the UK's earliest exponents of the approach – has expressed concern that it is simply 'a term taken on by columnists at *The Independent*, and has become rather meaningless now'.

'There's a fine line between psychogeography and tourism,' he told me. Arguably there is something akin to the guided tour about our 2008 'dérive', and there is certainly something of the tourist about my own HS2 route walk. I even wrote an article about it for *The Independent*. But Oldfield Ford argues that, 'for me, the term can't be used unless there is an inherent critique of urban planning and architecture'. Bale's bile-ridden bridge performance – he describes the 2012 site as 'a bloated desolation' – is just such a critique.

In a 2009 article entitled 'The Contemporary Dérive', Phil Smith – known on Facebook under the name Mythogeography – charts a history of exactly the kind of walk that I was attempting:

> The straight line has long been deployed by aesthetic walkers. Rather than following contours or increasingly institutionalised pathways like the official Coastal Paths in the UK or the ersatz, scallop-marked 'pilgrims' ways' in Europe (their symbols more likely to lead 'pilgrims' to local hotels than sacred places), the disruptively-applied straight line interrupts passivity and crosses boundaries, beating back at the beaten track.

Smith cites early twentieth-century 'trampers' like Stephen Graham, Geoffrey Murray and Charles Hurst, as well as the early work of artist Richard Long. More recently, we could mention Mark Mason's 2011 book *Walk the Lines*, in which the author travels the entire London Underground network on foot, overground. There are many others. Despite – or because of – their history and popularity, Smith seems not overly enthusiastic about these kinds of approaches. Partly, he believes psychogeography to have become divorced from its original focus on situation and spectacle. Partly, he denounces the 'tendency to solo walking', which, he points out, is mostly carried out by men. Instead, Smith espouses a collective, often undocumented, approach to psychogeography, which is much more likely to be gender-balanced, participatory and genuinely radical. Similar concerns have been expressed in the world of nature writing, or 'new nature writing'. In the *London Review of Books*, Kathleen Jamie famously summarised the figure of Robert Macfarlane as 'A Lone Enraptured Male'. It's worth noting here that Frederic Gros's *A Philosophy of Walking* features not a single woman.

I read Smith's article the week before I set off to walk the route of HS2. By then it was too late to change my approach – and I'm not sure I wanted to. Despite its political limitations, there is a reason why so many of these walks are carried out alone. Ever since I can remember, my father and I have gone on walks together: from strolls to the pub in Buckinghamshire to weekends in Oxfordshire or scaling mountains in Scotland. For this walk, I was keen to retain that sense of adventure, of an openness to the unknown which is basically indistinguishable from poor map reading. What I wanted to do differently was to really think about the places I was in and engage with those who lived or worked in them. Walking with my father is an act of companionship and conversation, also mild competition – neither of us quite willing to reveal if we're exhausted. It's silly, really, but fun. The side effect, however, is that we don't really notice where we are. For this walk, I needed to be much more alive to places and to people. Otherwise I'd be missing the details, and, after all, isn't it the details of a place which matter most? I felt – rightly or wrongly – that I needed to be alone.

In his fascinating book, *The New English Landscape*, Ken Worpole discusses the writings of Sebald and Sinclair, among many others. Their work, argues Worpole, relies on 'the principle of immersion', namely the idea that by immersing themselves deeply within a place, such writers are able to uncover what might otherwise remain hidden to the person simply passing through. That is what distinguishes such work from travel writing. My walk is based upon a similar principle, but this book is also an attempt to navigate a way between those two competing experiences of place – as somewhere to live in, or somewhere to pass through. To stay still or to keep moving?

In the meantime, it's worth noting how much contemporary nature writing focuses on what has been lost from our environment: once-common species of plant or bird, old buildings, paths or ways of living. There is arguably something intrinsically conservative or nostalgic about this kind of writing. Perhaps that's why I'm drawn to it and perhaps that's why I find it so limited. What such writing sometimes overlooks, to its detriment, is the people who are alive today. My walk is a journey of discovery not only of England's landscapes, but also of its diverse inhabitants: lost security guards and angry villagers, train enthusiasts and suicidal retirees, politicians, publicans, artists and farmers.

And it all starts here, in London. Whatever theory you have, whatever story you want to tell yourself – or others – in a place like London, the opposite is also almost always true. As historian Henry D. Smith II wrote in an article comparing Tokyo to London: 'The city is never what we think it is: it is always far more complex and changeable than our ideas about it.'

That is what Craig Taylor's 2011 book, *Londoners*, does so well: to convey the multiplicity of overlapping individual stories which may contradict each other but do not cancel each other out. Eighty individuals tell their tales of the city: from developers to sex workers, millionaires to market traders. Taylor's decision to privilege the oral – the voices of those whom he has interviewed – allows his book to avoid the imposition of a singular narrative which is so characteristic of certain kinds of writing: from the omniscient narrator of Victorian realism to the sensitive and literate 'I' of new nature writing.

In Ross Sutherland's 'Poem looked up on Google Streetview', from 2010, the poet broaches the fracturing of narrative that takes place when viewing London through the lens of Google Streetview. We are presented with an apparently simple scene (although perhaps Sutherland's introductory zeugma should alert us to the rhetorical and conceptual complexities to come):

> Two girls in sympathetic postures and winter coats
> are swapping stories about Northern cities ...

Or are they? The narrator is unsure of his own characters. Perhaps they are actually

> ... discussing granddads,
> or impractical music stands, or psychoholography

Which of these alternatives the two girls are actually engaged in – if indeed any – remains untold. And what of psychoholography? If psychogeography is a way of mapping the spirit of a place, then is psychoholography the same process transferred to the virtual world? An endless series of online wanderings running counter to the fabric of the Internet? This too remains unclear.

Sutherland goes on to describe the jarring nature of

attempting to follow a linear path on Google Streetview. Every so often there is a sudden shift in time or date and the flow of meaning is ruptured. 'The city resets at the crossroads, jumps back to 6am.' But what does it mean? The poet struggles to explain:

These empty moments
Are often the most complicated,
Where the thousandth analogy for London breaks down.
London is not a broken river, nor a waterlogged mirror,
Nor an ageing, racist, colour-blind boxer.
If we assigned a metaphor to it, we'd just end up
Talking about something else

To me, this is perhaps the perfect expression of the difficulty of saying anything about London. I love Sutherland's use of hypallage to convey the limits of metaphor: the transferral of expected epithets so that the mirror becomes waterlogged, and the river broken – not the other way around, as you might expect. The collapse of rhetoric expressed through rhetoric. And now I really am talking about something else … perhaps to talk about London is always to talk about something else. Perhaps that is why I'm walking away from London with an old walking stick in my hand.

Let's start again.

I first moved to London in 2006, as soon as I had graduated from university. Having grown up in semi-suburban, semi-rural Buckinghamshire, gone to secondary school in a village in Northamptonshire, and then on to university in Oxford, I had always lived within London's gravitational pull. Arguably all of England exists within it – economically, politically, maybe even culturally. That is what regional devolution has been conceived to address. George Osborne has argued that HS2 is part of the solution. Once I moved to London, I never intended to leave. All that has changed.

The area around King's Cross, near where this walk begins, has undergone significant redevelopment in the short time I've lived in London. If anything, it's a surprise that Euston, just a few steps west, has remained so long unaltered. This, despite the nearby presence of University College London and the Wellcome Trust, the offices of HMRC and Facebook's London HQ. Perhaps the vast red brick bulk of Colin St John Wilson's British Library put off developers. Now such functionalism is back in fashion and the area around King's Cross and Euston is changing fast.

In some ways, the work done here is undoubtedly an improvement. The 2014 restoration of King's Cross station removed the unsightly green-roofed shed and other clutter from the front. Now, Lewis Cubitt's nineteenth-century arches are displayed in their full magnificence, a striking counterpoint to the gloriously overblown Victorian Gothic of George Gilbert Scott's St Pancras Hotel. The area is beginning to look beautiful.

But it is to the north of the Euston Road that the real change is underway. Here is Granary Square – 'the canalside heart of King's Cross'. A nineteenth-century Grade II listed granary building and transit sheds have been converted into use as an art college by architects Stanton Williams and developers Argent. They are the new home of Central Saint Martins. On Google Streetview you can get right inside the main building's central atrium, but you cannot leave. Outside are fountains and cafes and restaurants. In the summer the steps down to the canal are coated in fake grass. What is gained is a kind of tranquillity (so long, of course, as you are paying for food or education). What is lost is any sense of adventure. The only thing to discover here now is a new brand of organic wine.

What is also being lost is the diversity of the area's existing communities. Back in 2006, developers Argent agreed to provide 40% affordable housing in this new King's Cross development. As reported in *The Guardian*, they are now trying to renege on this commitment. Green councillor Sian Berry has launched a legal challenge. Architecture critic Olly Wainwright has been particularly scathing of the concept of 'viability' – which frequently allows developers to backtrack on social housing commitments if their profits are under threat. Argent, he wrote:

> blames 'the economy, political changes [and] reductions in subsidy', which have all made the scheme 'unviable' – while conveniently ignoring the stratospheric rise in house prices over the last eight years. Flats recently advertised in the Kings Cross scheme include a one-bed for £985,000 and two-bed for £1.7m.

Such stories seem typical of London today. Established development narratives involve depicting an area as an empty wasteland waiting to be saved by development and made good and useful. King's Cross: nothing but a den of iniquity. This tactic is nothing new. The same line was employed in the nineteenth century when St Pancras was built. A population of labourers lived in the areas of Agar Town and Somers Town before they were sold to the Midland Railway, designated as slums, and cleared to make way for warehouses. Victorian writers described the area as the foulest slum in London. But historian Steven P. Swensen has contested this view, describing the area as 'a vibrant neighbourhood teeming with life and activity'. Whatever the truth of Agar Town, John Betjeman tells us that once the area was cleared, 'the inhabitants were not properly rehoused'.

King's Cross was not a wasteland this time around either. Or rather, where some see wasteland, others see wildness. Amid all the new developments, squeezed tightly between the Grand Union Canal to the east (which, like HS2 and me, goes all the way to Birmingham) and a bundle of train lines heading north, is Camley Street nature reserve. The site was once woodland; then used to store coal in the nineteenth century. By the 1970s it was a municipal dump. Then, slowly, nature began to return. 'In the mid-1980s,' writes Ben Campkin in *Remaking London*, 'as more and more plants, animals and insects appeared, local residents noticed the formation of a spontaneous urban park, and nurtured it into a thriving nature reserve.'

In 1981, local campaigners successfully opposed an attempt to turn the site into a lorry park. Subsequently, the Greater London Council acquired the land and paid for the creation of the nature reserve. Then, in 1984, management of the site changed hands again – this time to the newly formed London Wildlife Trust. Today it is one of 1,280 designated 'local nature reserves' across the UK, home to over 300 species of plants including the common spotted orchid.

It may be going too far to describe Camley Street as 'wild', as some have attempted to do, but Campkin notes how such places – born out of community collaboration and protected by community struggle – run counter to dominant narratives of top-down control. 'Interestingly,' he notes with well-weighted irony, 'the main developers in the ongoing regeneration, Argent, now promote it as an attraction.'

I first visited Camley Street nature reserve in 2013, when building work was in full swing: I recall the sound of drilling clattering through the air, even as a moorhen peered into algae-coated water, and an ungainly fat young blackbird disappeared into the bushes. I was there for the opening of a new art exhibition – *Wild New Territories* – and this disconnect between sight and sound was neatly exploited by Jamie Griffiths, Diego Samper and Rob Scharein, whose collaboratively-produced installation introduced the sounds of the Amazon rainforest into this little patch of north London greenery. At the same time, similar ideas of nature boxed up, packaged and commoditised were explored through Foreign Investment's satirical intervention, which offered visitors the chance to buy sections of the sky above King's Cross at £215.75 per square foot. That would probably be a bargain today.

I may have called London home for years now, but King's Cross has never meant much to me. I remember arguing about Gilbert Scott's neo-Gothic edifice with a friend visiting from Paris. I love it; she hated it. I remember going to a dubious party in a strange building masquerading as a hotel. Nobody ever slept in there. Now such places have been swept away, and those in search of illicit thrills must look elsewhere. More recently, I've reviewed exhibitions at the Wellcome, the Foundling Museum and the British Library. I saw a friend's band in a pub on Gray's Inn Road. In 2004, Larry Gagosian opened a massive gallery on Britannia Street. I've still never visited. King's Cross is a place I come to only in order to leave. This walk is a case in point.

King's Cross is unique; it is also utterly typical. As the glass and steel of government-endorsed, corporate modernity rises into the skies to be bought by overseas investors, soon London, so they say, will just be another Dubai. Government exists to oil the wheels of private enterprise, and to shoulder the risk. HS2 is merely part of the process. There have been fears that part of the project includes a large-scale land-grab around its end points in London and Birmingham. Not only do campaigners argue that Camden faces a 'decade of destruction' should the project go ahead, but even after building work has finished, the borough may continue to suffer. The Regent's Park housing estate next to Euston station is one of the last sites in the capital yet to be converted into investment apartments or 'mixed-use' commercial developments. The fears, it seems, are well-founded.

According to a 2014 article in the *Camden New Journal*, during an HS2 working group, Camden councillor Heather Johnson, chair of the local planning committee:

> made it abundantly clear her 'regeneration' aspirations, as feared, extend far wider than development of the Euston station site. Regent's Park estate, she argued, itself needed and wanted regeneration.

The estate lies pent between Regent's Park and Euston station, between the train lines and the offices of Facebook. The majority was built during the 1950s on land sold in 1951 by the Crown Estate to the Metropolitan Borough of St Pancras, following the destruction of most of the buildings during the London Blitz. The Luftwaffe had not done all the work, however: speculative middle-class housing designed by celebrated Regency architect John Nash was demolished to make way for the new estate. There were plans to bring down Nash's work at Cambridge Gate and Cambridge Terrace too, in order to 'remove a feeling of isolation', but somehow these two survived. As a result, the Regent's Park Estate is cut off from the park – whether pleasantly secluded or unnecessarily isolated is a matter for individual opinion.

Today, the area is a mix of low, medium, and high-rise blocks. In a characteristic piece of oddball place-making, many of the estate names come from the Lake District. There's Conniston, Cartmel, Ainsdale, Eskdale, Langdale and Silverdale. One hundred and sixty-eight of these homes now face demolition.

The area's population density is low for central London, but overcrowding in individual properties is comparatively high. Around a quarter of the homes are privately owned. According to local council statistics, 20% of tenanted households are over sixty-five years old; 16% are Bangladeshi. The percentage of those on Jobseeker's Allowance or incapacity benefits is higher than the national average. Housing and environmental conditions have been described as poor. But to its residents, this is home. The website *Inside Housing* tells of local resident Stan Passmore, 87, who lives in Eskdale, one of the blocks scheduled for demolition. 'I've been here fifty years. Everybody knows one another,' he is quoted as saying. Those shunted aside by HS2 would have to be rehoused. But where?

Councillor Johnson's statement suggests that an area can have desires independent of its population. This is a central tenet of the regeneration credo. But even if regeneration is an effective solution to the problems of an area, such solutions do not solve the problems of its people; as we will see along the route, they simply push such problems elsewhere. Unfortunately, local councils are parochial by definition. Their concern is not the people in their parish, but the parish itself – or, more accurately, their concern is only the people of the parish so long as they remain of the parish. Why should they care what takes place beyond their administrative borders?

It therefore comes as no surprise that the desire for 'regeneration' is not confined to the officials at HS2 Ltd. Camden Council, the Greater London Authority (GLA) and Transport for London (TfL) are jointly preparing a Euston Area Plan. Their 2031 vision is characteristically thick with development-speak buzzwords:

> The Euston area will be rejuvenated as both a local hub of activity and a gateway to London through new high quality comprehensive and transformational development above and around a world class transport interchange at Euston Station.

All this activity and rejuvenation, transformation and development: there is reference here to a geographical location, but not to its people. Those people are not impressed. A document posted to the St Pancras Church website describes the proposed redevelopment of Euston as 'a multi-billion pound profit opportunity for developers under the guise of "regeneration"'. It continues:

We have seen what regeneration looks like these last 30 years in Regent Square, and it is sterile and unfriendly, the only evening life is young professionals' bars, with new luxury residents in gated enclaves. High Speed 2 is not about speed, nor even about capacity, it is about profits for developers.

Their position could hardly be any clearer. Such regeneration is for a certain type of person; those who do not fit the demographic are not only ignored but actively shunted aside. A few short steps from Euston 'world class transport interchange' (i.e. station) I find myself facing the Regent's Park Estate for the first time. It's calm away from the commuter-hour rush and the buildings glow mauve in the soft morning sun. Children have been dropped off at the local school and pairs of women in brightly coloured silks stand and talk on street corners. They exchange friendly greetings and news. Their fuchsia hijabs are vivid against the lilac bricks of Woodhall. The statistics tell me it's an area with problems, but this morning it feels idyllic.

I feel a great warmth inside me – in part it's the excitement of the journey, but also the weather, and that semi-elation of being somehow cut off from all those around you. Maybe this is how spies feel? I ought to stop and ask somebody about their views on HS2, find out how they are being affected, be a journalist. But I'm not a natural conversation-starter and everyone seems involved in their own conversations. Besides, I'm enjoying this glow of self-containment. I fear it might burst if I start speaking. Predictably, it doesn't last.

Instead of talking to people, I head north, excited to be on my way, making sure I stop to take notes and photographs. In London there is much to see, and my progress is slow. Apart from the proposed developments around Euston station, by and large, the route of HS2 follows the existing train lines as they sweep north-west out of London. On the one hand, this reduces costs and disruption, but it does mean that HS2 will be unable to travel at anything like top speed until trains are well outside the city. As anyone knows who has been lured into paying the extra price of the Gatwick 'Express', inner-city overground trains can rarely travel at any great speed.

For the most part, I stay as close to the train lines as possible. I pass offices and churches, neat terraces and looming blocks. On the corner of Cardington Street and Hampstead Road stands an old hospital. It is the former National Temperance Hospital, originally opened in 1873 on Gower Street by the National Temperance League and managed by a board of twelve teetotal directors. Alcohol – widely used in treatment at the time – was discouraged. The hospital moved here to this once-elegant turreted building in 1885. According to website *Derelict London*, 'inpatients were admitted to the new hospital free by a letter from a governor, or on payment of a fixed amount.'

Like so many small-scale private health institutions, the National Temperance Hospital was incorporated into the NHS in 1948, then merged, then closed. Now it stands forlorn: parched and peeling, fenced off, boarded up. As I stop to take a photo, a pigeon appears to take the air on the balustrades of a third-floor balcony.

Further on, I stop again before the Peabody-owned Tintern House, a self-contained cuboid of brick. For some reason it reminds me of Marvell's 'Drop of Dew': 'Round in itself incloses' – disdainful and cut off from its surroundings, 'trembling lest it grow impure'. A little further on, and the contrast with the Regent's Park Estate grows ever more stark. Here stand the whitewashed cottages of Park Village East: Wychcliffe, Piercefield, Albany and Sussex. Each is a mini-dukedom in itself. These too were built by John Nash; the architect invested his own money in the scheme and subsequently profited from it. At the time, he was accused of professional misconduct by MP Colonel Thomas Davies, although he was acquitted and later published a lengthy apologia in which he repeatedly stresses that profit was never his main motivation. Nash was concerned above all to show 'the difference between zealous – I will say enthusiastic – affection for my profession, united to an earnest desire to complete the plans in progress for the improvement of the metropolis; and a grasping anxiety for unfair emoluments with which I have been so unjustly charged.' The language these days may be less ornate, but the debates about our cities have hardly changed, it seems, in over 180 years.

On the opposite side of the street, the railway passes unnoticed. Here will run HS2, slowly at first, any noise muffled for delicate residents by brick walls, exotic planting and double glazing. My mood is beginning to sag. Other people's wealth can have that effect. Plus I'm getting blisters. I really did over-pack – not only all those OS maps but books of poetry, binoculars, spare trousers and jumpers, a loaf of bread, apples, and a novel or two. What was I thinking?

Passing the nineteenth-century Gothic revival St Mark's church and gardens by the Regent's Canal, I emerge on to the cushioned quiet of Princess Road: wilfully quirky cafes and the council-endorsed graffiti on Regent's Park Road bridge. You can tell officially approved graffiti because the people are always happy. It's been brightly painted in the acid hues of London 2012, colours appropriated from a short-lived east London music and fashion scene known as 'nu-rave'. Nu-rave itself borrowed much from the rave culture of the early-1990s, although with any political activism removed. From grass-roots movement to hipster fad to government-endorsed branding campaign: perhaps the full cycle of gentrification is summarised right here. Over the top, somebody has sprayed 'Goon Sqad' [sic] in even more garish tones.

A few minutes later, I come across another weird piece of place-making – no doubt its originators found it amusing. A series of Edwardian semi-detached houses line Eton Avenue, Wadham Gardens, Winchester Road, King's College Road and Merton Rise. I wonder who owns this land. Hours of subsequent searching reveal nothing. On Fellows Road, a few coal tits flitter round a browning sycamore.

The mile or so further north is a slice through the recent history of England's residential architecture – the various attempts at providing adequate social housing which are now being abandoned in favour of commercial developments. Over the next half hour or so I pass, first, Regency Lodge – its brick 1930s curves striving for elegance and nearly succeeding despite the lace curtains and box privet. Nikolaus Pevsner described it as 'good though a trifle stodgy in the English Manner'. Then, in stark contrast, is a low-slung and oppressive estate just off Bolton Road: a maze of brick buildings and narrow spaces with no apparent way out. It's suffocating and fills me with rumbling paranoia.

Most striking, however, is the Alexandra Road Estate,

which I stumble into like it's an oasis of concrete and lush planting: 'the hanging gardens of Camden,' they called it once. The story of the Alexandra and Ainsworth Estate (to give it its full name) is fascinatingly told by Andrew Freear in a 1995 article in *AA Files*, the journal of the Architectural Association School of Architecture. It tells us much about attitudes towards housing in the capital – in that period when local authorities actually had authority (and resources) – and it shows how much has changed. It seems to me like another world.

The project was first conceived in the 1950s – a time when low-cost housing was a high priority, and government grants were widely available to local authorities. High-rise buildings were the latest innovation, although initiatives such as the Andover Estate in Holloway and the Alton Estate in Roehampton were to prove controversial.

In 1965, London's political boundaries were redrawn, and the boroughs of Holborn, St Pancras and Hampstead were merged together to form the new borough of Camden. 'Camden soon became known as the youngest and most progressive of the London boroughs,' writes Freear, who demonstrably admires the borough's 'unequivocal commitment to modernism'.

Sydney Cook was appointed as the borough architect while Bruno Schlaffenberg arrived as head of planning.

Schlaffenberg had previously worked at London County Council (LCC) and was an advocate of high-rise developments in line with the beliefs of the government, who were beginning to put pressure on local authorities to adopt low-cost, industrialised building techniques. Cook, however, felt differently, and not a single such scheme was implemented during his tenure. Both the architects and the planners were housed together in Holborn Town Hall. 'Needless to say,' notes Freear, 'their relationship became very frosty.'

One of Cook's first decisions was to hire New York-born architect Neave Brown. Brown believed that high-density, low-rise housing would 'address the problem of fitting housing into the environment'. He was surprisingly critical of a project by modernist master Le Corbusier, arguing that 'the work of many talented architects is seen to be more frequently an indulgence in individual virtuosity, rather than an attempt to correlate the problem at hand with the problem at large'. How relevant that sounds today in the age of the 'iconic' skyscraper.

Before Alexandra Road, Brown built a five-home development at Winscombe Street, followed by seventy-one further homes at Fleet Road. Alexandra Road was designed in 1968 to incorporate no less than 520 homes for 1,660 people into 6.47 hectares just to the south of the railway lines by Swiss Cottage. But there were problems: opposition from Schlaffenberg, delays with planning permission, issues with contractors and sub-contractors (175 in all), materials, widespread inflation, a burst Victorian sewer and lack of skilled labour. The story of Alexandra Road is a litany of bureaucratic in-fighting and plain bad luck. A change in local government to the Conservatives made Brown adapt his design to include one-third private properties.

Work commenced in 1972 and was completed in 1978. Initial estimates for Alexandra Road were £7.15 million. The final cost was £20.9 million. Local press at the time made much of the discrepancy, but Freear argues that the two figures are not really comparable: many elements were added to the original cost, including 'children's reception centre, a youth club, a play centre, a home for physically handicapped adults, a series of public spaces, and 42 additional sums for the foundation and sewer problems'. When Ken Livingstone took over as Chair of the Camden Housing Committee, he was highly critical and launched a public enquiry. According to Brown, in a recent interview, once the residents moved in and loved the estate, the enquiry was buried. Nonetheless, the controversy surrounding it was enough, Brown believes, to finish his career. He never worked in England again.

'Social housing presents fiendishly difficult design

problems,' architect David Kohn has said. But Brown thought long and hard about every aspect of Alexandra Road. His attention to detail is quite extraordinary: from sliding internal divisions to elegant staircases, and the position of living quarters. Public space was a central concern, and all of the different elements link together continuously. The estate is bounded to the north by the West Coast Main Line, and the desire to limit sounds and vibrations from passing trains was also a key consideration in the layout: an eight-storey block of terraced apartments acts as a noise barrier and its foundations rest on rubber pads to minimise vibrations. One wonders whether they will be sufficient to withstand HS2. There was an emphasis too on human scale and walkability. Schlaffenberg had designed a whole model for London based on the linking of buildings by elevated pedestrian walkways. It seems to have been one subject upon which he and Brown agreed.

What especially interests me about projects like this is not only the convoluted process by which they are conceived and executed, but also the manner in which they are subsequently managed. Alexandra Road has endured a number of problems – especially with regards to its heating system and glass lift-shafts – but the architecture press was largely positive. Freear tells us, however, that during the 1980s very little maintenance work was carried out; planting and landscaping were especially neglected. Nonetheless, he observes 'a very strong sense of community' on the estate. In 1989, the residents voted to form a tenants' co-operative in order to take over management themselves and hire architects to restore the estate to its original condition. However, Camden Council got wind of their plans and took over the four-year £8 million contract. 'Recently,' writes Freear, 'it was revealed that the grant for the first-stage repairs was being siphoned off by the Council to pay interest charges on their capital loans.'

It was at this stage that English Heritage became involved, awarding the estate Grade II* listed status in 1993. On the one hand, this reflects a renewed affection for such projects in certain circles. On the other, it constitutes a further removal of agency from the estate's residents: several of those whom Freear spoke to expressed concern over the changes being made. Freear also observes that 'a universal complaint was the simple lack of maintenance, care and upkeep, over the last two decades'. It seems that whoever decides what is best for residents – governments, local authorities, architects or heritage groups – it is rarely the residents themselves.

That said, to me today, Alexandra Road is a fantastic sight. I approach, the estate presenting itself as a snaking valley of interlocking white reinforced concrete blocks. As I walk through, a slim black cat lopes down the concrete banisters that form the valley's textbook V-shape – carved out of the land by a river of modernity, its riverbed tiled in terracotta. To either side, gentle curves of spacious terraces overhang with greenery. Two women have stopped for a chat, while a workman enjoys the morning sun. Another man walks his trolley and his dog along the raised walkways. Pinned to a lamp post is a handwritten advert for an African drumming group. It feels like a place in which people want to live.

*

If Alexandra Road provides an education in the complex history of residential buildings, then a similar lesson might be gleaned from the two libraries I pass on this first morning. First is Swiss Cottage Central Library, an inspirational 1960s design by Sir Basil Spence. As professor of architecture at the Royal Academy from 1961 to 1968, Spence was one of the great figures of Brutalist architecture. In the 1960s and 1970s he designed a number of buildings across English university campuses – including Liverpool, Nottingham, Queen's College, Cambridge, Exeter, Southampton and Sussex. But he is probably most famous for his design of Coventry Cathedral and New Zealand's 'Beehive' Parliament building.

The library at Swiss Cottage was first opened in 1964 and

was originally intended to form part of a new civic centre. But the plans were abandoned and only the library and adjacent swimming pool were built. The result is a kind of bizarre, concrete zoetrope – those circular spinning devices used to give the illusion of motion to horses or to people. In 2003, the library was remodelled at the same time as the new purpose-built Hampstead Theatre was opened nearby. As I walk by the rectangular pool and stepped lawns, a fountain sprays up in front of the theatre's wooden cladding, and the capital H glyph stands out against a grey backing. It feels like I've walked into the architect's render.

More recently, a neon 'outdoor gym' has been deposited outside Swiss Cottage Library. It looks like a half-hearted relic of the Olympics, when the government tried to encourage us to do more exercise. At the same time they were selling off school playing fields to developers, and McDonald's was the Games' official restaurant. On the day I pass, the gym stands alone: wet, leafy and unused. Opposite is a piece of Modernist bronze, *The Hampstead Figure* by F. E. McWilliam, dated 1964. One wonders what the two make of each other.

Further on in Kilburn, a library is no longer merely a library. Here we find Kilburn Library Centre + Sanctum. Milk-toned sheets of frosted glass form the front of a clunky curve alongside luxury serviced apartments. If a society can be summarised by its libraries, then I wonder what this says about London today.

I stop to sit down in a Lebanese restaurant opposite. I order an orange juice and try to think. On the one hand, it's the first new library in Camden for nearly fifty years. It contains a recording studio, advice centre, IT training centre and a cafe managed by the Camden Society as a training facility for young people with disabilities. On the other hand, such projects say so much about the state of public finances today, the porousness between public and private, the sop of a 'library centre' in order to construct 'luxury hotel apartments' that nobody in the area can possibly afford. Between 2007 and 2012, full-time library staff in the UK fell by 18% to under 22,000. For the first time ever they were outnumbered by volunteers. As a result, all these new buildings are quickly becoming redundant. In recent years, so much public money designated for art or culture, education or healthcare has simply been spent on buildings. Although the construction industry fared badly during the recession, with output falling faster than the whole economy in 2008, successive governments have made its recovery a priority. It has largely worked: in 2014, the industry was worth £92 billion, or 6.4% of the total economy – less than its 2007 peak but well up from 1997 when New Labour swept to power. It is the only secondary industry that is actually growing. Building aside, the UK is a service economy. For comparison, in 2014, financial and insurance services contributed £126.9 billion, or 8% of the total. Tourism contributed £126.9 billion, or 9%. Banking, building and tourism: this is the economic future.

Construction is everywhere along the route of HS2. By Kilburn High Road station is Coventry Close housing development. A little further along is Canterbury Works – its brick arches boarded up for development by Claridge Architects. On the junction of Albert Road and Salisbury Road, just near Queens Park station, are advertising hoardings for Queens Park Place, a forthcoming development from Londonnewcastle. My wife runs a blog collecting images and information about development hoardings. I stop to take some photos.

A little further down the Harrow Road is the main entrance to Kensal Green Cemetery: a stone Greek-style archway from the 1830s when the cemetery first opened. My uncle is buried in here somewhere. I step inside. It is at this point that the preferred route of HS2 turns away from the Bakerloo line and various Overground lines and dips south-west towards where Old Oak Common station is planned. The line is due to run right under here, and there have been various news reports of graves being destroyed and bodies exhumed. Fifty thousand was the number being bandied about by *The Telegraph* in 2012, although, despite the misleading headline, that figure actually relates to the number buried in London's public gardens rather than those likely to be dug up for HS2. HS2 Ltd has repeatedly stated that graves in Kensal Green will not be affected. 'The preferred route for consultation goes under Kensal Green Cemetery,' said a spokesman in the *Evening Standard*, 'between 80 and 115 feet below. Because of the depth of the tunnel the graves will not be disturbed.'

Today it's bright and sunny as mourners and sightseers walk the cemetery's wide straight paths. Green parakeets shriek from amid the remaining yellow foliage above. On the ground below, the fallen leaves are amber and leathery. I walk vaguely south-west, following the line on my map as it heads down towards Wormwood Scrubs. The skeletal cylinders of Kensington gasworks are straight ahead of me. So too is the Grand Union Canal, blocking my path. I turn westwards, hoping to find an exit on to the Harrow Road.

This route takes me through the rose gardens: row upon row of little trees each in its own plot. Each body buried here becomes its own rose. They are simple and bright. There's a sense of the future, and of hope, quite different to all the lumpen Gothic-revival mausoleums that loom across much of the rest of the cemetery. It is here, I think, that Counter's Creek once ran, but the upper reaches of this little river have long since been drained or redirected. Its only remaining open watercourse is the quay of Chelsea Creek. The ground feels soggy, however. I wonder if the waters are rising again? Perhaps I'm just imagining things.

Lost in thought, I come across a chair, standing beneath a budding cherry tree and facing out over the canal. On its arms are tied an array of gently coloured ribbons: mauves, purples, dusky pinks, sky blue and cornflower. It is dedicated simply to Charlotte Horricks – 15th July 2012, aged 24. Nearby, the sun reflects off the inky indigo canal. A duck honks, then a train.

I stop to take a photograph and watch a goldfinch dance a little jig upon the ground. It occurs to me that I don't know how to get out of here. The walls are high and all the gates seem locked. I'm loath to ask anybody for fear of interrupting their personal moments of grief or remembrance. I continue to wander. In the distance is Wembley's angled arch.

Eventually I find a way out, through an iron gate, on to Scrubs Lane and past the high, heady stench of London taxis getting a respray. I cross an old iron bridge and look up, its faded livery of bright blue and rose-pink against a sky of rich azure.

As I continue towards Wormwood Scrubs, this begins to feel less and less like London. I look back down the road towards the city – down the canal towards the cranes and the

BT Tower. It occurs to me that I'm part of a pattern. The month after my route walk, a feature was published in *Vice* arguing that it was time for artists and their ilk to leave the capital and embrace England's other cities. In the same week, an article in *The Guardian* suggested that this demographic shift was already underway. Subsequently, several newspapers have published pieces complaining about costs of living in the capital. Many have been written by people who have lately fled to Brighton or to Birmingham. As journalist and science-fiction author Cory Doctorow wrote about his own departure from the city: 'We're not poor. In any other city, and by national standards, we are the one percent. Low-income people we know and live near are in much worse shape. For one thing, they can't leave.'

It's an important observation – one that reminds me of that east London drift walk. 'They never had us in mind.' Robin Bale's bile-flecked lament has stayed with me. It is exactly the sentiment that seems to sum up the state of the capital today. It is underpinned by a resignation to the politics of division, in the face of which we feel so powerless, and our art and literature so futile. But, then again, who is this 'us'? And who are 'they'? And which side am I on? What is this politics of division, and – childishly perhaps – who started it? They did. No, they did.

On the one hand, it seems, 'they' are those in power –

the people who make the decisions about what happens in and to a city: CEOs and local councillors, architects and developers, politicians and police chiefs. 'They' are also, of course, the rich and the landed. London is still largely owned as a series of ancient estates. The Crown Estate owns Regent's Park, for example; the Duke of Westminster has 300 acres in Mayfair and Belgravia, worth around £10 billion. Marylebone is split between the Portman Estate and the de Walden Estate. The Cadogan estate consists of ninety acres of Chelsea and Knightsbridge. The Corporation of London runs the City; Oxbridge colleges own land across the country. Knowledge of exactly who owns what is slim, and these landowners are notoriously secretive – perhaps that's how they've managed to retain control for so many hundreds of years.

These, then, are the 'they'. On the other hand, well, who are we? Arguably, perhaps, everybody else. But 'we' are not united as one body with clear aims and strategies – nor is it entirely clear whether we ought to be. Do I feel like one of 'us'? Not really. I may not have power over the lives of others, but, like Doctorow, I'm privileged enough to have a degree of agency over my own. Perhaps that is the legacy of identity politics: every 'community' must speak for itself – but who will hear them above the din? Or perhaps it comes down to the permanently problematic notion of 'the people'.

So many claim to speak in their name: that is democracy. Whether this is a subject for lament or an opportunity for fertile new ground to be cultivated elsewhere remains to be seen. In the meantime, London is not for 'us' any more. Perhaps it is no longer for me either – but at least I have a choice.

This is not the first time I have left London – I wonder if it will be the last. In 2013 I was made redundant. That same month a change in the law meant that we had to move out of our flat in Bethnal Green. It was time to go: five months in South America turned out to be cheaper than life in the capital. Then, no sooner had we returned than it was time to leave again – this time for Helsinki, where my wife had been accepted on a Fine Art Master's course.

Now, on the first day of this walk, I have nearly left London again. I enter Wormwood Scrubs. Bins and benches are evenly spaced around its perimeter: bin, bench, bin, bench … Apparently part of the area is a nature reserve, home to lizards and butterflies and a hundred species of bird. It looks like a desert to me: a long and empty expanse of green, mown to within two inches of its life. Goalposts bereft of netting lurch across it in ungainly fashion. A lone dandelion has managed to flower beneath the level of the lawn. On the right as I walk a channel of longer grass has been fenced off and reserved for model aircraft flying. To the south stands the prison. In the middle distance is a scattering of big and glossy blue-black crows. They glint silver as they take off towards the sun.

As I continue, a dog-walker greets me with a silent nod. This is the very edge of the capital.

Up ahead, a pug shits in the longer, wetter grass. Two lads discuss their new motorbike.

A little further, two walkers recognise each other's dogs.

'Percy!'

'Stitchy!'

They both turn to say hello to me, out loud this time. They are the first people who've spoken to me today. It's not yet lunchtime, but it's clear I'm no longer in London. Nobody says hello out loud in London. Farewell, then, to the city. Beyond lies suburbia, and lunch.

II
The Sounds of the Suburbs

Acton – Park Royal – Perivale – Northolt –

South Ruislip – Ruislip Gardens –

West Ruislip – Colne Valley Regional Park –

Denham

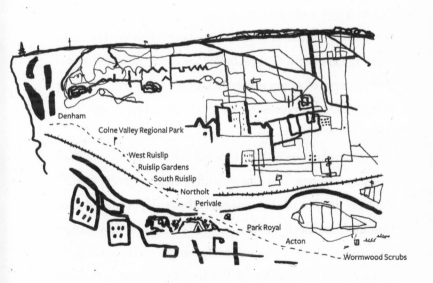

The sun has shone on the city; it is on the suburbs that the rain will fall. This may still be London, but the city feels far behind. It's only the first day of my attempt to walk the proposed route of HS2 from London to Birmingham, but in five hours of walking I've seen the city change: from commuter-hour Euston, through Brutalist housing estates, past closed-down pubs and boarded-up hospitals, and endless, endless construction. Each day, it seems, the city must make itself anew.

I've crossed the vast empty expanse of Wormwood Scrubs. I'm now in Acton, among residential estates pinched between train tracks – sweeping grey lines on the map heading out west and north-west, inhaling and exhaling commuters as the city takes its daily breaths. The lines converge above the Scrubs, below the canal. Row upon row, the residents of Acton present a crumbling civility. Nothing happens in this corner of west London; there is no 'I' in Acton.

For the planners of HS2 Ltd, suburbia is little more than a place to change. The first stop after Euston station is to be built on the site of the existing railway depot at Old Oak Common, just north of Wormwood Scrubs. This new station will form a major transport interchange, with connections to Crossrail and the Great Western Main Line. Old Oak Common is not good enough any more: the station is to be renamed New Queens Park. But the decision-makers at HS2 are not the only ones to ignore the suburbs. For decades, planners, politicians, artists and architects have all turned a blind eye to the same old blandness of English suburbia. But today's walkers are discovering something new behind the mock-Tudor beams of sundry neat little crescents. Might there be more to suburbia than meets the eye?

Since the psychogeographic drift walk which I attended in 2008, artist Laura Oldfield Ford has turned her attention from the sedimentary layers of east London's architectural and (anti-)social landscape towards a new subject: the suburbs. 'The suburb is the new inner city,' she wrote in a text that accompanied her 2014 exhibition at the Stanley Picker Gallery, 'a reversal has taken place.'

Oldfield Ford is not the first to have identified this pattern. US academic Aran Ehrenhault, for example, has described it as 'the great inversion' – from inner-city areas of deprivation surrounded by affluent suburbs in the twentieth century to the exact opposite in the twenty-first. Some of Oldfield Ford's analysis may be reductive or overstated but it is hard to resist the precision of her rage. The text continues:

Once maligned areas like Brixton, Hackney and Clapham have become the chic residences of a new bourgeoisie;

spaces once open for experimentation and drifting have been locked down and sealed off ... time has been co-opted, we no longer have time to wander and dream in a city where exorbitant rents take all your wages.

As the city has continued to grow, areas that were once suburbs came to be associated with the worst of inner-city deprivation. Now they have been gentrified, and the poor pushed once more to the margins. According to Oldfield Ford, the working classes 'have been programmed out, subjected to an intense campaign of social cleansing'. In 2013, a map was published online that detailed 'the Heygate Diaspora' – the places to which leaseholders from the now-demolished Heygate Estate in Elephant and Castle were relocated. In every case, they were moved away from the centre of the city towards the suburbs, and often beyond. 'These suburbs are the new transient zones,' continues Oldfield Ford, 'where architecture is provisional and lanes behind rows of semi detached housing reveal gardens sprawling with camps and dormitories.' She points to the riots of 2011 as evidence of the consequences. It's either violence, or self-medication.

Then again, hasn't suburbia always fostered forms of discontent? The Clash may have spoken for the punks of inner-city south and west London – 'Guns of Brixton', '(White

Man) in Hammersmith Palais' – but many of the bands that came in their wake had distinctly parochial origins. Sham 69, The Members and The Jam were all formed in Surrey. They even sang of Surrey subjects, in songs such as (respectively) 'Hersham Boys', 'The Sound of the Suburbs' and 'The Eton Rifles'.

In 1937, John Betjeman published *Continual Dew*, in which appeared the poem 'Love in a Valley' – a characteristic homily to suburbia. Gas-fires, train lines, tennis courts and pine trees: all lit with the warm, sad glow of melancholy.

Take me, Lieutenant, to that Surrey homestead!
Red comes the winter and your rakish car,
Red among the hawthorns, redder than the hawberries
And trails of old man's nuisance, and noisier far.
Far, far below me roll the Coulsdon woodlands,
White down the valley curves the living rail,
Tall, tall, above me, olive spike the pinewoods,
Olive against blue-black, moving in the gale.

Deep down the drive go the cushioned rhododendrons,
Deep down, sand deep, drives the heather root,
Deep the spliced timber barked around the
  summer-house,
Light lies the tennis-court, plantain underfoot.

What a winter welcome to what a Surrey homestead!
Oh! the metal lantern and white enamelled door!
Oh! the spread of orange from the gas-fire on the carpet!
Oh! the tiny patter, sandalled footsteps on the floor!

Fling wide the curtains! – that's a Surrey sunset
Low down the line sings the Addiscombe train,
Leaded are the windows lozenging the crimson,
Drained dark the pines in resin-scented rain.
Portable Lieutenant! they carry you to China
And me to lonely shopping in a brilliant arcade;
Firm hand, fond hand, switch the giddy engine!
So for us a last time is bright light made.

Betjeman's idiosyncratic syntax is prominent in almost every line here. Lines 5-7 are exemplary: each begins with a single-syllable adjective, like a drumbeat launching the line ('Far', 'White', 'Tall'). Then follows an expanded descriptive phrase ('far below me', 'down the valley', 'tall above me'), before the main verb (here often one of movement – 'roll', 'curves', 'spike'), then, and only then, the subject of the sentence, delayed right to the end of the line. The rhythm and repetition create a sense of stability. In the last four lines this structure is largely abandoned, as security gives way to loneliness and uncertainty.

Just forty years later, The Members cited the proximity of Heathrow airport (a small rural airfield when Betjeman was writing) and Broadmoor psychiatric hospital to recast the same Surrey suburbia in a very different light.

Every lousy Monday morning, Heathrow jet goes
  crashing over my home,
Ten o'clock, Broadmoor siren driving me mad, won't
  leave me alone.

Paul Weller shouts about 'a row going on down near Slough'. Sham 69 live 'so close to the city, we ain't got much choice'. Those lines are just as distant to us (and just as close) as Betjeman was to punk. The gap is only forty years or so.

In a 1989 article for *The Town Planning Review*, academic J. W. R. Whitehand wrote of the suburbs: 'Outwardly stable and with an image of middle-class respectability, they apparently lack major problems.' But, as Whitehand was aware, suburbia has never existed in a fixed state. Perhaps the most significant change has been less a question of class than of race. Suburbia, traditionally, is a bastion of whiteness. Punk may have drawn upon black music, the Clash may have envied black people's response to social problems ('they don't mind throwing a brick' – 'White Riot') but there are few things whiter than three-chord guitar bands. Author, editor and activist Trenton Oldfield has described gentrification as 'whitetrification': in a 2014 interview I edited for the Institute of Art and Ideas he argued that, 'white communities come in and literally drain the colour out of the area – physically and metaphorically.' The implication would then be that 'the colour' flows to the suburbs. According to Graeme Archer's 2013 article in *The Telegraph*, Enfield's white population has dropped by nearly twenty-five percentage points in ten years. For Archer, this is a cause for concern; for others, it's a sign of the times. 'London's soul is in the suburbs,' wrote Rupa Haq in a 2013 article in *The Guardian*.

Such complexities may be overlooked in Oldfield Ford's analysis. As we saw in the last chapter, it is hard to argue against her assertion that London has now become a brand. The capital's priorities are finance, tourism and overseas investment. The people who made the city unique are on the way out. Interestingly, Oldfield Ford also accuses psychogeography of being 'appropriated' by 'a sanitised heritage industry'. Is this a rejection of earlier methods? Or is it simply the word that has been co-opted, not the act itself? The ease with which psychogeography may be appropriated has been a perennial concern. I wonder to what extent my own walk is a sanitised version of a once-radical strategy: at what point does psychogeography become tourism? At what point does the descriptive become prescriptive? These are questions which I will return to again and again.

In the meantime, I'm in need of lunch.

In his 1885 essay, 'One of the New Voters', Richard Jefferies describes what it is that draws rural labourers to the public house: not alcohol or tobacco – these are merely sidelines – but 'the magnetism of company and conversation'. But, notes Jefferies, in a move that marks a division between author and reader on one hand and the subjects of his writing on the other: '*Their* conversation, not *your* conversation.' Jefferies is attempting to convey to his readers (the piece was first published in the *Manchester Guardian*) that there are limits to our understanding. Social superiority, education, literacy: these things close certain doors as they open others. 'We have not been through the same circumstances,' he continues, 'our day has been differently spent, and the same words have therefore a varying value.'

I'm not sure how much this is in my mind as I peer through the barred windows of a tiny workers' cafe by the railway lines in North Acton. I'm not sure how much this is in my mind as I struggle to heave open the ten-tonne iron door. But it is there, I think, in my face. The rucksack, the walking stick, the haircut: 'I am not one of you'. Faces twist up from plates piled with beans and bacon, egg and chips. A flicker of reaction perhaps, then back to breakfast – served all day. I order a fried egg sandwich with hash browns.

'Hash browns *in* the sandwich?' The man serving me sounds horrified.

'No, on the side please,' I hasten to explain.

'Thank god for that,' he seems to say.

I find a space by the radiator in the corner of the cafe. I sit and listen as a meal is finished.

A man with grey sideburns turns to his mate: 'Right, come on then. We gotta keep going.'

'You gettin' all of it?' says the man behind the counter.

'Looks like it,' he replies. And then, as if by way of explanation: 'Gotta keep going, that's the thing. Gotta keep going.'

From another man nearby: 'Life's difficult enough without being a bomb disposal expert.'

Nobody disagrees.

'Right then, let's get back to it.'

I am one of the last to leave, my lunch not constrained by the schedule of a working day. As the rush subsides, a middle-aged woman emerges from the kitchen. She stands and chats with the two men who work here. Both have thinning grey hair and wear glasses. She is married to one of them; I struggle to work out their relationship with the other.

'Where are you off to then son?' she asks.

'Birmingham,' I say, and pause, waiting to see the impact of this outlandish answer. Not a flicker of surprise. I explain the nature of my journey: 'I'm walking the route of HS2.'

'Good for you mate,' says one.

He's not rude or dismissive, but certainly not particularly interested. Perhaps there have been dozens of us – route-walkers trekking endlessly up and down the line. This cafe has been here fifty-two years. They've seen it all.

'You'll be going by Denham then?' asks one of the men.

'I hope so.'

'I should take the canal if I were you,' he says. 'It's lovely along that canal near Denham. You could take it all the way to Birmingham if you wanted.'

He's right. The Grand Union Canal stretches some 137 miles from London to Birmingham; it's not much less direct than HS2, which is 119 miles. Opened on 1 January 1929, it was formed from the amalgamation of several different canals with the aim of competing against the recently improved roads and railways now connecting the country. Over the next two days my route will intersect with the canal from time to time, but it cuts north earlier – heading up the Colne Valley, then through Tring and Leighton Buzzard and Bletchley. Thereafter, it is not until the outskirts of Royal Leamington Spa, where Longhole Bridge carries Ridgeway Lane over the canal, that our paths will cross again.

'The canal is very nice,' he says.

'Thank you,' I say.

I lug my rucksack on to my back, stagger to the door, heave it open, and head back out into the quickly chilling, after-lunch sun.

Right then, I think to myself. *Let's get back to it.*

*

My post-hash-brown high does not last long. As the weather cools, I find myself trudging endlessly in an interminable nowhere land. Is this suburbia now? Vast storage units and car dealerships line the A40. Burger King, Screwfix, Staples, Tenpin Action. Crescents of semi-detached housing have seen better days.

Park Royal tube station presents a semblance of architectural consideration. Part of the mid-war extension of the Piccadilly line, it was designed by Herbert Arthur Welch and Felix Lander in the style laid out by the Underground's principal architect, Charles Holden. Technically, it's known as the rather effete-sounding Streamline Moderne – effectively Art Deco with all the edges rounded off. Many of the buildings in this style look like cruise-liners. But the L-shaped Park Royal is not glass or bright white; it's made of brick. A tower rises from a gently curving base of shops, displaying the Underground's patriotic roundel for all to see. The principal flourish of modernity is the ticket hall – double-height and drum-shaped. The building was given Grade II listed status on 28 January 1987.

A few yards on, a grand old Art Deco cinema stands closed and dilapidated. Not even Wetherspoons are interested. What could be more depressing than Premier Inn, Hangar Lane? I turn swiftly off the A40 on to Connell Crescent, the outermost ring of concentric roads around Chatsworth Woods. A majestic weeping willow cascades over the corner. A large rat lies face-up on the pavement, dead, its mouth open in final surprise. Connell Crescent is a street of red brick and pebble-dash. For one resident, the red bricks were just not red enough: each has been painted even redder, the grouting marked out in bright white.

At the council-run Alperton Sports Ground, a battalion of starlings invades the grass from the telephone wires above. 'Pit-pinging Perivale' is all I can decipher from my notes of this great event. I have no idea what it means.

Momentarily, I'm distracted by a door's exquisite rust. Framed beautifully against the brown-painted brick of a substation or outbuilding, the door's whole centre is a rich, crusty russet. Each layer of paint above is still visible: from pale turquoise to grey-mauve to an oily top-wash of smeary black. Over the years it's been graffitied and cleaned, graffitied and overpainted, painted and cleaned and left to the wind and rain. Tiny etched markings are just visible in its surfaces – symbolising what, I'll never know. A whole swathe of contemporary abstract painting falls just short of this door. The rusted bolt no longer fits in its rusted lock.

Unsurprisingly, I'm making much slower progress than I had imagined. And then the rain begins.

I decide I need to find somewhere to sleep.

Before setting off I had done a limited amount of research on the subject of 'wild camping'. My fellow man, it seemed, would be my greatest enemy. This is not rural Russia or the wild frontiers of North America. Much to the chagrin of George Monbiot and the proponents of rewilding, there are no bears or wolves in England. Not even a wild boar. It was humans that I was advised to fear most: the drunk, the ne'er-do-well, and, of course, the angry farmer. 'Gerroffmoilend!' etc. My research yielded the following advice, not all of which, I was rapidly realising, would be all that helpful:

1. Get in early, get out early.
2. Avoid being seen.
3. Aim for somewhere sheltered and concealed – like a forest.
4. Stay away from built-up areas.

Stay away from built-up areas? I'm in Perivale! The wood I had planned to spend the night in is in Ruislip, still far off at the rate I'm going. The rain isn't stopping and I'm not convinced about the waterproof qualities of my rucksack. Rather stupidly, I was sure to keep myself well insulated from the rain – waterproof jacket, waterproof trousers – but had neglected to take the same care over the pile of stuff on my back.

I make a decision: Ruislip, in this weather, is too far. The rain is becoming heavier and I need to stop. It's only 4 p.m. but darkening fast. I stop and take out my map. Near to my current location, among the curling rows of neatly arranged houses, there's a nature reserve! In Perivale? That's what the map says, and I've not yet learnt to distrust it. Nearby is a small street named after the famous nineteenth-century naturalist whose writing has provided inspiration to so many contemporary nature writers: Gilbert White Close. It has to be a sign.

I turn right into a housing estate, bound for Gilbert White, thinking of bird-spotting and lush prose, trusting in the great man to lead me into the secluded safety of the nature reserve. It turns out, inevitably, to be a mistake. Omens, I realise, even ones as auspicious as Gilbert White, have no place in the business of map-reading. The road itself is hardly a cul-de-sac, a strip of tarmac in an estate of beige brick neatness.

It leads directly to nowhere, and I'm compelled to turn around, retrace my steps and seek an alternative point of entry. All the while the rain comes down.

Walking back the way I came, I notice a small patch of grass. In one corner, by the road, a large playground; in the other, a low-slung community centre of some kind. I walk quickly, trying not to look suspicious, across the open grass towards a corner of soggy autumn trees. A quick turn to check I've not been spotted, and in. Through the trees, however, is a fence that separates me from the safety of the nature reserve beyond. It's too high to climb.

I take off my pack and set it down amid the damp and muddy bed of leaves. I stand beneath the half-shelter of this semi-wooded corner, and dither. The rain gathers on branches and drops on to my head. *This is it*, I think. *Home for the night*. Is it? Is it really? Am I actually doing this? My stomach is a tangled dance of nerves and indecision. I could just walk around the corner to Perivale, get the tube home. It's not even 5 p.m. I'd be back in time for supper. No. I'm doing this. This is only the first day of ten – I can't give up already. I unzip my rucksack, take out the tent. The ground is sodden and leafy, grainy with muck, twiggy with fallen branches and sprouting woody growth. It's no campsite. Perhaps the wood was a mistake after all, but at least I'm concealed – sort of.

I try to think strategically. On the one hand, I'm relieved to be this side of the fence as it limits the directions from which unknown dangers can approach. On the other, it also cuts off any potential escape route. I'm trapped here. For now, I curse this fence. Why must nature be cut off like this? Boxed off, untouchable. Even here, in the heart of suburbia, nature is put in its place – over there. In due course, however, I will have cause to be thankful.

My fingers are wet and numbing fast as I struggle with clips and clasps. I try to work quickly but I don't know what I'm doing. The strange, silken nylon of the tent grows slimy as the trees drip their accumulated wetness. I haven't put up a tent in two years. It's dark in here now and I dare not use the torch in more than small bursts. I'm terrified of being seen. I know that if I were asked to move on now my resolve would crack and I'd simply get the train home. What if a policeman comes? What if … worse? This is ridiculous.

Eventually, after snapping branches out of the way, the tent stands. It's distinctly misshapen where I had to squeeze it between two young trees, but it's standing nonetheless. I climb inside, pushing through branches in order to do so (the entrance is not where I'd expected it), bringing in mud and leaves. Without unpacking anything I sit in the darkness. It's not even 6 p.m. There is a whole evening ahead, and then the night. I have never felt more vulnerable.

I sit and write, amazed by how much my mood has changed during the day: from low-level anxious exhilaration at Euston to genuine warmth and goodwill through the housing estates nearby. Hatred of humanity in the pompous environs of Primrose Hill, with its endless parade of cutesy shops where everyone looks like they were nearly on the telly. After the great happiness of a lunchtime fried egg sandwich and hash browns (a plateful of joyful beige), the mood lowered through industrial estates and interminable suburbia – a place for cars now, not walkers. I've felt the same intensity of attention as when I'm writing about art. It's like a switch flicks and you're 'on' – attuned to every detail and its impact upon your thoughts and feelings. Now, in the darkness, I'm unable to switch it off. I feel lost and vulnerable, buffeted by moods. I wish my wife were here. I wish I were at home. All of a sudden I miss her horribly and think I'm going to cry. My torch seems to be running out so I continue writing in the murky, fuzzy dark. I think and write.

In circling footsteps the rain treads ever nearer and fuels my growing paranoia. What am I doing here? I feel like a child again. My thoughts turn inwards, back to that first night of boarding school – alone and afraid and knowing all the time that it is irrational. My ears are sharply attuned to the amazing array of rain noises: pins and needles; gentle crepuscular cracklings; insistent drumming; and, as it stops, the water gathering slowly at the point of a leaf before tipping, now, to fall hard and fat on the tent's taught skin. Each noise is a bestiary of night-time potential: a fox pawing delicately past; the rustle of a grey squirrel up above; a landing owl. But worst of all, my nameless fellow man. Sitting upright, fully clothed in my sleeping bag, I realise I am shaking.

I must have fallen asleep at some point, because in the deep still of the night I'm woken by a spluttering burst of breath – a big, sudden sound, right there outside the tent. A living, breathing thing is maybe two yards away. My nerve endings fray with alertness. Fight or flight? Or neither: characteristically, I freeze. It comes again – that noise. The air, pulled out through giant nostrils … a little further away this time. Slowly, as silently as possible, I inch down the zip of the tent. I wince at every scratch of tooth. First the inner lining. Then the outer lining. I peep out among wet dark branches and pale-glowing indigo sky. Nothing. I slip on my boots and creep to the fence – managing for the first time not to snap a twig or crunch against the branches. It is surprisingly light out. I peer through the fence into the flat channel of grass beyond. I hear the soft steps of something much, much bigger than me. Then, all of a sudden, I realise: strolling slowly past, it's none other than the apparition of a white horse – a real white horse! Its flank and neck and hindquarters glow low like lilac, silver-tipped in the electricity of a moment and this cold suburban moonlight.

It hasn't seen me. Or, if it has, it isn't interested. For a moment, I'm in awe. Then, a heartbeat later, there's a careful crash in the trees opposite. A little larger, a brown horse noses its way through the branches to join the other. I feel an amazing sense of exhilaration, so privileged to have witnessed this, here in Perivale. I am electrified. Suddenly, this whole ridiculous undertaking feels right. I remember too the fence which separates us. I give thanks and feel safe. I return to my tent and sleep soundly until woken by the pre-dawn freeze. Evening passed and morning came. That was the first night.

*

Packing up my tent in the moistness of a November morning, I startle a fox. Like me the night before, he freezes – torn in a moment of indecision. For some reason, I find this reassuring: sometimes even foxes don't know what to do.

I look at the fox, russet against damp russet leaves. He looks at me. 'Boo,' I say, to break the tension. Relieved, he springs into action, and darts away across the grass to another small patch of trees on the other side. Foxes are to be a constant presence throughout this journey.

*

A short walk down the road, I stop in the morning glow of Perivale station. Designed in 1938, Perivale was not completed until 1947. A planned tower and extended wing were never constructed, so the result is less striking than Park Royal. The characteristic curved exterior is concave rather than convex but, like Park Royal, the building is Grade II listed. At 6 a.m. it glows blue under its own signage and dusty pink from the car park lighting. Hunched-over commuters and smoking workmen eye me with suspicion as I stop to take a photo.

Just down the road is one of my favourite buildings in the country: the Hoover Building. As a child I remember looking out of the back window to catch a glimpse of this strange white edifice as we drove home from London along the A40. Turquoise window-leading and red go-faster stripes complete its outré appearance. It was built in 1933 for the Hoover Company, and later bought by Tesco in 1989. Wallis, Gilbert and Partners were responsible for the design. Apparently they also designed a bus station in my home town of Amersham. Unfortunately it was closed in 1989, five years after I was born, and later demolished. All that exists now is a photo of a cardboard model. It reminds me of Neasden depot: there's just something slightly perfect about that font against low, oblong brick buildings.

Unfortunately, I have a schedule to keep, so a close-up of the Hoover Building must wait for another day. Because of yesterday's early finish I have a lot of ground to make up. At 11 a.m. I'm supposed to be meeting with Stewart Pomeroy, Green Spaces Team Manager at Colne Valley Regional Park. From Perivale station I get repeatedly lost in tired-looking suburban housing estates. Men troop out of front doors into their cars or towards the tube station. They look at me like I'm an alien. A man in a newsagent's asks me if I'm a wildlife photographer. Clearly I must look the part. I later realise I have half a bush sticking out the back of my rucksack.

Tiring of cul-de-sacs, I descend to the Regent's Canal, where a raft of little coots also begins its morning commute, plopping one by one from the verge into the water. They jangle by as if on rusty bicycles. A little way behind, two pairs of swans – stately, sedate – make their way along the canal. Birds cry in the hedgerows and the swans look from side to side, regally acknowledging the fanfare that is their due. Further down stand the remnants of industry: fenced-off buildings edged with rusted-out corrugated iron and ventilation shafts – the waves of corrugation doubled in the wavy reflection. Nearby, a log lies suspended in the cloudy olive aspic. On the water drapes the greyness of the sky and, briefly, the short-lived reflection of a cormorant as it sails by overhead. I keep walking.

Conscious of time and the weight on my back, I decide to cheat. What's the point of simply walking from one tube station to another? Besides, no one need know, I reason to myself. I nip on to the tube at Northolt and get off again a few minutes later at West Ruislip. Few things can compare to the illicit exhilaration of this tube ride – after all my walking, the speed of the train is scarcely credible. Maybe this is how the Metropolitan line's first passengers felt. 'Early Electric,' as Betjeman declaimed in *Metro-Land*, 'punctual and prompt. Off to those cuttings in the Hampstead Hills ...'

Outside the Ruislip Conservative Club, I stop to ask a hearty sort of lady for directions. She seems delighted. Then, finally it's time to put aside my *A-Z*, and take out the OS map. Goodbye, London. Hello, countryside. Straight away, I spot a green woodpecker in the grass by John O'Neill Walk; in the mid-distance a grey heron stands among the bulrushes. But the transition from suburbia to countryside is a slow one. Golf marks the division: not one but two courses must be crossed. One early morning golfer ignores my request for directions – perhaps my footwear does not meet the club's requirements. Another kindly obliges. After the golf courses, I come across a sign: 'GRID LOCK HERE,' it proclaims. '800+ LORRIES A DAY. STOP HS2.' I cross a rolling field – suddenly the air feels different, the sky big and open. I climb over a stile and into the Colne Valley Regional Park. I'm right on schedule.

The river Colne is one of the principal tributaries to the Thames (the others being the Churn, the Thame, the Leech, the Windrush, the Evenlode, the Cherwell, the Kennet, the Ver, the Wey, the Mole, the Medway, the Lea and the Roding). There are other river Colnes too – in Essex and West Yorkshire – as well as Colne Water, which runs through the Lancashire town of Colne. The word seems to derive from the Latin noun *colonia* – meaning a colony or settlement or a possession of land. *Colonia* in turn comes from the verb *colo* which means not only to till or cultivate but also to inhabit, protect, nurture and even to honour or worship. Perhaps the entire ethics of our relationship with the land could be reconfigured in line with the multiple meanings of this little word.

The Colne itself rises perennially from a subterranean river in North Mumms Park, Hertfordshire. From there it flows west and south through Colney Heath, London Colney and Colney Street. It runs under the M1 and A41, down through Watford, then just south of Rickmansworth, where it starts to split into a series of large lakes. This is the start of Colne Valley Regional Park.

According to a 2014 article in a local newspaper, 'The concept of the Colne Valley Park has a long history.' Between the two world wars, the idea that London was in need of a 'green lung' began to gain traction. Local authorities responded by beginning to acquire large tracts of land in the area under the 'Colne Valley scheme'. This became formal policy in 1935 as part of the larger green belt scheme; in 1938, the green belt was legally instituted under the London and Home Counties Act. Some of this land is still available for public use (such as Black Park near Slough and Northmoor Hill Wood in Denham) although, the article notes, some local authorities have been selling off land acquired under the scheme once the lease has expired.

The land that was acquired includes gentle chalk hills, ancient woodlands and sunken lanes. What makes it distinctive, however, is the string of over sixty lakes that runs north to south along the side of the river. Most have been formed by gravel extraction and subsequently filled in with water. It was these that first kindled the idea for the regional park. In 1965, the town clerk of Hillingdon submitted a report suggesting that the large pits which lined the Colne ought to be used for water recreation, which was becoming increasingly popular. Following a conference of nine local authorities later that year, the Colne Valley Regional Park was established. The boundaries were drawn to include all the open land visible from the valley floor between Rickmansworth and Denham, limited to the east by London and to the south by the Thames. These boundaries remain largely the same today, although the total area of the park has expanded from 25,000 to 27,500 acres.

But Colne Valley finds itself at an administrative confluence. It spreads across five local councils – Buckinghamshire, Hillingdon, Berkshire, Hertfordshire and Surrey. London looms to the east, Heathrow airport to the south. HS2 threatens its very future. On the edge of the park I think I spot a nuthatch – its black and white head slinking up and down an oak tree. A little further on, a sparrowhawk comes to rest in a tree overlooking the river. I stand and admire its rose-buff front and wings of military grey. I move a little closer and it flies away. On one lake bob a number of ducks – do those have blue beaks? Am I going mad? I've been walking for six hours.

Thankfully, my early start means I'm exactly on time. Stewart had emailed me before I'd set off on the walk and we'd arranged to meet at the visitor centre. 'Colne Valley is on the edge of Buckinghamshire, Slough, and London,' he tells me over a cup of tea in the foyer, 'so the focus often goes elsewhere.' I nod my head in agreement: I've lived in London and Amersham, never more than a few miles away, and have never heard of the place. 'But it is a coherent landscape,' he continues. This seems to be an important point for Stewart, although I'm not 100% certain what he means. I wonder what an incoherent landscape might look like? It sounds appealing. 'A trout moving up the Colne,' he explains, 'is not going to worry about moving from Buckinghamshire to Hillingdon. Administrative boundaries are an accident of history, and don't make sense.'

One such boundary separated the Saxon kingdoms of Mercia and Wessex and is thought to run through the Colne Valley, along what is now known as Old Shire Lane. Today it's a popular route for walkers but during HS2's years of construction this will be the site of one of the 'sustainable placements' that punctuate the route. What the phrase 'sustainable placement' actually means is rubbish dump. It's a classic example of the duplicitous language wheeled out by such organisations. 'The area will just be trashed,' says Stewart. Because of its in-between location, he believes that Colne Valley stands to be one of the worst affected areas in the country should HS2 get the go-ahead.

Colne Valley is an unusual area. On the one hand this is the kind of liminal space that fascinates today's breed of nature writers. 'Urban fringe,' Stewart calls it. But it is very different to the kind of post-industrial spaces regrowing with buddleia so beloved by the poets. A brick viaduct, its arches overflowing with brambles and nettles, is the closest I get to this kind of edgeland. A few yards further down the canal a door has been attached to a trunk of an oak tree.

Elsewhere this is carefully managed land. Our interaction with it has been planned and directed – along footpaths by neat signposts and next to lakes by prohibitive posters: 'private fishing'; 'members only'; 'no day tickets' and the like.

Colne Valley Regional Park is a Community Interest Company (CIC) which doesn't own any of the land it manages. Instead, Stewart and his team must work in partnership with their many members in order to achieve their goals. These include maintaining and enhancing the landscape, safeguarding the countryside, conserving biodiversity, providing for countryside recreation and achieving a sustainable rural economy and community. The Park's members include between fifty and sixty very different organisations numbering tens of thousands of people: from the Environment Agency and National Trust to parish councils and local businesses like Hillingdon Outdoor Activities Centre or Denham Waterski Club.

Stewart emphasises the importance of usefulness, something I have in the past been highly sceptical of: the reduction of nature's great complexity, its vast unknowability, to the level of a resource – to serve a single purpose or function. Nature as utility, valued only insofar as it serves a human purpose. It makes me uncomfortable, for example, to read on the park's website that 'Wildlife,

Conservation and Environment' comes under the heading 'Things to Do'. But then this is a straightforward position to adopt from the security of a desk. For somebody in Stewart's position, fighting at every moment to safeguard the land he lives to protect, proving utility is a vital political strategy. In the age of management, that which is not useful is simply going to waste.

And Colne Valley is greatly used. Three million people live within ten miles of the park. A large school group arrives while Stewart and I are talking. Ramblers' groups walk past regularly. The park's website includes details for guided walks, self-guided walks, angling, canal activities (such as boat hire and yachting), cycling, flying, golf, horse riding, lake activities (sailing, canoeing, even water-skiing) and orienteering. But this is not just about human uses. Stewart repeatedly points out how wildlife 'uses' the landscape here. The lakes are now important sites for breeding wetland birds and wintering water birds such as tufted ducks and gadwalls. During especially cold spells, rarer species such as the red-necked grebe and the great northern diver have been known to visit. Large flocks of lapwings and geese congregate in the fields, while redwings and fieldfares search the hedgerows for berries.

All of this is under threat. According to Carol Gibson, Director of Colne Valley Park CIC: 'The Colne Valley

Regional Park is under siege.' She identifies four main threats: HS2, of course, but also the proposed new runway at Heathrow, an expanded freight exchange in Slough, and the expansion of Pinewood Studios in south Buckinghamshire. All of these may seem unconnected, but, Gibson argues, they are connected – 'through landscape and the facts of geography and history'. Already pressure on development and the relaxation of planning restrictions under the coalition government have pushed up the price of land in the area. One fear is that farmers and other sympathetic landowners may be pushed out: as Stewart tells me, 'farmers help keep the green belt green'.

These are indirect effects; the impact of HS2 will be direct and permanent. Even if a tunnel is built under the Chilterns, Colne Valley will find itself sandwiched between two portals. A huge viaduct is to be built across the valley, cutting straight through Broadwater Lake nature reserve. Hertfordshire and Middlesex Wildlife Trust has said that it will 'devastate habitats and wildlife'. European protected species such as Daubenton's and pipistrelle bats could be threatened too. 'We will be left with a lake that is cut in half by a viaduct,' Stewart tells me, 'and now doesn't have a use.'

As Gibson has put it: 'The damage to local landscapes, rivers, biodiversity and communities will be hard to overcome without substantial support from developers to provide an equivalent or better environment.' But according to Pomeroy: 'decent mitigation and compensation are not on the cards. Colne Valley is a gateway to the Chilterns,' he continues. 'It's a buffer. The more urbanised this gets, the more vulnerable the Chilterns becomes. The urban fringe is going to change significantly over the next four decades. Nobody is looking at the overall cumulative impact.'

*

As I leave Colne Valley, I follow the path of the Misbourne as Stewart has advised. I see, or think I see, a kingfisher – a dark streak low across the water. It leaves a shimmer of iridescent blue trembling in the air. I'm still unsure if what I saw was only what I wanted to see.

Walking up Old Shire Lane, I gaze out across the valley and gently sloping farmland. I try to imagine what HS2 will look like as it rushes through the countryside, fifteen metres above the ground. A long, straight line across a curving vista. In some ways it's the antithesis to much writing about landscape, which, as we shall see, often enacts a process of excavation and remembrance. In the fields where the tracks will be, poppies are growing – commemorating their own future obliteration. A barbed wire fence is strung with spiderwebs. I cross the M25.

*

It suddenly occurs to me that I've been here in Colne Valley before. Yes! I remember! Or think I remember: Rickmansworth aquadrome, as if in another life. As I child I was taken here for afternoon walks with my ever-dapper grandparents – Nanny swathed in camel cashmere; Grandpa, beige and practical in showerproof car-coat. We would stroll along as Nanny tutted at the Canada geese – so loud, so messy, so foreign. Canada geese, which were introduced into London's St James's Park back in 1665, had apparently not assimilated to their new habitat – not, I would come to realise, like my grandparents.

Few people have quite so typified for me a certain kind of Englishness. There was their vague and glamorous past – flights to America, a fleet of vintage cars – but in the years I knew them it was a sensible, English life of golf clubs and gardening. Glamour still clung to them – Nanny's big gold medallion; Grandpa's moustache – but only just. Leaving London, they settled in Moor Park, where they built a spacious bungalow. The front garden had an enormous pond framed by leylandii and a plastic heron. The back garden sloped down from the house with a maze of semi-secluded paths providing scope for great childhood adventures. In spring, these paths were filled with bluebells.

They wore sensible, well-tailored English clothing, and only ever bought the best. My grandfather used to have his hair cut at Burberry. He donned his tweed flat cap to play golf at Moor Park (he was terrible). My grandma played tennis there and met with friends in its ludicrous clubhouse – a Grade I listed Palladian mansion, whose interiors are coated with Italianate depictions of Ovid's *Metamorphoses*. Up in the ceiling a *trompe-l'œil* dome is painted. It enchanted me as a child and I've been fascinated by that effect ever since. It enchanted John Betjeman too: in his 1973 television film *Metro-Land*, Betjeman visits Moor Park:

> Did ever golf club have a nineteenth hole as sumptuous
> as this? Did ever golf club have so fine a hall? Venetian
> decor, 1732
> And yonder dome is not a dome at all
> But painted in the semblance of a dome

And then, a little later:

> What Georgian wit these classic Gods have heard,
> Who now must listen to the golfer's tale

As a failed golfer, I can testify to the tiresomeness of the post-round anecdotes. On Sundays and special occasions we came here to eat roast lunches in hot rooms. I remember the textured wallpaper and the chandeliers. What could be more English?

I know now that my grandparents were Jewish. Grandma's maiden name was Levy. In the late nineteenth century, the family had fled the pogroms of Imperial Russia (present-day Poland) and moved, like so many, to east London. It was only in 2013, on a walking weekend in Oxfordshire with my father, that he told me the origins of our surname, Jeffreys. The family name was in fact Jaffe, but was changed in 1927 to help my grandfather get into Mill Hill school in north London. My brother, Henry, knew this for years but never mentioned it. I only know most of these things from an article he wrote in *The Guardian*. It's a strange way to discover your own past.

I knew bits and pieces before that: there was a speech given at my grandmother's ninetieth birthday by a cousin of hers. He talked about the Levy family, the flight from Poland and the founding of Ealing synagogue. When my grandmother died, I was given some of her prayer books. The inscriptions inside are in Hebrew. No wonder the family has always voted Conservative: according to Rupa Haq, 'One of the reasons Thatcher was selected by Conservatives in Finchley in the '50s was her pledge to end the ban on Jews joining Finchley golf club.' At school I was mocked for being Jewish – it's the nose, they said – but I always denied it. That feels strange now.

From east London, the family moved west, to Ealing, then gradually out into Buckinghamshire: my grandparents to Moor Park, then my parents to Amersham. The line of this journey away from London is the same as that followed by HS2, and therefore by me on this walk. It's hardly surprising – for this is a journey shaped by transport. The same train that took Betjeman to Moor Park took my grandparents and many others: the Metropolitan line.

The Metropolitan line began life in 1863. At first it connected Paddington with Farringdon Street – it was the world's first underground railway, with wooden carriages and steam locomotives. Drivers were allowed to grow beards in the belief that this would filter out the worst of the fumes. What women drivers were to do remains unclear – one assumes there simply weren't any. The Metropolitan's owners described the atmosphere as 'invigorating'.

Under the chairmanship of Edward Watkin MP, the Metropolitan line reached Harrow in 1880, Rickmansworth in 1887, Chesham in 1889 and Aylesbury in 1892. At its peak, the line extended out as far as Verney Junction in Buckinghamshire, fifty miles from Baker Street. The trouble, as Clive Foxell notes in his book, *The Metropolitan Line*, was that very few people actually lived in these places. But that was about to change. The building of the railway had required the purchase of large areas of land along the line. These were now ripe for development. On the back of having to pay for the demolition of a large building in the City, Watkin had been able to get a series of Acts through Parliament which allowed Metropolitan Railways to develop this land as they saw fit.

In 1881, a small workers' estate in Neasden was the first step, but it was not until 1910 that Robert Selbie, then General Manager, commenced a major programme of land development. As the Met began to build – in Moor Park and Rickmansworth and Uxbridge – so too did speculative developers. The pre-railway population of Rickmansworth was just 5,500. By 1939 it stood at 47,700. Passenger revenues doubled between 1913 and 1939. The suburbs were on the rise, and there was money to be made.

According to Foxell, the term 'Metro-land' – now so closely tied to Betjeman – started as a marketing term but gradually became 'accepted as the generic description of a lifestyle'. What Metropolitan Railways knew is what today's property developers know too: selling property is not just about facilities or location, but lifestyle. You can see the appeal to those, like my grandparents, who wish to buy into an entire way of living. Much of their tailoring may have been bespoke – and Grandpa may have built his own house – but the lifestyle they were buying into was off-the-peg English.

The Metropolitan line has been a common thread throughout my life – first connecting me from Amersham to London, then from London to my family. As we shall see in the next two chapters, the line has had a significant influence not only on lifestyles but on landscapes. On revolutionary politics too. It will continue to be a significant presence along this walk.

Rickmansworth aquadrome encapsulated the Metro dream. Foxell describes the allure of Metro-land as being that of 'a tamed semi-rural environment'. In his book is a wonderful map entitled 'Metropolitan Railway and Connections'. Marked in red against the black and white of roads and countryside, the Met line extends from London like a vital artery. The only other details picked out are golf courses: few things epitomise the taming of the landscape quite as neatly as golf. But then so does the aquadrome: its pond and concrete, birds and ice-cream – perfect for a Sunday stroll. In some ways I can hardly really remember it at all, but then sometimes it's the haziest memories that we cling to most closely.

This is the dream that was sold and bought. Metro-land.

But suburbia is changing now. Somewhere along the line, this is the dream that died.

*

On a residential street in Denham, a dog is killed. I'm walking up a gentle slope. Two houses side by side sport posters of bluebells, 'Save Newstead Wood from Development' emblazoned across them. On the other side of the road a little dog darts under a parked car, into the road, and back on to the verge again. It's a tiny thing, hardly a toy even – bred for delicacy, it wouldn't survive a second outside its owners' arms. Wouldn't? It doesn't – the proof is there in front of me. I shout across. 'Your dog is in the road!' I'm ignored. I signal to a car driver. She sees the dog and slows down, driving carefully around and past it.

Thirty seconds later, I am further along the road. I look back. As the dog darts out once more, a second driver fails to see it. It crumples under the wheels. The sound is like boot on snow – soft, then hard. The man disappears inside the house. The woman, in a dressing gown, holds her hands to her head in the horror and grief of a soap opera. I keep walking.

III

Not Quite Suburbia /
Home County Blues

Chalfont St Peter – Chalfont St Giles –

Amersham – Little Missenden – Hyde Heath –

South Heath

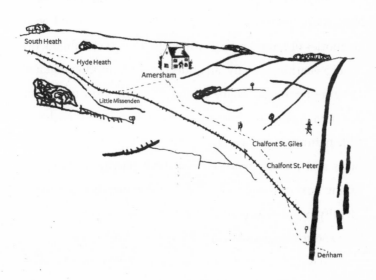

At around 6 p.m. on the second day I find myself walking towards home. Dusk has already descended over Little Chalfont as the fields – dotted with dog walkers – glowed mauve in the day's dying embers. Now, in the hills overlooking Old Amersham, it is dark. Even with my torch I can't see more than a yard or so in front of me. It's easier to see without it, as my eyes adjust to the gloom. For nearly the first time on this walk I know where I'm going. Memory, and the slowly nearing lights of a vast Tesco, guide me homewards.

Writing about place seems now more popular than ever: men (and it is so often men) alone with nature and their thoughts. So often this kind of writing is tinged with memories of home and a yearning after a lost childhood, or, if not a yearning exactly, an undeclared assumption that it is our childhoods that shape us, the places we grew up in that are permanently central to our identity. All these budding little nature writers wandering through the woods, spotting birds and picking wild flowers. Then moving to London, railing against the glass and steel of free-market modernity, identifying the weeds at the side of the road. Reading graffiti tags and fox tracks and calling it psychogeography.

Such writing is rarely shy to name its influences. The likes of Richard Mabey and Roger Deakin are often cited, while Deakin in his turn was influenced by the father of landscape history, W. G. Hoskins. Theirs is an approach to place that privileges the rooted. In *Wildwood*, Deakin quotes Hoskins admiringly when he writes of ancestry as something that keeps us connected to place: 'the immemorial, provincial England, stable, rooted deep in the soil, unmoving, contented and sane'. How are immigrants and their offspring supposed to respond to this kind of writing? Later in the book, Deakin goes to meet the artist David Nash, well known for his wooden sculptures. He praises Nash's work and finds in it further justification for a life lived within limits. Deakin lauds Nash's 'commitment to a settled life in one place'. A little later, he describes Nash's charcoal and pastel drawings of 'sheep spaces' – 'the hollows that animals wear and harden into the ground in their own image over generations'. Deakin sees these marks in the ground as 'signs of settling, of the intimate, long-term connection with the earth that is Nash's own way of life too'.

I read such works with my own sense of loss, or perhaps, of missed opportunity. I've never felt this way about a place. If only I'd had one of those childhoods – filled with hours of carp fishing or building forts in forests. But Amersham, or more specifically Chesham Bois where I grew up, never felt like that kind of place. As a child, the back garden provided my environment for adventure – but always curtailed by already-internalised convention, and laurel hedges. A gap in one hedge in the back left-hand corner of the garden provided a threshold of unbridled excitement. On one bold day, I even ventured through – only to find that the neighbour's neatly mown lawn and flower beds were exactly like those on our side of this no-longer great divide.

Instead, my memories are of helping to dig the local pond – my first (and still only) use of a pickaxe on frozen mud; of chatting happily to Roger the Butcher; of defending the yew tree from marauding aliens; of the lady in the fruit and veg shop with her mittens that were also fingerless gloves. They blew my mind. But not for me those formative adventures – alone amid the vast mystery of an unknown nature. No wilderness. No sublime. Not here in this not-quite-suburbia.

The changing history of landscape aesthetics, as we shall see, has seen nature idealised first as rigidly ordered gardens, then as the lonely mountain-top sublime, and now as hybrid landscapes of industry, memory and wilderness. But what of Buckinghamshire? Nobody writes of Bucks today – except of course to note the influence of the great garden of Stowe. How, then, should I look to write about the places I call home? Might the environmental case against HS2 provide me with a clue?

I had originally decided to pitch my tent in one of the small patches of wood south of Old Amersham – Roger's

Wood or David's Wood – but as I draw near I change my mind. It seems churlish to sleep in a tent when I'm so close to my parents' house. My wife is there too, and by now it's too dark to set up the tent. Besides, I need to lighten the load. I'd completely overestimated the amount I could carry and need to jettison as many unnecessary items as possible. This rucksack weighs a tonne and the excess weight is causing blisters the size of tennis balls across the soles of my feet. I can feel them rub with every step.

I tell myself all of these things, but in truth I just want to be at home. I hate camping.

*

One of the great local controversies of my childhood was the arrival of Tesco. Old Amersham is a historic market town and there was considerable local opposition. Tesco arrived at the tail end of the 1980s. I can't have been more than five or six but I seem to remember my parents talking of little else for months. They were staunchly loyal to the independent village shops, and Waitrose. Tesco – vast, open 24 hours per day – represented the invasion of a vulgar, commercialised modernity. It was not wanted here. Planning permission, my parents told me, was denied by the local council. Tesco appealed at every stage and eventually some Westminster

MP approved the scheme.

Today, Tesco sprawls across the valley to the south-east of historic Old Amersham. It is a village in its own right with petrol station, banking and Fox's outdoor centre. The Fox family has run businesses one kind or another on this site since 1953: first a motoring school, then clothing and army tents, more recently gear for outdoor leisure pursuits. The acquiescence to Tesco of Mr K. Fox lent the supermarket's arrival a veneer of local approval. Rumour has it that he was paid a lot of money. The building's ochre-tiled pitched roofs were conceived as a nod to architectural sensibility. It feels more like a mockery – a reminder that sensitivity to the local vernacular is rarely a concern of those with power and money: now it's merely an aesthetic gesture adopted by a faceless giant.

At all hours of the day, the car park is full; the checkouts never cease to bleep. I cannot find any information online about the political machinations through which Tesco secured planning permission. Neither is there much on what was there before – a meat factory, apparently, and a bus garage. The collective memory is short when the archive is hidden from view. This was twenty-five years ago. In the subsequent years, local shops have predictably closed. The fruit and veg shop I remember so clearly as a child has long gone. With it went the lady with the mittens.

To the west of the Tesco, Old Amersham, with its ramshackle rows of sixteenth-century cottages and the wide high street of a coaching town, is a beautiful place for a Saturday afternoon stroll. Today, its high-end jewellers, tailors and womenswear shops have been supplemented by generic chain restaurants and cafes. All the pubs have been tidied up and ruined. As a young child, Old Amersham's Tudor gables and pubs and shops were of little interest, and the only time I was keen to visit was for the annual Christmas fair, with its bustling crowd and fairground rides. One year, catastrophe almost struck as one of the generators exploded, and a local man became a national hero by leaping into the blazing lorry and driving it to the safety of a nearby field. But that's another story …

The only other occasion for a trip to the old town would be for a haircut. 'Bomber' Harris had his little barber shop on Whieldon Street, just next to an upmarket silversmith's. Their emblem was the glis glis, like a cross between a dormouse and a squirrel, accidentally introduced by the second Baron Rothschild, whose collection forms the basis of the nearby Tring Museum. It's not the only strange species roaming the proudly mown gardens of Buckinghamshire. Muntjac – like squat little deer – are regular visitors to my parents' garden, always chastised for nibbling the wrong flowers. Red kites, too, are a common sight in the skies across both Bucks and neighbouring Oxfordshire, following an intensive re-introduction programme by the RSPB. In a sense, their frequency detracts from what was once a splendid sight – although perhaps that reflects a misjudged appreciation of nature, whereby scarcity equates to importance, within the skewed economics of the collector.

The Amersham of my childhood was therefore 'top' Amersham, Amersham-on-the-Hill, or simply 'the new town'. The early years of the twentieth century saw the town grow up around the station, which was built in 1892. But the arrival of the train here is a little more complicated than it may first appear. Why, for example, would Metropolitan Railways not open a station in Old Amersham, where people actually lived? There was no such place as Amersham-on-the-Hill until the trains came. The reason, as so often with English history, is one of land ownership. The Tyrwhitt Drakes – the local lords of the manor – lived in nearby Shardeloes. They objected to the idea of a railway running through their land: they were worried about their precious view.

The Met, a private company, was forced to alter its route. HS2, with compulsory purchase orders and a compensation budget of at least £10 billion, has no such problems. As rail transport overtook the horse and cart, one side effect of such proprietorial intransigence was the economic stagnation of Old Amersham: arguably it is this that has helped to maintain the old market town so charmingly 'untouched'. It also explains the lack of Victorian terraces anywhere in the Amersham area. Economic growth and architectural preservation rarely make happy bedfellows.

Prior to the arrival of the trains, the area around Amersham was known as Amersham Common. This common land stretched all the way from Little Chalfont to where my cricket club is in Hyde Heath. Farm expansions and the enclosures gradually ate away at this shared grazing land. In an age that only valued the environment on what it could provide for man – crops or hunting or elegantly landscaped vistas – that which was not turned to profit was deemed waste. It's a familiar attitude today. The Commons were broken up and taken over, and the age of land ownership was consolidated. An Englishman's home is his castle, so it's said. The phrase, or something similar, comes from Cicero, but one of its earliest expressions in English comes from William Blackstone's *Commentaries on the Laws of England*. The book was published in the 1760s, shortly before the first Inclosure Act of 1773.

Ownership of land – for some – became enshrined in our laws and in our national psyche. Perhaps it already was: Sir Roy Strong, art historian, curator and landscape designer, has argued that land ownership was an integral part of English national identity since it was first defined in the Elizabethan age. In an article for *The Telegraph*, he wrote:

In England land ownership embodied economic wealth, social status and political power. Unlike on mainland Europe, where kings were absolute, we were a parliamentary democracy and the basis for power was not living in town or attendance at court but in the country where landowners built houses and were buried in their parish church.

Gradually, more and more people came to own their own land. In his early conservative years, Richard Jefferies argued that a 'sense of ownership engenders a pride in the place'. Something similar underpinned Thatcher's policy of right-to-buy. The flipside is what has come to be known, thanks to American ecologist Garett Hardin, as the tragedy of the commons. If pride in a place comes to be defined in relation to the sense of ownership, then those places which are not owned by any one individual or group are easily overlooked, neglected or simply exploited. Once that happens it is easy for somebody to step in and take ownership – especially when those charged with protecting common land (the government, local councils) find themselves strapped for cash. That is what is happening to public space in London, and our realisation comes too late.

Today, it is the manner in which HS2 rides roughshod over an individual's long-established right to ownership that is such an affront to so many. In part that explains why opposition to the project unites both left and right, the Green Party and UKIP. This strikes me again and again when I speak to those affected further along the route. Today Amersham Common exists in name only.

It's hard to see how anybody could have strong feelings for a place like Amersham these days. It is simply a satellite – a place for people to live and raise families. While, at one time, the growth of suburbia was an arrow to the future (according to the prophet Betjeman), now it seems in terminal decline. No new restaurant lasts more than a year. The charity shops and estate agents slowly multiply.

I often try to imagine what Amersham must have been like when my parents first moved here. A little slice of the neatly nearly-rural to call your own. A place to raise a family and easily leave. I've always found it hard to see the allure, but it must be there: the surrounding towns of Beaconsfield, Gerrards Cross and Chalfont St Giles are some of the most expensive in the country. Easy access to London is a significant factor. So are the local schools. The average price of a house in Chesham Bois, where I was born and brought up, is £832,000. The Metro-land dream may have long faded, but the lifestyle it created is still a desirable one.

Amersham, however, has changed significantly since then. There are more people, for a start, and there's more traffic. In a 1989 article for *Town Planning Review*, J. W. R. Whitehand produced a pair of maps to demonstrate the extent of the change. In 1960, the area around Chesham Road was chiefly comprised of large, detached houses, each some way apart from the others. By 1987, these have nearly all been replaced by estates of smaller dwellings more tightly packed together. One major cause of the change has been infilling, by which new properties are built on the spare land between houses. In other cases, existing houses have been demolished to be replaced by flats or several smaller houses. In part this is down to the restrictions on developing in the green belt. It is also due to the desire for profit. In a 1990 article also for *Town Planning Review*, Whitehand demonstrated that much of this activity was initiated not by developers, as might be assumed, but by existing homeowners, seeking to maximise the value of their land. Home may be a castle, but not when there's money to be made. Often, explains Whitehand, estate agents would encourage individuals to seek planning permission for their land in order to then sell to a developer, who would profit in turn from increasing the number of properties on the land. Today, the streets are busy with cars, a succession of mini-roundabouts clogged at all hours.

Intriguingly, Whitehand is critical of the slowness with which the local council processed planning applications. Those from individuals, he points out, usually moved considerably more slowly than those from developers. He cites the example of Oakfield Corner in particular: 'Some of the formal reasons for rejecting applications appear to have had little justification and others were evidently spurious.' At some stage, the council clearly ran out of reasons to say no: in the late-1990s, Berkeley Homes built a number of new flats on Oakfield Close, just back from the roundabout at Oakfield Corner. Locals harrumphed about it for months: more homes, more people, more traffic. Oakfield Corner is home to one of John Kennard's distinctive mock-Tudor designs with its white walls and black beams. It's been a charity shop for as long as I can remember. Opposite is a curved brick building from the 1930s that possesses, now I think about it, an understated kind of style. It is currently a NatWest bank.

In 2012, Tesco made a second foray into Amersham in the form of a new coffee shop. The arrival of Harris + Hoole was the talk of the town: finally, an alternative to Costa – a little slice of London hipster culture right here in Amersham. Serving flat whites and artisan sandwiches, Harris + Hoole was welcomed with open arms. Named after two coffee-loving characters in Samuel Pepys' diary, the company was set up by Nick, Andrew and Laura Tolley, who previously founded Taylor Street Baristas in 2006. You wouldn't know it to visit, but the company, it turns out, is also 49% owned by Tesco. This news took a while to filter through: the place is still packed. There's no such thing as local any more, but instead of multinationals taking the blame, it's immigration.

On the prow of the hill just behind Amersham station stands High and Over, a pristine white tranche of continental modernism glimpsed through the trees and the 1960s dwellings of Station Road. It was built in 1929 by acclaimed architect Anyas Douglas Connell for Bernard Ashmole – war hero, archaeologist and art historian. It was featured in *The House Book*, published by Phaidon in 2001. 'The last great British country house,' it said, 'and the first modern house in the English countryside.' I never noticed it.

Strangely for somebody who has yet to learn to drive, as a child I was far more interested in the turquoise Chevrolet we occasionally used to see parked in one of the driveways. Usually all that was visible was the fleeting glimpse of an all-American tail-fin glowing in a dark garage. One memorable day it was parked out on the road in all its ludicrous exotic glory. After that, I never saw it again.

A more lasting fixture is just around the corner from the station: my father's office, with its stuffed owls, ten-tonne fax machine and the strange smell of old filing cabinets. On the wall, a black and white photograph of a young boy running around with arms outstretched, clearly pretending to be an aeroplane. 'Can you ever remember anyone playing chartered accountants?' reads the caption. No, was dad's answer to the rhetorical question. His was not a profession I ever seriously considered.

*

My wife takes pity on me and picks me up in the car outside Tesco. We drive up the hill, past my father's office, past Oakfield Corner, and home.

*

My walk resumes at 6 a.m. The sun is rising, cold and bright over the frosty fields of the Misbourne valley. I've never realised how beautiful this area is. Bright browns of autumn, rich wet greens silvered over by the sparkling frost. Mist rises in clouds from the Misbourne. A Maginot Line of molehills weaves across a frosty front lawn by the cricket club. My footsteps crackle and pheasants trundle away across the cricket field and into the hedgerows. Birds chatter in the trees. I walk by the banks of the river, putting up grouse and a shapely grey heron. I look left up to creamy-stoned Shardeloes, the ancestral home of the Tyrwhitt-Drake family, smartly overseeing its prospect.

From as far back as 1626 and for over 200 years, there was rarely a period when at least one of the two MPs for Amersham was not a Drake or a Tyrwhitt Drake. Under the family, Amersham was what is known as a 'rotten borough' – it had a tiny electorate and the landowners could effectively control who their two MPs would be. This they duly did to gain unrepresentative influence in the House of Commons. Not that they used it much: neither of the Tyrwhitt Drakes bothered with Parliament, except to oppose Catholic emancipation and the Reform Act which eventually abolished their seats in 1832.

Shardeloes was built between 1758 and 1766. There had previously been a manor house on the site but it was demolished by William Drake, Sr to make way for his new one. The building was designed in the Palladian style by Stiff Leadbetter, one of the most successful architect-builders of the period. Robert Adam provided the interiors and Humphrey Repton configured the grounds in classical English landscape fashion. The lake I pass on my right, misty and evocative in the cold November morning, was formed by Repton after he dammed the Misbourne. Shardeloes itself was requisitioned for use as a maternity hospital during

World War II. It was later saved from demolition by The Amersham Society with help from the Campaign to Protect Rural England. It is now luxury flats.

HS2 will run right through here – whether overground or under is yet to be decided. An access shaft is to be located a few paces west of where I am now. The lake and this gentle slope may seem fixed, eternal, 'natural'. But nature here has a history – a beginning under Repton, and now, it seems, an end.

For the first time I'm hit by a palpable sense of loss, or imminent loss – for what, I'm not entirely sure. Nonetheless, the feeling is there. It runs hand in hand with my delight in this early morning beauty, filling the centre of my senses with a cloud of sadness (present and future) that, if anything, crystallises the landscape's gentle-sloped, mist-tinted wonder. I stop walking. I take photos: a rook high and alone in an ancient oak; a wooden stile, straight out of a Constable painting; the sun gleaming over frost-furred farms; the footsteps of a fellow walker marking rich green in the silver slopes as he heads east away from me – side by side along the river and away, over the gentle hill and out of sight. Constable's paintings of Dedham Vale on the border between Essex and Suffolk were in part an attempt to preserve a landscape threatened by the industrial revolution. Perhaps I'm trying to do something similar by photographing the landscapes of my home. In 2010, Transport Secretary Philip Hammond described this precise area as 'not some Constable country'. Although my carefully composed photos suggest otherwise, Hammond is right: the A413 runs parallel to the Misbourne just a few yards away from me. It's easy to ignore if you're used to it.

When Hammond's comments were reported, locals were incensed by what they saw as a slight on their beloved home county. But what bothers me is the implication that the UK's only landscapes worth saving are those that fit within the aesthetics of the late Romantics. Campaigners have cited the presence nearby of rare wildlife such as Bechstein's bats and great crested newts. But they do not prove Hammond wrong; rather, it demonstrates that, like the trout swimming up the Colne, animals have very different criteria of value than our own.

Despite the beauty of landscaped grounds such as those here at Shardeloes, architect and critic Sam Jacob has gone so far as to describe the picturesque as 'dangerous'. In fact, it is its very beauty that makes it so:

the picturesque is dangerous because it presents seductive pictorial views that look entirely natural yet cloak immense power. Even more – the picturesque naturalises power by producing images which look naturally immutable.

Such criticisms apply especially to the kind of landscaping carried out on behalf of the landed gentry by Repton, Capability Brown and others in the name of the picturesque. I know that my understanding of what is natural has been shaped by this history. I know that it is an understanding tethered to a particular history and a particular politics. But right now I couldn't care less. Right now, I feel alive with an ecstatic sadness as I enter Little Missenden. It was here, I think, that the idea for this walk first crystallised. It is here that my father walks every Saturday to meet his two closest friends at the pub. He wears his StopHS2 jumper with pride. By a bridge over the Misbourne stand a pair of brick houses that I've always loved. Nearby, mud-spattered and dimly lit beneath the trees, a sign: StopHS2. Such signs are dotted throughout this charming village. I walk on, upwards towards South Heath.

In nearby Hyde Heath, a last vestige of common land remains: a sloping expanse of grass framed by woods on three sides and a road on the other. In the north-east corner stand a slide, some swings and a climbing frame. I've played cricket here since I was fifteen, but it's only been in the past six years or so that I've started to play more regularly. From early May to mid-September, I'm there almost every Sunday, embarrassing myself on the village green, afterwards reliving it all in the downbeat surrounds of The Plough across the road.

People always ask what the appeal of cricket is, and to be honest I'm not entirely sure. But I've come to love the club. In 2013 I tried playing for a team of London journalists, but spending hours standing around in a field with a bunch of people you don't know is simply tedious. The fun is sharing in the success of friends you've known for years, but also revelling in the fractious arguments of people who know exactly which button to push to piss each other off. Lately, I've discovered wild garlic in the surrounding woods and started bringing bunches back to London. As soon as he found out, our strike bowler, whose parents live right on the common, promised to piss on it whenever he remembered.

The Plough is a pub that clings on – how, I'm not entirely sure. But where so many village pubs have slowly died or been unceremoniously knocked down and converted into flats, The Plough somehow survives. Lager, ale and crisps. Cigarettes, a fruit machine. The new landlord and his wife actually seem to enjoy running a pub. They bring in guest ales and organise events. They do lock-ins. There is still the sense that the pub serves food only because it has to. Lone local men perch at the bar, waiting for the company of their fellow man and offending him when he arrives.

In some ways it's a dispiriting place; in others, it has the perfect balance. It serves the needs of its community. Thankfully, there's no competition. The cricket club is part of this community and this community crystallises in the pub. This is important.

Other clubs drink their after-match pints in their pavilions: cut off from their surroundings, the talk can only ever be of cricket. Hyde Heath cricket club is a part of the community – there are other people here, and other ideas. It is in pubs like this that world views collide and must attempt to justify themselves. Most of my friends have similar backgrounds or similar interests; arguably, Hyde Heath is the melting pot that London likes to think it is. How often do Hackney's graphic designers interact with the local Turkish men, beyond ordering a kebab or a haircut? How many of the artists meet people from the estates if it's not to produce an Arts Council-funded project about them? In the village, the CEO of a global multinational plays alongside a local taxi driver; privileged white males alongside Pakistanis from Chesham; Londoners, locals, teenagers, adults with young children, retirees: all converge in cricket and The Plough.

It's very different to The Red Lion, a pub in nearby Chesham Bois that I worked in for several months in an endless summer between school and university. I lied my way into that job: 'Yes, of course I've worked behind a bar before.' How hard could it be? As my first pint of Carlsberg Export exploded all over the floor I was an easy target for the assembled barroom wits.

'Can you put a whiskey in the top of that?' was a favourite quip.

That evening I was a sitting duck: the new boy, the posh kid – fair game for the pub jesters and easy prey, I must have seemed, for a lusty-minded Canadian lady of sizeable dimensions. With little alternative, I was paid the princely sum of £5 for a kiss on the lips. It was my first and only foray into the world's oldest profession. 'If you come back after tonight,' said Len the landlord, 'you'll be here for a while.'

He was right. I grew to love that place and its cast of bizarre characters. Never before had I encountered such people – it's hard now to think they were even real. There was Terry, whose Carling was always to be poured into a special glass, ready and waiting just as he reached the bar. He was a bag of tricks, with his fake £50 notes and semi-amiable deception: 'I gave you £20.' 'No, Terry, it was definitely £10.' There was something threatening lurking beneath the surface jokes. Then there was the drunken couple who sat and slurred at the bar all day, while a vast greyhound lolled at their feet. They told me the same anecdote every single day – something about smuggling a hip flask into a tea party at Buckingham Palace. I rarely ever understood a word they said. Then there was Jumbo – aptly named – who came in one night as his marriage collapsed and ordered the whole four-and-a-half-litre bottle of Famous Grouse from behind the bar and took it home. 'That'll be his supper,' said Len. He wasn't joking.

Then, finally, there was the local poacher – or so I liked to think of him. Maybe he was the gamekeeper. Dan, I think. I'm surprised I can't remember his name, so clear is his visage etched upon my memory: thick, dark sideburns, checked shirt, faded green gilet, quilted and patched. Each evening he came and perched at the corner of the bar – the same spot every time, from 6 p.m. until closing. Carefully he counted out his change, asked if I was free and requested another Carling. The last of the Buckinghamshire accent: a rural burring slur, now gone for good. There was genuine affection on my last night of work as we said goodbye. It was only then that I realised he had been standing up all this time – every night for a timeless life.

It was so tight-knit, that place, that it was almost violent. It was an uneasy atmosphere that accompanied the exiles from Amersham's Boot and Slipper, at that time undergoing 'improvements' courtesy of Chef and Brewer. It is now one of those pub-themed pubs with 'home-cooked fare' and hops in the hallway. The Boot lot drank ale and smoked cigars. They probably vote UKIP now. The Red Lion locals were Carling drinkers, Bensons on the go at all times. Now I think of it, they probably vote UKIP too. The smoking ban would have hit that pub hard. It has now been knocked down and converted into flats.

The Plough is not so extreme. The locals don't go silent when a stranger enters. I like to think the cricket club helps with that. There are always new people coming and going and keeping the regulars entertained. Every August bank holiday, staff from the Bank of England come to play against Hyde Heath. After the match, they dress up like idiots and head to The Plough. Blacking up is not unknown. I'm surprised the *Daily Mail* hasn't sent a photographer along.

Apart from my parents, this cricket club is my strongest link to the local area – the only thing that ties me to a sense of community here. Why then is it always closest to home that I get the most lost?

I've walked up the hill from Missenden towards South Heath. On the OS map a motte and bailey is picked out in evocative Gothic script – a historic monument of some significance I imagine, right here on my doorstep. Why did I never know about this? I'm excited to see the remnants of this ancient fort, a clue to the area's past lives. I peer through a hedgerow where the map says it ought to be. I see nothing. There is nothing but a gentle grassed mound, maybe a couple of feet higher than the surrounding lawn. This, it gradually dawns on me, is it. This is the great relic of South Bucks pre-history. On top of it stands a goalpost. A yard or so away lies a football, half-deflated.

This is not the only time on my journey that such apparently historic sites prove more impressive on the map than in person. Were it not for the OS map, who would know about such things, or care?

Head full of thoughts, I take the wrong footpath and end up walking in the wrong direction – heading north and east when I want to stick north-west. I can see the wood I should be aiming for, but I'm the wrong side of a thick and prickly hedgerow. Spotting a gap, I struggle through and head across the open field in what I think now must be the right direction. It is once inside the wood, however, that things start to go wrong. I decide to attempt a clever shortcut – how hard can it be? – but it's not long before I realise my error. There may be footpaths in this little square of woodland, but this is pheasant territory and each path is simply a spoke outwards from the central feeding station. Time and again I arrive back in the middle, where birds eat from blue plastic containers to get fat and get shot. It is the only reason the pheasants are here; indeed, it is the only reason the wood itself is here. Otherwise, this too would be fields. After half an hour or so of aimless tramping, I rather wish it was open fields.

I walk in circles, crashing through bracken and old beech trees, wading through brambles and nettles, intent on taking the most direct route from one side of the wood to the other.

Why I'm being so pig-headed about this is unclear, even to me. I eventually emerge on the wrong side, walking up the wrong road. I've been walking now for two and a half days and I'm two minutes away from the pub I drink in every Sunday. My lack of progress could hardly be more stark. I begin to feel ridiculous again. I can only hope – as I trudge along the road – that I'm not spotted by anyone I know.

From one woodland to another: just to the south of South Heath, on the left of King's Lane as I walk up it, is Sibley's Coppice. This ancient woodland will be decimated by HS2. According to a report on the Chilterns AONB website, the south-west corner of the wood will be destroyed by 120 metres of the line. 'Although there will ultimately be a green tunnel here,' it says, 'the construction of the cut and cover tunnel could cause a wide corridor of damage and a greater loss of habitat.' The report goes on to detail the likely indirect impacts, including changes in hydrology, habitat fragmentation, noise disturbance, dust and air pollution from the cutting – particularly during construction – and even changes in air flows ('due to passing of trains and structural change in woodland canopy').

The report is typical of so many attempts up and down the line to highlight the destruction to be wrought by HS2 on a local area. Characteristically, it attempts to underline the unique importance of this particular woodland habitat.

'This acid oak and beech wood,' it says, 'has 17 ancient woodland indicator plants including several which are rare in Bucks, namely sessile oak, southern woodrush and remote sedge.' The report is thick with the language of conservation management: 'Biological Notification Sites', 'BAP priority wood-pasture', 'ancient woodland indicator plants'. This is of course a strategy designed to underscore value through the use of independently established criteria, rather than, say, appeals to emotion or justice or ethics. For such things cannot be measured. But this kind of approach runs the risk of playing into the hands of the politicians and the developers: ancient woodland is no longer only identified by its indicators but defined by them. Tree species may come to seem valuable only insofar as they have been designated 'truly ancient' or 'valuable'. In Sibley's Coppice, thirteen such trees stand to be destroyed by HS2.

This is not dissimilar to the approach taken by Stewart Pomeroy at Colne Valley. It is a widespread tactic in conservation. Another tactic that has gained ground in recent years is attempting to translate such values into financial ones. In 2013, for example, UK charity the Game and Wildlife Conservation Trust (GWCT) announced the launch of a pan-European research project to detail the economic benefits of nature. The ongoing project is being funded by the European Commission, with the intention of examining 'how we can best protect vital natural resources, across Europe'.

The study – entitled the QUESSA project (which stands for Quantification of Ecosystem Services for Sustainable Agriculture) – aims to identify 'natural key habitats' and develop conservation systems for farmers and policy-makers. QUESSA will take four years, is receiving €3 million from the European Framework's 7 programme, and involves research partners from France, Italy, Germany, Netherlands, Switzerland, Estonia, Hungary and the UK.

The argument made by GWCT is that, by understanding the natural environment in terms of its economic benefits, we will be better able to protect our natural resources. At the time of the project's launch, GWCT's press release cited DEFRA figures to argue that 'pollinators alone are worth £430 million per year to British agriculture'. A 2015 article in *The Telegraph* observed that this made bees more valuable to the UK economy than the royal family.

At the time, in 2013, Dr John Holland, an entomologist with the GWCT, said:

With wildlife declining across Europe, the QUESSA project will help to identify areas ... that need to be targeted and improved to maximise their use by pollinators, natural pest controllers, wildlife or to help improve soil conservation and provide clean water.

We will be particularly looking at how we can improve semi-natural habitats outside and within crops in order to provide a true value on the natural services that each habitat provides.

To those who feel that nature should be valued for its intrinsic importance, rather than for the effective delivery of 'natural services', this kind of consultant-speak approach could be considered a part of the problem, rather than a potential solution. Such an approach follows the logic of the cost-benefit analysis, a logic that will come to seem deeply flawed.

It is this – or something like it – that bothers me here in Sibley's Coppice. What strikes me reading the Chilterns AONB report is the way in which, by adopting the strategies and language of the planner or developer, the argument is already made vulnerable. The loss of thirteen trees, however old they may be, whatever it is they might indicate, hardly seems especially significant in a project of the scale of HS2. Besides – and more importantly – the value of ancient woodland is not necessarily related to the age of the individual trees within it.

The concept of ancient woodland was developed by the ecologist Oliver Rackham in his 1980 book *Ancient Woodland, its History, Vegetation and Uses in England.* According to the Woodland Trust, 'ancient woodland is woodland which has been continuously wooded or managed since 1600'. These habitats develop slowly over time, creating unique and complex ecological systems of fungi, lichen and other plants. As Rackham wrote in a 2008 article for *New Phytologist*: 'Ancient woodland does not necessarily involve ancient trees': it contains some of the most biologically diverse and threatened species of both plants and animals in the whole of the UK. According to the Chilterns AONB report, in Sibley's Coppice this includes sessile oak, southern woodrush and remote sedge, as well as, in its wetter corners, wavy bittercress and soft rush. This is why simply planting new trees – as espoused by Boris Johnson – does not work. Nor does the transplanting of old trees to new locations. As Sara Maitland noted in *Gossip from the Forest*: 'We tend to think of "forests" or "woodlands" as places for trees ... but it is whole habitats, not individual trees or even species, that we need to conserve.'

In a 2012 letter to Cheryl Gillan, the local Conservative MP for Chesham and Amersham, then-Transport Secretary Justine Greening sought to assuage the concerns of Gillan's constituents over the loss of ancient woodland. One solution, she said almost unbelievably, might be 'transplanting woodland to an adjacent site'. Predictably, there was widespread outrage when the contents of the letter found its way into the media. The important thing about ancient woodland, argued many, is that it's ancient. The clue is rather in the name. Arguments like Greening's are practically beyond parody, but they do contain a certain kind of rationality. If ancient woodland is valuable only insofar as it contains various 'indicator species', then surely you can simply put those indicator species somewhere else? That is the logic of the zoo.

I wonder if there is an analogy to be made between the transplanting of such ancient ecosystems and the systematic removal from the capital of communities such as those in the Regent's Park Estate and the Heygate. Or rather, I wonder how far such an analogy may be pushed? In an article for *The Observer*, Rowan Moore described London as the 'city that ate itself'. 'It is suffering a form of entropy,' he wrote, 'whereby the distinctive or special is converted into property values.' As writer and curator Isabel de Vasconcellos commented: 'A city is an organism. If you carve it out, there'll be nothing left but a beautifully embalmed body.' Strikingly similar is Rackham's description of the attempt to relocate or recreate ancient woodland. It is, he says, doomed to failure:

Some features, like giant coppice stools and the creatures that live on them, can be created only through the passage of time. The result, at best, will be pastiche: it will be like throwing away a painting by Constable and substituting a painting by Tom Keating in the style of Constable.

That is why the effort has been made to emphasise the uniqueness of Sibley's Coppice. But the indicators through which to underscore the wood's irreplaceability are at risk of being the very things that enable its replacement. Gradually awareness is rising that this approach to valuation is hugely problematic. Perhaps it is this realisation that has fuelled the current interest in writing and thinking about place – as tangled knots of relations that cannot be reduced to a single building, species, story or method of evaluation. As then-Green Party leader Natalie Bennett argued in an article for the Institute of Art and Ideas: 'we must avoid the current approach of putting a monetary value on nature. The implication then is always that it can be traded off, that nature fits within economics, when in fact it's the other way around.'

She goes on to allude specifically to HS2 and effects on places like Sibley's Coppice:

I'm very much opposed to biodiversity off-setting, because the fact is, if you have an ancient forest, for example, you cannot replace that. It is literally irreplaceable. The true value is just beyond valuation. Planting a thousand trees somewhere else simply doesn't make up for the whole ecology that you're losing if you're going to, say, stick a high-speed train through it.

It is hard to argue with Bennet here. But it is also hard to see how values 'beyond valuation' could make themselves heard amid the din of modern market economics that so fills the ears of our leaders.

What such debates draw our attention to is not only the difficulty in protecting ancient woodland, but exactly what it is that we're trying to protect. For there is no consensus here. In recent years, there have been growing calls for what has come to be known as rewilding. The term was coined by activist Dave Foreman in 1990, and entered the mainstream in 2013 with the publication of *Feral*, George Monbiot's personal manifesto on the subject. The idea of rewilding is that nature is best left to its own devices. Humans should think long term, step back, and stop attempting to manage nature. Monbiot describes it as 'the mass restoration of ecosystems': it is, he argues, 'an opportunity to reverse the destruction of the natural world'. Rewilding is often accompanied by the human-instigated return of large predators such as bears and wolves in order to initiate what are known as trophic cascades – effects in the food chain that see those at the bottom blossom because predators start to keep grazers like deer, sheep and rabbits in check.

The idea that nature flourishes best when left alone is not new. The tidiness of those who supposedly look after our landscapes – and especially our woodlands – has been under attack for decades. I can't help but think of the man with the leaf-blower outside Euston station. In an 1881 essay entitled 'Trees About Town', Richard Jefferies urged his readers:

> Do not clear away the fallen branches and brown leaves, sweeping the plantation as if it were the floor of a ball-room, for it is just the tangle and the wilderness that brings the birds, and they like the disarray.

What is natural for Jefferies is aligned with what is untidy. It is only humans who seek after order. This line of thinking continues in the writings of Roger Deakin. In his posthumously published 2007 book, *Wildwood*, Deakin criticises humanity's attitude towards the environment as one of 'too much management and not enough informed neglect'. This chimes closely with the views set out in *Feral*. Monbiot is highly critical of what he sees as 'the desire for tidiness' among the UK's landscape managers. 'Even by European standards,' he writes, 'the UK has a peculiar fear of nature, and its conservationists a peculiar fear of letting go.'

Again, there is a striking overlap here between the language of woodland management and the language of urban management. Like our woods, our cities have been places of neglect. If woodlands thrive by being left alone, might housing estates too? This is not to advocate for neglect – we have seen the problems that can cause – but for the empowerment of community groups and residents' associations. As we saw at Alexandra Road, councils have historically been reluctant to do this, but maybe it's time for a rethink. Perhaps pride in a place need not be dependent on ownership: perhaps Deakin's idea of 'informed neglect' could be translated to the urban context by empowering and financing local residents and then, where possible, leaving them alone. This may be the logic that underpinned David Cameron's 'Big Society' – at least as it was originally conceived by theorist Phillip Blond.

It is interesting here to contrast Monbiot's sentiments with those espoused by John Betjeman. In his essay 'Middlesex', from 1963, Betjeman worries about the loss of 'the delicate attractions of the county'. His affection, characteristically, is for the human-scale: 'old brick walls, inns and farm buildings'. He writes:

Unless there is public will to preserve and maintain the wild and the natural, the old and the gentle, then all the Home Counties will suffer the same fate.

The idea that 'the natural' is something that needs to be preserved and maintained is increasingly out of favour amongst those who, like Monbiot, advocate rewilding. Monbiot, I imagine, would baulk at the use of 'wild' and 'natural' in such a context – the old buildings of the Home Counties! He would baulk further at the equation of 'wild and natural' with 'old and gentle'. Monbiot's nature is not old; it is ancient. And it is by no means gentle; it is violent and dangerous and thrillingly so.

But Monbiot's view is also a controversial one: increasingly popular among the radical left, but less wholeheartedly embraced by certain conservationists. Like Monbiot, Oliver Rackham, one of the most influential ecological thinkers of the last fifty years, has also been critical of aspects of woodland management, especially in relation to how we conceive neglect. In 'Landscape and the Conservation of Meaning', published in the *RSA Journal*, Rackham wrote that:

Neglect is too often presented as an aspect of the bad old days which will somehow not occur in the future, rather than as a neutral aspect of human nature whose effects should be understood, provided for and turned to advantage.

Where Rackham differs from Monbiot, however, is in the nuance of his argument and his comparative lack of ideology. Where Monbiot has a vision and is writing for a non-specialist public, Rackham is able to be more sensitive to the individual characteristics of place. Monbiot, for example, advocates for the return of wild boar. 'Boar,' he writes, 'are the untidiest animals to have lived in this country since the Iron Age. This should commend them to anyone with an interest in the natural world.' Rackham, meanwhile, is more equivocal. In a 2008 article for *New Phytologist*, he points out the destructive impact that such animals can have: 'In North America feral domestic pigs and European wild pigs, let loose in a pigless continent, have reinforced the proliferating deer in eliminating woodland herbs.' I don't pretend to know which side I ought to be on in such discussions. Perhaps it's not a matter of taking sides.

I had just finished reading Monbiot's book before setting out on this walk. My head was full of huge, dark woods, full of latent danger and excitement. Perhaps it's for that reason that, to me, Sibley's Coppice feels distinctly tame. It is, as the name suggests, a coppiced wood – it has been managed in the same way for hundreds of years. Today it seems neat and tidy and rather pretty as the sun shines through the burnt ochre oak canopy. But exciting? Or even unique? Hardly.

Monbiot would not be interested in a place like Sibley's Coppice. But Rackham might be. For the act of coppicing is another point of difference between the two. Rackham seems largely in favour. He acknowledges that 'English ancient woods have all been managed and exploited for centuries or millennia' – but, he says, they are still 'natural vegetation and are not artefacts'. It is complex issue: what exactly is natural? At what point does human intervention become unnatural? Rackham himself seems to struggle. His attempt to differentiate between the 'normal dynamics' of a woodland ecosystem and changes that might be more threatening are never entirely clear-cut. For Rackham – and arguably this is both a strength and a weakness – there are no hard and fast rules. What he is especially attuned to is the importance of analysing individual cases – their unique histories, locations, microclimates, ecosystems – and how they relate to the larger whole. He is not, as far as I can see, attempting to fix a generalised law of conservation.

Monbiot, however, is more critical of the practice. He uses coppicing as an example of the self-fulfilling nature of much UK conservation: 'Woods are coppiced … to sustain the past impacts of coppicing.' It may even harm the uniqueness of an ecosystem. He cites Clive Hambler and Martin Speight, who argue that while the practice may favour butterfly species which can thrive in many habitats, it 'harms woodland beetles and moths that can live nowhere else'. Earlier in the book, Monbiot does betray a brief fascination with coppicing – namely the idea that it may only succeed because of an evolutionary response developed by certain species of tree to the presence of large mammals such as elephants. Intriguingly, it is Rackham who Monbiot cites for this idea.

Perhaps the origin of these differences between Rackham's approach to management and Monbiot's espousal of rewilding is the state held by each to be ideal. While Monbiot acknowledges early on in *Feral* that '[t]here was no state of grace, no golden age in which people lived in harmony with nature', he nonetheless seeks a return, in certain areas, to a conception of nature that precedes the presence of mankind.

But how far back should we go? It's worth pointing out that humans have been trying to manage nature since our early years as a species. Even before the dawn of organised agriculture, humans may have been altering their habitat through the planting of favoured trees, the 'beating' of game, herding and husbandry. Indeed, biologist Colin Tudge has written that we ought to refer to the first humans not as hunter-gatherers but as 'wildlife managers'.

Rackham, however, limits his scope to the last few hundred or thousand years. He draws a distinction between 'ancient woodland' and 'virgin forest' or 'wildwood', which he describes as 'ecosystems that have escaped human intervention'. For Rackham, the environment is a collaboration in which humans are involved. Monbiot comes very close to advocating the removal of people altogether. This is where he gets into trouble – both with a Welsh farmer called Dafydd, who is a recurring presence in the book, and with his own sensitivity to the vexed history of similar undertakings. In Slovenia, rewilding has come about accidentally as a direct result of human atrocities – first Nazism, then the ethnic cleansing under Marshall Tito. As Gary Budden commented in an essay on the subject: 'Clearly, an environmentalist's delight can also be a humanitarian disaster.'

Dafydd, whose ideas are addressed at some length in *Feral*, feels his way of life is threatened by Monbiot's advocacy of rewilding. 'Conservation,' he says, 'should be about how we can live in nature. When it deviates from that, you forget that you're still looking at it from a human perspective. I think rewilding is an oxymoron. As William Cronon puts it, if you argue for wilderness for its own sake, you're still imposing a human point of view.'

Dafydd is probably right, so too Cronon. There is a

paradox at the heart of rewilding, and at the heart of much contemporary thinking about the environment. It is ultimately impossible to move beyond a human point of view. But does that mean we ought not to try? We have imaginations, after all. I'll be forced to think more about this in a field north of Aylesbury. For now, I'm reaching the far side of Sibley's Coppice. It's tiny and neat and pleasant: perhaps an inappropriate receptacle for all these debates about wolves and Nazis and anthropocentrism. But it's places like Sibley's Coppice and Burnham Beeches – managed by the City of London Corporation since 1879 – that informed my childhood understanding of what nature is. That it could be so much more – indeed, that it once was – I have only recently begun to learn. That is why I will never be a nature writer. That, and I don't know the names of half the things I'm looking at. I hear a bird shriek somewhere up in the trees. I have no idea what it is.

To walk in such places now is to be confronted by a lack of knowledge: not only in the larger, conceptual sense of the limits of human understanding – there are some things we will simply never know – but in the more immediate sense – more personal, more real – that I simply don't know very much about nature. I don't know the names of these trees that I walk among. I don't know which are ancient and which are merely very old, which have been carefully coppiced and which left alone. I'm not the only one: councillors, planners, developers and politicians are all making decisions about the environment with as little knowledge about it as me. For much of the rest of the walk this will colour almost all of my thoughts.

In his seminal 1955 book, *The Making of the English Landscape*, W. G. Hoskins writes that 'The English landscape itself, to those who know how to read it aright, is the richest historical record we possess.' I'm increasingly worried that, in the language of landscape, I may be only semi-literate. Without the knowledge of the nature writers, my experience, it seems, is a narrow one. Without knowledge of nature, says Hoskins, 'the enjoyment may be real, but it is limited in scope and in the last resort vaguely diffused in emotion'.

As I walk, something cries out overhead with a shrill and joyous call. Once outside the coppice, I catch sight of a kite. *Did you make that noise?* I wonder, almost out loud. Perched in ungainly fashion on the crest of a fir tree in the front of somebody's garden, the kite looks away from me, and declines to answer.

IV

Chilterns:
Any Other
Nature Business

Wendover – Aylesbury – Waddesdon –

Quainton

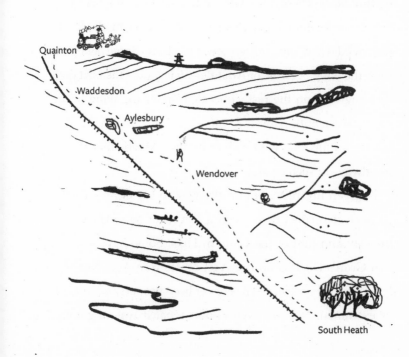

In a hedge outside Aylesbury I spot a firecrest. Or at least I think I do: a tiny glint of flame zipping through a dark green block of privet. But I may just have imagined it; I had firecrests on the mind ahead of my scheduled meeting with Roger and Jenny Waller in a pub of that name on the A413 south of Wendover.

At just three and a half inches long, the firecrest is one of Britain's smallest birds – weighing about the same as a knob of butter. Pale green and grey and white and plump, it gets its name from the shock of red and yellow jutting up from its tiny head. There is something manic about the firecrest, but also something regal. In a moment of lyricism, the RSPB described it as a 'tiny, restless jewel of a bird'. Some believe it to be the 'king of birds' of Aristotelean legend – the bird that flew higher than the rest, concealed under the wing of an eagle. Its scientific name is *Regulus ignicapilla*, which literally means 'a little king with its hair on fire'. Maybe that's why it's always in such a panic.

Between firecrests, I'm on the way to see Grim's Ditch, an ancient earthwork stretching eleven or so miles across the clay and flint of the Chiltern Hills. Some have argued that Grim's Ditch is Bronze Age, others Iron Age. Nobody knows for sure because it has never been properly excavated or examined. Nobody even knows what it was originally for, or even why it is called Grim's Ditch. In places, these earthworks are large, visible structures in the landscape. To walk the Ridgeway through Oxfordshire, for example, is to be acutely aware of the labourers of the past – building this vast spine across the countryside.

Here, in the Misbourne Valley, however, Grim's Ditch is only noticeable because it's marked on my OS map in evocative Gothic script. Here be history, such fonts denote. But amid Wendover's gentle slopes, a little to the north of the humming A413, there is very little evidence of anything out of the ordinary. A large pylon looms above. The electricity fizzes and crackles along the slung-out cables. Up and down goes a tractor in the middle distance. I get as close as I can to this small stretch of ancient history, but it's overgrown with bracken and largely impenetrable. The discrepancies between the map and the experience of this walk are becoming increasingly obvious to me, and increasingly important. Down at eye level a wren flits away into the brambles and nettles and disappears. Here, the stories of the past are hidden from view. Perhaps they will stay that way forever; if the plans for HS2 go ahead, this 120-metre section of the ditch will be destroyed.

Projects like HS2 display an unexpected ambivalence to both the landscape and the people who inhabit it. As I shall learn around Aylesbury, society can be shaped for the better by new modes of transport. So too can our understanding of our environment and our history. New roads and new railways can force us to rethink our relationship to places – both in society and in the world. As we shall see, a division has emerged between the literature of travel and the so-called 'nature writing'. Will this prove to be a mistake? Archaeologists, for example, have a more open-minded relationship to infrastructure projects. On the one hand, such large-scale upheaval threatens to destroy valuable evidence that can help them flesh out their theories and gain new insights into our past. Robin Summer addressed this issue in a 2014 article in *The Observer*:

Singled out for criticism by English Heritage is HS2 Ltd's lack of detailed work on the historic environment in the Chilterns, an area of outstanding natural beauty and an archaeological hotspot. 'Discussion of it is limited to two paragraphs, and the impacts on it limited to three,' says English Heritage.

Buckinghamshire county council has estimated that around 7,000 designated heritage assets could be affected by phase one of HS2 – the route between London and Birmingham. This includes ancient tracks and field boundaries, historically significant buildings and important archaeological sites.

The actual figure is likely to be far higher. Much of our past stands to be lost, and we do not even know what or how much.

On the other hand, projects like HS2 often involve allowances in both time and money for archaeology. As birds follow behind the plough, the archaeologist precedes it, grubbing up shards of the past as the bulldozers approach. A friend of mine – now an archaeology professor at Sheffield University – once told me that archaeologists secretly delight in big infrastructure projects. It is a discipline reliant on the same extractive logic as modern industry. More construction means more work; in a recession, archaeology also suffers. In *The Observer*, Summer described HS2 as a 'bonanza'.

*

Once upon a time, the Firecrest used to be what they call a real pub. Now it is a 'Vintage Inn' – owned by Mitchells and Butlers, formerly a brewery with a cricket ground in Birmingham (now being redeveloped by Warwickshire cricket club). Today, they are the largest pub operator in the UK. Their other subsidiary brands include all the usual roadside suspects: Harvester, Toby Carvery, All Bar One and Browns restaurants. Inside, the Firecrest is blandly anonymous. Outside, away from the road, is a large and pleasant garden. Roger, Jenny and I sit outside, in part because Roger has brought with him a month-old puppy. In part because it's simply nicer. Roger and Jenny are residents of the nearby village of Dunsmore and committed opponents of HS2. Before I set off on this walk, I emailed several anti-HS2 organisations to tell them about what I was doing and to see if there were people who might be interested in speaking to me along the way. I was amazed at the speed and quantity of responses: this is a well-organised network of campaigners. Roger and Jenny are the first of several I will meet along the route. She is a retired NHS speech therapy manager, he a retired dental surgeon who ran his own practice in nearby Hemel Hempstead. In many ways their story is typical.

'I remember the moment we first heard the announcement,' says Jenny. 'We were at a meeting of a local conservation society. I still feel so angry. We live in an Area of Outstanding Natural Beauty and had recently formed the Dunsmore Conservation Society in order to become more proactive about protecting local footpaths and open spaces. Then this happens.' Jenny describes the prospect of HS2 – its viaducts and embankments cutting through the countryside – as an 'iconic scar'. 'To propose that in an AONB,' she says, 'is scandalous.'

This is a point made up and down the line, and in

some ways it's understandable. The countryside of Buckinghamshire and Oxfordshire is populated by a large number of people who have chosen to live here because they like the landscape. They are proud of it, and loyal. Any threat is to be resisted at all costs. Roger tells me of a friend who built a house in Dunsmore specifically for its views down the valley. HS2 will blight that view with two viaducts and a large embankment.

The construction period is perhaps the greatest fear. 'It will be seven or eight years of mess,' says Jenny. 'The valley will be a building site. It will take twenty years to recover and we won't be alive to see it.' This is the same point made by many of the retirees I meet. While they see the countryside they love as eternally self-renewing, their time within it is limited to a single lifespan. 'We have to enjoy it while we still can,' says Roger.

It's funny though; one of the things that has struck me most immediately over the course of this walk is how unlovable parts of the countryside already seem. Having emerged from London and its suburbs, the landscape is largely agricultural – bland expanses of lifeless fields. Oilseed rape and feed crops. Already the slopes are marked by pylons, busy roads, towns and train lines. This may be an Area of Outstanding Natural Beauty, but there's little that is really 'natural' here, and any moments of beauty are few and far between. Or maybe I'm just reading it wrong.

As we talk, a train rushes by at the end of the pub's garden. 'See, that train is OK,' says Jenny. I can't help but smile to myself. Proponents of the project cite such attitudes in order to argue that people will eventually get used to the noise of HS2 as well. It's hard not to think that the arrival of electric trains was treated with the same suspicion. But HS2 may not be so straightforward. Once the line is fully operational, eighteen services per hour will travel each way at speeds of up to 225mph. Aerodynamic noise, I'm told, increases to the 6th power of speed, which means that trains running at 225mph sound five times louder than those at 175mph. Currently, trains on the Chiltern Line rarely exceed 100mph. There is no question that HS2 will be much, much louder that existing trains. To complicate matters, the sound maps published by HS2 Ltd do not currently include peak figures, so it is very hard for local people to know the extent to which they will really be affected.

Later on my walk, I am given one of the publications from the draft environmental statement, produced by HS2 with engineers URS and Arup in 2013. It's a map book for 'Community Forum Area 11 – Stoke Mandeville and Aylesbury' and it's utterly baffling. Close-ups of the line have been rotated to fit the landscape format of the booklet rather than to aid legibility. Pages are out of order. In *The*

Power of Maps, artist, author and cartographer Denis Wood argues that 'maps facilitate the reproduction of the culture that brings them into being'. A map's effectiveness is the product of selectivity – what to include and what not to include – which is itself the product of a certain interest. Wood continues:

Because these interests select what from the vast storehouse of knowledge about the earth the map will represent, these interests are embodied in the map as presences and absences. Every map shows this . . . but not that, and every map shows what it shows this way . . . but not the other. Not only is this inescapable but it is precisely because of this interested selectivity – this choice of word or sign or aspect of the world to make a point – that the map is enabled to work.

Maps, in short, have power. Looking at these HS2 maps, it's clear that important information about transportation routes, visibility or footpath access is barely mentioned. But, more than that, what is left out is people. There are embankments and cuttings, 'landscape character areas' and borough boundaries, materials stockpiles and satellite construction compounds. There are temporary earthworks and temporary mitigation earthworks. There are watercourses, and rights of way, and community forum boundaries; local nature reserves, special protection areas and sites of special scientific interest. But there are no people: there is nothing about what people do or think or value. There are no animals either. Instead we have maps of many colours and wide-angle panoramic photomontages showing what HS2 might look like in 2026 – barely a hump on the horizon, several miles away.

What is missing from such maps matters because it's possible to argue that the impact of HS2 is really less about the countryside – which is likely to recover in the long term – than it is about the people who live here. Up and down the line I'm told stories of people's health ruined by the worry of HS2 and the stress in having to fight it. Financial difficulties have long been linked with suicide rates, something only exacerbated by the recession following the 2008 banking crisis. With many people along the route facing severe financial losses in the form of plummeting house prices, it's hardly surprising that there is not only anger here, but sadness too. Jenny tells me of two men who are now on sleeping tablets and anti-depressants. A farmer killed himself in Warwickshire. In a few days' time I will meet a woman who admitted on national television to seriously considering suicide. That moment was the first her husband knew of her feelings. He had felt the same.

The implications are not just personal, but political too. While UKIP's stance on immigration has drawn the headlines, it's arguable that their surge in votes across the country in the 2015 general election can be explained in part by projects like HS2 and what they suggest about the attitudes of politicians towards their electorate. Retired, white, middle-class, rural: this is the traditional Tory heartland. These people have worked hard, earned money, bought houses in attractive areas and retired to enjoy their leisure. They have done all that this country's political and economic system has asked of them. In return, these are the people that the system has served. Until now. Now, they feel frustration and anger: the democracy that they believed in has failed them. The political classes, it turns out, don't care about them. Local politicians may be nice, but they are useless. Suddenly these people are talking the language of protest, a language more associated with industrial workers and students. 'Everyone round here is disillusioned with politics,' says Jenny. 'Nobody believes anything that politicians say any more. We're totally disillusioned.'

Across the UK, people are tiring of being forgotten, of being left off the maps produced in London to be perused in London for decisions made in London. It's the same story throughout the affected countryside. Nigel Farage, former banker, man of the pub, has positioned himself as something different, something authentic. In the 2015 general election, UKIP received 12% of the national vote. It was only Britain's first-past-the-post system that prevented the party winning even a solitary seat. It is the same disillusionment that has fuelled the rise of the Green Party and, more recently, the election of Jeremy Corbyn as leader of the Labour Party. Of course, 2016's vote to leave the European Union can be seen, at least in part, in this light. Finally, a chance for voters to express their frustrations in a referendum where every person counts.

While such disillusionment has seen a rise in support for the political fringes, the sense of adversity seems also to have brought people together. 'The really good thing is the people we've met,' says Roger, 'people who are not going to sit back and allow something like this to happen.' Again, this is a story that repeats itself along the line – of local people coming together to fight against HS2. It makes me wonder if we can only really form a meaningful sense of community in the face of a shared enemy.

*

Getting cold outside, Roger, Jenny and I drive to another pub in Wendover for some lunch. Then, full and gently woozy after a couple more pints, I set off again, from Wendover towards Aylesbury. Here, the fight against HS2 converges with another, again involving disenfranchised members of the middle-classes – not home-owning retirees this time, but women. In 2013 the Reverend Colin Cartwright of Chesham published *Burning to Get the Vote*. The book is a history of suffragist activity in Buckinghamshire in the decade leading up to World War I. On the very first page, Cartwright dedicates his book to 'the people of Buckinghamshire and the campaign against HS2: "No backwards step!"'

In the early years of the twentieth century, Cartwright tells us, Aylesbury was a hub of suffragist activity – not as much as nearby High Wycombe, but significant nonetheless. Much of it centred on the prison, built in 1847. 1909, for example, saw the foundation of the Women's Tax Resistance League, which took up the arguments of the American revolutionaries: 'No taxation without representation'. The League was also inspired by local hero John Hampden, who refused to pay King Charles I's ship tax, and whose attempted arrest in the House of Commons helped spark the Civil War in 1642. The ship tax was Charles's attempt to raise sufficient income to become independent from the parliament of landowners and merchants who opposed him. Hampden's refusal was that of a wealthy landowner fighting for the power of money over the power of the monarchy. The significance, according to Marxist historian

A. L. Morton, was that, 'The divine right of kings was squarely opposed to, and finally broken upon, the divine right of private property.'

Like George Washington's, Hampden's actions came – inaccurately perhaps – to be associated with a wider conception of democracy and social progress. Hampden lived near Aylesbury, in the village of Great Hampden, which was named after his family. His silhouette is on the logo of the district council, and a statue of him was erected in the town square in 1912.

That same year, Amy Hicks, a member of the League, was sent to Aylesbury prison for refusing to pay taxes and went on hunger strike. Further hunger strikes took place in the prison throughout the year and were countered by the still-controversial strategy of force-feeding. Cartwright quotes a letter from one of the hunger-strikers, Ada Cecile Wright, in which she describes the horrific process in detail:

The door of my cell was flung open and 4-6 or seven officers entered and seized me. There was a deep, breathless struggle as I clung to my iron bedstead … I was tied down into a chair, hands and arms held firmly by the wardresses either side. The two doctors began their objectionable work. They forced open my jaws and a steel gag was inserted between my teeth and my mouth was then prized open and kept so by the doctor behind. The doctor in front rammed the stomach tube down my throat (unspeakable instrument of disgust and torture) ... We rub our eyes and ask if this is Christian England in the 20th century?

Rebecca Solnit has described the force-feeding of such protesters as 'a new form of institutionalised rape'. Certainly, Wright's description is one of violent openings (of the cell door, of the prisoner's jaws, of her mouth) and forcible insertions. Solnit links the struggle for the right to vote to the battle over a woman's right to walk in public. She describes how, simply by being seen walking in public, women were assumed to be prostitutes, and either harassed by men or oppressed by the state. Women were therefore removed from public life – both physically and politically. Solnit goes on to describe the way in which the suffragette movement re-appropriated the power of walking through marches and public demonstrations.

Solnit may link suffragism to walking, but others have linked the movement to other forms of transport– bicycles and, here in Buckinghamshire, the railway. In 1912, the year of Wright's horrific treatment at the hands of the state, Aylesbury saw a number of protests and riots, as well as a visit by none other than Sylvia Pankhurst, who spoke before a crowd at the station. As Cartwright notes, the suffragettes were not the first in Aylesbury to rebel against the political establishment. The town, like several others in Buckinghamshire, has a long history of nonconformism and antipathy towards the aristocracy. During the Civil War, for example, Aylesbury became a stronghold for the Parliamentarian forces. In 1642, the town's Parliamentarian garrison defeated a much larger Royalist force at Holman's Bridge, a few miles to the north.

Suffragism was always closely linked with the railways. As Cartwright argues, the opening of a line between London and Chesham in 1889 'made it easier for high-profile speakers to visit the area'. In addition – and even more significant, believes Cartwright – was the exodus of people moving from London to live in places like Buckinghamshire: 'Many of the later recruits to the women's suffrage movement in the county were from this growing number of people, who were either pioneering commuters, or those seeking to settle in a more rural location.' So those early years prior to the official adoption of 'Metro-land' saw the arrival in Buckinghamshire not only of those in pursuit of the suburban dream of golf and gardens, but those of a more radical political mind too.

There is a certain irony about this link between protests and the railways. As Clive Foxell notes in his history of the Metropolitan line, much of the early opposition to the railways was based on exactly this concern. The army, in particular, feared that railways would be a threat to national security. Foxell cites the case of the Duke of Wellington, a leading general at the time, who had arrived by train in Manchester in 1830 only to be met by 'a large and hostile crowd wearing the tricolour cockades supporting the French Revolution'. The event caused the Duke to observe, rather memorably, that 'railways would simply encourage the lower classes to travel about'. Egads! Yet, as Foxell notes with pleasure: 'within a few years the army itself was using trains to transport troops to quell the Chartist riots'.

Throughout his history of Buckinghamshire suffragism, Cartwright clearly differentiates between the peaceful protests and political rallies of the suffragists and the more extreme tactics employed by the controversial suffragettes. Perhaps unsurprisingly for a man of the cloth, he disapproves of the latter: 'eventually,' he writes, the suffragettes 'found themselves chained, not just to railings, but also to a politics of despair and impotent fury'. It is interesting to compare this to the approach taken by anti-HS2 campaigners, which has so far been peaceful, proper and largely ineffective. Further up the line, after the general election, there will be rumblings of more radical action.

*

Aylesbury is, in several ways, a watershed. This area of Buckinghamshire consists largely of layers of different rocks, running south-west to north-east, almost exactly perpendicular to HS2. Towards London are the younger layers – sands, silts and clay around Slough and chalk around Amersham and the Misbourne. Aylesbury, however, is part-sited on layers of limestone – the two northernmost outcrops of Portland stone in England. The town sits atop what nineteenth-century topographical publisher Samuel Lewis described as a 'gentle eminence'. Around it and below lies the Vale of Aylesbury, made up of slow-draining clays, ideal for pastures and brooks.

But Aylesbury is a watershed in another way too. It marks the limits of my knowledge: the boundary between the region I feel I know – London, the suburbs, the Buckinghamshire Chilterns – and the blank expanse of OS maps beyond. Once upon a time the Metropolitan Line ended here at Aylesbury. My knowledge now ends with it.

But this is not just an observation of ignorance; when it comes to writing about place, such knowledge is important. There is something of a methodological divide observable in recent literature of place. On the one hand is the travel writing of the likes of Paul Theroux and, of particular interest to me, Bruce Chatwin. These men travelled alone, and ill-equipped, to far-off places – Africa, Australia, South America. They went with specific aims: to escape and explore and have adventures and then, safely back at home, to write about them. They are educated observers. They write with precision and flair. They are outsiders.

By contrast is what has come to be known as 'nature writing' or 'new nature writing' or even, following *Granta*, 'the new nature writing'. Such writing is often marked by a belief that one can only really write about those places that one really knows. Such knowledge takes time to accrue. This latter approach is most clearly expounded by W. G. Hoskins and subsequently demonstrated by the likes of Roger Deakin and, to a lesser extent, Richard Mabey. It is an approach that has been gaining prominence lately, perhaps as a reaction against the increasing ease and frequency of foreign travel and its environmental costs, or the proliferation of the exotic via sundry Attenborough-narrated documentaries. Perhaps it's a response to the increasing conception of travel as commodity, packaged up as fast and convenient, repackaged back in an instant via Facebook photos or Instagram. Books, of course, take time to write; nature writing suggests that the wisdom they contain should be slow-learned too.

In his introduction to the 2008 *Granta* magazine that kickstarted widespread interest in this type of writing, Jason Cowley specifically pits his 'new nature writing' against travel writing. Although both may consist of 'narratives told in the first person', Cowley is explicit in his rejection of the old in favour of the new. Travel writing is 'a debased and exhausted genre'; this new nature writing, meanwhile, is 'urgent, vital and alert to the defining particulars of our times'.

The collection included works by the likes of Robert Macfarlane, Kathleen Jamie and Roger Deakin: the big names of the then-emergent form all present and correct. Today, just a few years later, the genre – if it can be called that – is a packed one. In 'Highways and Byways', the afterword to a 2012 collection entitled *In the Company of Ghosts: Poetics of the Motorway*, cultural geographer Stephen Daniels writes: 'so called edgelands are now where the literary action is, crowded with a varied cast of deep topographers, new nature writers, literary cartographers and psychogeographers.'

This proliferation of monikers points to a problem. Like any good rock band labelled with the latest genre tag ('emo', 'grime', 'nu-rave' etc.) the current slew of nature writers all seem to bridle at the term. How anyone can ever find the energy to get worked up about the name of a genre is beyond me. But they can and they do. In 2015, Jamie Doward wrote an article in *The Guardian* tackling this exact question. It's interesting to note, in light of Cowley's statements, that, according to Doward, 'Robert Macfarlane prefers travel writer'. The article goes on to quote Richard Mabey:

'I have very mixed feelings about what is happening,'
Mabey said. 'I'm delighted that there is more writing
about nature going on, but I'm increasingly confused by
what this genre tag actually means. Nature writing ought
to be writing about nature. I'm not sure books about pets
ought to qualify, nor do I think books that are principally
about the nature of the self ought to qualify.'

At the risk of over-analysing what may well have been a
throwaway phone conversation with a journalist, it's worth
thinking about what Mabey seems to be saying here. First
is the idea that books must somehow 'qualify' as nature
writing – as if it is the exclusive domain of learned experts
(rather than a convenient tag for publishers and journalists).
Second is the implication that pets are not 'nature'. Surely,
the very thing that characterises the most interesting
'nature writing' is a considered uncertainty about the very
concept of 'nature' and humanity's relationship to it? Esther
Woolfson eloquently ponders the status of the pet in *Corvus:
A Life with Birds*, for example. So too does Helen Macdonald
in *H is for Hawk*. We'll come back to these later.

For now, let us focus on what such writing does well. In
Wildwood, for example, Deakin recounts his own feelings of

shame and embarrassment upon an encounter with a family of mice. Responding to an 'impulse', Deakin picks up a piece of driftwood in the New Forest, only to find the nest of a field mouse concealed beneath. While her young escape, the mother stands her ground. Deakin continues:

> Embarrassed to have disturbed the family in so remote a spot, I gently returned their roof into position, wishing there were some way of reassuring them that this was a genuine mistake and they were quite safe.

Deakin here is ashamed at the impetuosity that caused him to pick up the driftwood. His gentleness is an attempted reparation, but he can never know quite what effect his initial action has had, or whether his subsequent remorse means anything at all to a little field mouse. Perhaps it is this inability to know the mind of the other that causes this singular moment to linger on in the memory:

> The look of hurt, uncertainty and puzzlement in the mouse's face has stayed with me. So has her courage in standing by the nest, decoying us from her young.

It is a lovely description both of the connection between humans and animals – like us, mice feel fear and confusion, they make decisions – and of the division that separates us: ultimately, Deakin cannot communicate his apologies to the mouse. There is perhaps a lesson here. We like to think of ourselves as in control of our actions, but there is a limit to how much we can manage our impact on others. 'It is salutary,' Deakin continues, 'to be reminded of the extent of your own power and your potential for accidental brutality.' I can't help but think of Lennie in John Steinbeck's *Of Mice and Men*, who accidentally kills his puppy while stroking it. Sometimes we are all powerless to limit the impact of our own power. Technology has only accentuated this fact. In *The Day Before Yesterday*, biologist Colin Tudge wrote of anthropogenic climate change: '"Influence", of course, emphatically does not mean "control".' Then again towards the end of the book: 'although our influence is huge, our control is minimal'.

Later in *Wildwood*, as we have already discussed, Deakin goes to meet the artist David Nash. As if in response to this moment of 'accidental brutality', Deakin is full of praise for the still and humble life – what he describes as Nash's 'commitment to a settled life in one place'. In Deakin's mind, there is a parallel between Nash's life and that of the sheep whose marks in the landscape the artist is so drawn to. They are, for Deakin, 'signs of settling, of the intimate, long-term connection with the earth that is Nash's own way of life too'.

There is certainly something admirable in this privileging of the small-scale and undemonstrative relationship with the earth. It calls to mind W. G. Hoskins' evocation of a phrase employed by artist, craftsman and font designer Eric Gill – that of the 'handmade world'. Deakin himself praises the 'small-scale people's landscape'. It is a world that is within our understanding because our bodies have helped to shape it, in a small and humble way. We have not mediated the world through tools and technology – and language – or sought to conquer it and, in so doing, found ourselves irrevocably cut off from our environment and our fellow creatures. We have not left our problems behind by moving ever onwards, but sought to tackle them head-on. As I walk, I carry with me a copy of a new novel by Honor Gavin. *Midland* tells the story of the bombing of Birmingham and its subsequent post-war redevelopments. It seemed an appropriate book to bring with me. Early in the book, the narrator criticises one of her classmates for leaving Birmingham behind in favour of southern Africa:

> To our young woman that option seemed more a cop-out than it was laudable … staying put, to her way of thinking, was the better endeavour. To stay put was heroic in its foregoing of heroism. It was inconsequential.

It is exactly this elevation of the inconsequential that interests today's writers. The heroic writers of today are the likes of Gilbert White or J. A. Baker – those who have seldom travelled, and have instead focused their keen eyes on the minutiae of an individual location. In so doing they have been able to accrue insights that would be unthinkable to the traveller simply passing through. And while this is surely to be praised, there is, it seems to me, a danger. Encouraging us to be content with what we have, to focus only on what lies before our eyes, to take pleasure and interest in the minutiae – regardless of what may be happening on the larger scale – risks obstructing the desire for change where change is needed, and risks reinforcing the powerlessness of those without power. There is something both limited and limiting about this approach to thought: man as farmyard animal, bred to become stupid, docile and delicious.

This is the criticism levelled at Western middle-class environmentalism by academic David Pepper in his book *The Roots of Modern Environmentalism*. He argues that such an approach is reminiscent of the 'lifeboat ethics' espoused by US ecologist Garrett Hardin (and before him, English political economist Thomas Malthus). Hardin's parable describes a lifeboat of limited capacity in a sea of drowning men and women. The metaphor is based on the assumption (first espoused by Malthus) that the earth has capacity for only a finite number of humans. Hardin uses the analogy to argue against foreign aid, immigration and food banks. Malthus, in his era, did the same. Helping the poor only makes their problems worse. Are today's nature writers retreading this dangerous territory?

When Cowley takes aim at travel writing, he specifically targets the 'lyrical pastoral tradition of the romantic wanderer'. I wonder whether this is intended to include Bruce Chatwin. Interestingly, while Macfarlane embraces the 'travel writing' tag, Chatwin rejected it. When his book *The Songlines* was nominated for the Thomas Cook Travel Award, he requested that it be withdrawn from consideration, on the grounds that it was a work of fiction. Nonetheless, like Deakin, Hoskins and others, Chatwin admires those whose relationship with the land is intimate and meaningful, where there is a connection. In *The Songlines*, for example, Chatwin writes about Aboriginal tribes in Australia – and a relationship to the land that is ancient, complex and sustained through the retelling of myths and songs along unseen pathways that criss-cross the country.

The truth of Chatwin's writing has long been debated. The brevity of his visits to Australia and Patagonia has been widely criticised. But what is clear is that Chatwin's writing is shot through with a kind of disdain for the settled existence engendered and enabled by agriculture. Chatwin sees the process by which humanity gradually abandoned nomadic hunter-gathering in favour of settled agricultural society as the origin of our subsequent subjugation. He observes that the word 'nomad' comes from the Greek νόμος meaning 'pasture'. The Nomad is the clan chief who 'presides over the allocation of pastures'. Therefore νόμος also came to mean 'law' or custom, 'and so,' argues Chatwin, 'the basis of all Western laws'. Chatwin also argues, debatably perhaps, that the state formed 'once it was realised that the techniques of animal coercion could be applied to an inert peasant mass'. The oppression of humans, for Chatwin, stems from our control of animals. In that light, the urging of the new nature writers for us to live more like animals suddenly has very different connotations. Deakin's comparison between Nash and the grazing sheep seems like an extension of this process of subjugation.

For Chatwin, both agriculture and settlement represent deviations from the true path of human nature. What is natural is to wander the world. He points out, for example, that the best way to silence a screaming baby is to rock it at walking pace. 'The human gait is a long, lilting stride,' he writes, '1 … 2 … 1 … 2 – with a fourfold rhythm built into the action of the feet.' It's the same rhythm as the iambic pentameter. Why else would we have metrical feet?

It is in this celebration of what he calls 'wanderlust' that

Chatwin differs from Deakin. Chatwin's work – especially *In Patagonia* and *The Songlines* – consists in a working over of the division between the rooted and the rootless, the farmer and the nomad, Cain and Abel. Chatwin's confused admiration for the Aboriginal way of life is set in opposition to the white, Western settlers whose conceptions of land ownership are rooted in agriculture and settlement. He speculates that human civilisation was a mistake – something unnatural against which we have been subconsciously fighting ever since it occurred. This is why the story of Cain and Abel is so important. For Chatwin, it is not only a story of brotherly squabbling but a telling tale of victory by farmer over hunter. It is an allegory for the early development of civilisation and the violence with which it was instituted. That one brother could murder another points, for Chatwin, to the unnaturalness of civilisation itself.

At the risk of a simplistically biographical reading of Chatwin's work, it is worth pointing out that he was bisexual. He married Elizabeth Chanler in 1965, but had a number of affairs with men throughout his life – most notably with film director James Ivory and, later, fashion designer Jasper Conran. Although, according to Nicholas Shakespeare's biography of Chatwin, Elizabeth is said to have tolerated these affairs, by the late 1970s their relationship had deteriorated and she asked for a separation in 1980. While researching *The Songlines* in Australia, Chatwin first read about AIDS, the fear of which urged him to seek reconciliation with Elizabeth.

It's hard not to read some of Chatwin's work in this light. Women are associated with ideas of security, domesticity and permanence. While he acknowledges that the idea that 'men are the wanderers and women the guardians of hearth and home' is nothing more than a 'commonly held delusion', he nonetheless ties women to the home: 'women, above all, are the guardians of continuity: if the hearth moves, they move with it'. Women are associated with 'the old ways' (the title of a Robert Macfarlane book, incidentally): 'country', health, hearth and home. Although he denies it, it's hard not to read Chatwin's opposition between agriculture and hunter-gathering as a gendered one. It is certainly autobiographical. Is the wanderlust upon which he is so fixated a defining characteristic of mankind, or merely the projection of one man's obsession on to the vastness of human history?

Where nature writing and travel writing differ in their approach to settlement, both share a love of first-person narrative. Both also rely for their force on what Ken Worpole, describing the writings of W. G. Sebald and Iain Sinclair, named 'the principle of immersion'. Chatwin, for example, declares his desire 'to learn for myself, and not from other men's books'.

My walk is, I suppose, based upon the same principle – that direct experience is the best teacher – and this book is the subsequent attempt to navigate a way between the two approaches, the rooted versus the rootless. Or rather, the aim is to move from one to the other: from London, a city I've lived in for years, through parts of Buckinghamshire I've known my entire life, and gradually on into parts of England that I've never even heard of, let alone visited. For better or for worse, Aylesbury is perhaps the point when all this becomes travel writing.

*

It's 9 a.m. on the fourth day as I head west from Aylesbury station out towards the countryside. The town is proof that housing and transport are closely linked. As we saw in Chapter III, this was certainly the case with the Metropolitan line, and it could well be the case with HS2 here too. There have been rumours of accompanying housing projects in Birmingham and Camden, which critics have described as a 'land grab'. Here in Aylesbury, a new station was opened in 2008: Aylesbury Vale Parkway followed the construction of 15,000 new houses on the town's outskirts. As I head west towards the countryside, I pass a brand new village. On the corner of the roundabout are the telltale words – Taylor

Wimpey – spelled out in big red and blue letters on a fake grass ground. Pebbles and a few small plants frame the sign against the evenly sloping lawn. Dozens of red brick boxes line the street. Their front doors are red and blue. Paradise Orchard is the name of the street, the development itself is New Berry Vale. Newly planted trees stand in rows. The verges have not yet been grassed. Away from the main road, the building work continues.

Taylor Wimpey was created in 2007 from the merger of former rivals Taylor Woodrow and George Wimpey. It is one of the largest house-building companies in Britain. According to a map on the company's website, this development outside Aylesbury will consist of ninety properties, mostly two- and three-bedrooms. Twenty per cent of properties have been designated 'affordable'. Four-bedroom detached houses are currently listed at £310,000. This is how Taylor Wimpey describes the development: 'Surrounded by beautiful countryside yet with excellent transport links, a new-build property in Aylesbury at New Berry Vale offers the very best of well-connected country living.' It sounds an awful lot like the early descriptions of Metro-land. Perhaps the dream is alive after all.

From here, it's not long until I pass through another planned village, but one of a rather different nature. Six miles from Aylesbury, along the A41, is Waddesdon. On the outskirts of the village I stop for a cup of tea at Porky's Café – a roadside portacabin advertising breakfast and 'hot-meals' on signs made from number plates. Here, in the late nineteenth century, banker, politician and art collector Baron Ferdinand de Rothschild purchased a large estate and set about building Waddesdon Manor on a hilltop overlooking the village. Ornately designed to look like a French chateau, with formal gardens and landscaped park, Waddesdon Manor is one of the grandest country houses of the era. As I walk past the gatehouse, a red kite soars overhead.

The Rothschilds are quite the dynasty. Ferdinand's father, Nathan Mayer Rothschild, was the first Jew in the House of Lords. His son, Walter, built up a zoological collection that would later become Tring Museum. A descendant – Lionel de Rothschild – was MP for mid-Bucks and a prominent opponent of women's suffrage. Ferdinand's great-nephew, James Armand Edmond de Rothschild, was the last private owner of Waddesdon Manor: when he died in 1957, he bequeathed the house to the National Trust.

It was Ferdinand, however, who had most impact on the immediate area. Not content with his manor and gardens, he set to work building houses in the village for his employees and tenants. He also built a school, a pub, a cricket pavilion and a village hall. Ferdinand's taste was for the elaborate, faux-medieval. In fact, he was a pioneer in what became known as the Tudor Revival. As a result, there is something faintly ludicrous about Waddesdon. At one end are the twentieth-century houses, a car garage, a roof-rack business and various boarded-up buildings. 'This property has been shut down in line with Operation Falcon,' reads a sign in one window. Operation Falcon is an initiative from Thames Valley Police to tackle drugs and drug-related crime. Meanwhile, at the other end of the village, is the full splendour of Rothschild's idiosyncratic taste: a row of neat stone almshouses on one side; on the other, a large house with complicated patterns of wood and brick and curving, tower-like faux-fortifications. Further along, the Five Arrows hotel boasts pitched gables, a carved porch, half-timbering and at least a dozen tall, differently patterned brick chimneys.

In her seminal book *Villages of Vision*, first published in 1975, Gillian Darley traces a history of such planned villages across the UK. The book is subtitled 'A study of strange utopias' and Darley's interest is as much in the intentions that lay behind such initiatives as it is in their effects on the people who subsequently lived in them. As a result, *Villages of Vision* is full of eccentric characters – fashionable landlords and benevolent industrialists, religious nonconformists, Chartist co-operatives and utopian dreamers.

Across Buckinghamshire, the Rothschilds were

particularly active village-builders: not only here in Waddesdon, but also in the nearby villages of Aston Clinton, Cheddington, Halton, Hulcott and Mentmore. Elsewhere in the county, Darley notes examples of planned villages from Jordans (an early twentieth-century Quaker garden village) to Wotton Underwood, where a terrace of eighteenth-century cottages was built after 'emparking'. Emparking was the process by which the landed aristocracy – aided by the Parliamentary Acts of Enclosure – shunted aside long-standing tenant dwellings because they got in the way of a newly landscaped, picturesque view of nature. Sometimes these new buildings saw an improvement in living conditions; sometimes they merely looked more pleasing to the eye of fashion. In such instances, there is a privileging of aesthetics over functionality – a lack of consideration for the needs of the people who are actually going to live and work in these villages. This is exactly the point Sam Jacob was making about the dangers of the picturesque, and the naturalisation of power – both psychologically and literally.

In some ways, such planned villages are not so different from the kind of Taylor Wimpey development that is popping up on the outskirts of Aylesbury, and on areas of cheap land across the country. Here, the motive is not public health or the picturesque, but profit. As we shall see in the next chapter, the 'vision' is equally myopic.

As the rain starts to fall, I duck into the parish church for shelter. Inside, I get chatting to two women. Neither seems especially worried about HS2, but they wish me luck on my walk. As the rain eases I set off towards Quainton through two long, brown fields, just ploughed and mud-clogged. The women in the church had advised me against going through them. I thought I knew better. I was wrong. My boots are still heavy with lumps of gluey mud as I arrive at what was, once upon a time, Quainton Road station.

Of all the railway lines that once criss-crossed the Buckinghamshire countryside, Quainton Road station was at the epicentre. In *Lost Railways of the Chilterns,* Leslie Oppitz calls it 'a fascinating reminder of the many branch lines that once crossed the counties surrounding the Chiltern Hills'. The station was first opened in 1868 and the buildings that still stand today date from 1896. Three lines converged at Quainton: the Aylesbury and Buckingham Railway, which was taken over by the Metropolitan in 1891; the Great Central Railway, which – like Chiltern Rail today – connected Marylebone with the Midlands; and, lastly, the Wotton or Brill Tramway – a private line that connected the Duke of Buckingham's estate at Wotton Underwood with Brill, to the south-west, with stops further north at Waddesdon Road and Quainton.

From its apex as a central hub in the late nineteenth

century, Quainton began to decline in significance. The Brill Tramway was taken over by the Metropolitan, but other, more direct lines to London were built in the 1910s, and it went into financial decline. When Metropolitan Railway was taken into public ownership as part of London Transport in 1933, Quainton Road became part of the London Underground – despite being some forty miles from London and not underground. In 1935 the Brill Tramway was closed. Quainton Road station followed, after the publication of the Beeching report, in 1966.

Three years later, the Quainton Road Society was formed, and today Quainton Road has been preserved as the Buckinghamshire Railway Centre. As I cross the bridge over the old line, beneath me are Royal Mail train carriages in their livery of bright scarlet, an old engine, slickly painted in deep pine green, and – incongruously perhaps – a small tank, the barrel of its cannon pointing up towards me. The station itself is neatly preserved, with vintage signals, lamp posts and signage. An old Metropolitan Railway poster displays a painting by Douglas Constable to advertise the pleasures of 'fishing in Metro-land'.

After scraping the claggy, clinging lumps of mud from my boots, I head inside to meet Aidan Aylward, the centre's commercial manager. Aidan is the first person I meet who is pro-HS2. It's not surprising really: he's a train enthusiast.

'Our official view as a railway preservation group,' he tells me over biscuits and strong, sweet coffee, 'is that we broadly support railway development. But we don't want to be involved politically.' That's the official view; his personal opinion is a little more forthright. But because I'm writing a piece for *The Independent*, Aidan is keen to separate his views from those of the museum. 'The local village are very much against it,' he says. 'There's been lots of hype in the media and HS2 haven't put their case across very well. But I appreciate the need for it.'

Aidan worked under British Rail and then Freightliner. For seven years, he tells me, he was what's known as a 'shunter' – the person responsible for moving trains between yards and platforms and ensuring their safety. His relationship with Quainton began when he visited as a twelve-year-old train enthusiast, and he has been working here since 2010. We talk about HS2 and Aidan tells me about the history of the West Coast Mainline. The line's origins date to the 1830s and it contains 'lots of twists and turns'. Such 'pinch points' at Berkhamstead or Weedon Bec cause speed to be reduced, and traffic is now at capacity. 'The idea of HS2 is to take the longer journeys in order to free up West Coast for freight and local services. I'm not saying that where it is is right,' he continues, 'or how they're going about it. But something needs to be done.'

We talk about the history of the museum, and the traces of the trains that used to run through the countryside here. Aidan tells me that an old trackbed is now being used as an access road to a new incinerator further north near Calvert Green. 'Did you notice the wide grass verges along the road as you walked here?' he asks me. I did indeed. 'That was the old Brill branch.'

HS2 is planned to run through the centre's overflow car park. It misses the main building by just 200 yards. I wonder how enthusiastic Adrian would be were HS2 to run straight through the middle. 'With any big project nowadays, there are always a lot of environmental issues,' Aidan tells me. 'We've had lots of surveys here – for fish in the lake or bats by the pond. That's why it's costing so much – all these endless surveys. They have to pay the landowner for every one – all the way up the line from London to Birmingham. We've had half a dozen.'

He tells me about one group of surveyors who arrived in waders and life-preservers to check for fish in what they thought was a large expanse of water nearby. 'They didn't realise it was just that ditch across the field,' laughs Aidan. 'That tickled me.' Such anecdotes aptly demonstrate the discrepancy between top-down planning and detailed local knowledge. It is the latter to which today's nature writers are committed. Does that align the grand sweep of the travel writer with the centralised planners of HS2?

*

Even after I've said goodbye to Aidan, and let him get on with his work, I spend the next few hours thinking about trains. I think of something Stephen Daniels wrote in *Poetics of the Motorway* about the idea of 'byway sensibility' or 'branchline pastoral' – the way in which writers start to idealise forms of transport just at the point at which they begin to become outdated. As HS2 looms, will we start to romanticise the suddenly old-fashioned Virgin Pendolinos? After all, nothing ages faster than modernity.

I start thinking too about straight lines in the landscape – HS2 of course, but also about hedges and canals, roads, pylons, and ancient earthworks like Grim's Ditch. We used to think that nature needed man to straighten it out. That was when the wild was something to be feared. Now we imagine nature as curvaceous and soft or random and chaotic; only man's industry and architecture is hard and straight and logical. But there are straight lines in nature too – the edges of a crystal, a ray of light, the walls of a cell. Animals too can reason. We just tend to ignore them.

Over the next hour or so I criss-cross train lines that criss-cross the landscape. In places it's possible to trace the raised ground along the line of a hedgerow. No trains now; just a long, mounded ridge, half-hidden by bracken and gorse, with spiky hawthorn clad in mustard-yellow lichen. I stop for a moment outside a small house. The tracks are long gone, but the raised ridge makes for a neat little front driveway. Parked atop it is a Mini Cooper. The name of the house? Railway Cottage.

V

New English Landscapes

Calvert Green – Steeple Claydon

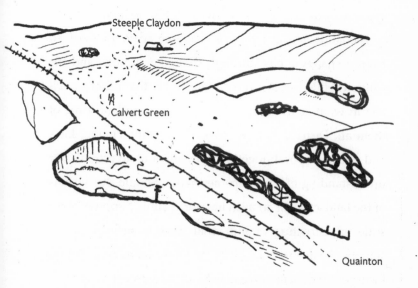

A few miles north-west of Aylesbury, a man traverses the fields with a half-cocked shotgun over his arm. As the wind begins to rise, I stay out of sight and stop for some lunch in a little apple orchard. Sheltered by a sturdy hedgerow, I sit down carefully on my waterproof map cover. I eat the heel from a loaf of corn bread, squashed from four days in a rucksack, and hacked-off hunks of cheddar. I've been walking for hours. I couldn't imagine anything more delicious.

Suddenly the wind changes direction and I'm buffeted from the side. Cheese flies everywhere and lands in lumps on the damp grass. As I rise to leave, I disturb a large brown buzzard, who rises and sails away, stately, to another port.

The landscape, as I walk, is changing again. I've walked from a changing city, through changing suburbs and the Chiltern Hills, but it is on the fourth day that I find myself lost in what is arguably the most interesting landscape of them all. Disused railway lines and landfill, circling kites and waste disposal: together, they force us to rethink our understanding of landscape aesthetics. Should our visions of the landscape, in art as in literature, simply oppose large-scale infrastructure or industrial projects such as power stations, incinerators or HS2? Or might there be a way of incorporating them into a new kind of landscape vision?

In 2013, Ken Worpole published a book entitled *The New*

English Landscape. It's a slim, beautiful volume – the result of ten years exploring the landscapes of East Anglia, combined with extensive reading and thinking. Supplemented with photographs by Jason Orton, Worpole's wide-ranging essay touches on some of the key issues in the nature literature of the last seventy-five years. It charts a shift in the centre of gravity of English nature writing: from the wild sublime of the Lake District, as conceived by the Romantic poets, to the tranquil idyll of the upper Thames. He cites Simon Schama's observation that the area most associated with Englishness during the Edwardian era was along the river from Hammersmith to Oxford. Peter Ackroyd makes a similar observation in. Since World War II, however, so-called nature writing has begun to focus on Essex and East Anglia. Where artists like John Nash and Eric Ravilious led the way in the 1930s, writers like J. A. Baker and W. G. Sebald followed in the 1950s and beyond. 'British topographical writing has been dominated in recent times by the landscapes of East Anglia,' writes Worpole.

Worpole believes that the east functions as an effective synecdoche for the rest of the country. He argues that Essex has been utilised 'as laboratory and site of experiment for changes in land use subsequently seen across much of the rest of the UK'. From swampland to industrialised agriculture and urban sprawl: the result is that the literature of the area is also becoming (or is already) the literature of England. In many ways it's hard to disagree. These days, literary-minded Londoners go not to read poetry on Oxford punts, but to walk amid the flats of the Essex estuary. In 2013, the Shorelines festival in Southend was curated by Rachel Lichtenstein, and saw the likes of Iain Sinclair, Robert Macfarlane, Caroline Bergvall and Worpole himself all gather for a weekend of sea-themed writing and events. In 2014, Essex was the first county to be the subject of a Rough Guide. You can now do an MA in Wild Writing at the University of Essex. The writings of W. G. Sebald continue to cast a long shadow.

The celebrated *H is for Hawk* is a case in point. Helen Macdonald's memoir is a tale of grief following the death of her father, and of the relationship between the author and a goshawk which she names Mabel. The book opens with Macdonald in Breckland, to the north of Cambridge where she works. It is characteristic of contemporary nature writing's interest in the hybrid landscapes of the east: Breckland, writes Macdonald, 'feels dangerous, half-buried, damaged. I love it because of all the places I know in England, it feels to me the wildest.' She goes on to clarify what she means by 'wild': 'It's not an untouched wilderness like a mountaintop, but a ramshackle wildness in which people and the land have conspired to strangeness.' She refers not to the Lake District of the Romantic poets, but to Essex and East Anglia.

Paul Kingsnorth makes a similar point about the Amazon rainforest in Issue 3 of *Dark Mountain*:

> The Amazon is not important because it's 'untouched'; it's important because it is wild, in the sense that it is self-willed. It is lived in and from by humans, but it is not created or controlled by them ... This is what intelligent green thinking has always called for: human and nonhuman nature working in some degree of harmony, in a modern world of compromise and change in which some principles, nevertheless, are worth cleaving to.

For the majority of these writers, landscape aesthetics are inextricably linked with ethics. What we value in a landscape is based on how – and how much – our impact is felt within it. In addition, the privileging of certain landscapes over others is never simply descriptive; it is an act of selection that is both personal and political. 'The requirement to interpret and re-evaluate contemporary landscapes – especially those which resist traditional categories of taste – is therefore vital,' argues Worpole. New approaches are required to move beyond the carefully framed pretence of purity espoused in nature magazines, and instead embrace the warts and all of the English landscape today: abandoned industrial sites, military fortifications, landfill.

Macdonald follows a similar path. She loves Breckland because: 'It's rich with the sense of an alternative countryside history; not just the grand, leisured dreams of landed estates, but a history of industry, forestry, disaster, commerce and work.' Worpole, too, emphasises the importance of work: 'Working landscapes create their own aesthetics,' he writes. In *The Roots of Modern Environmentalism*, David Pepper argues, following Karl Marx, that man's relationship with nature is defined by labour. It is labour through which we transform nature into something useful, and through which we also transform ourselves. This understanding of the importance of labour underpins Pepper's critique of the picturesque, which 'excluded not only agricultural workers but also the ploughed field and in general the works of man, which were considered distasteful. In this way the patrons of such art were not reminded of the more baleful aspects of the production from which their wealth came.' The ethic of the new landscape aesthetic is built upon this knowledge – that to exclude human labour is to reinforce existing structures of power and exploitation. This will become clear to me over the course of this afternoon.

Of course – and both Macdonald and Worpole are alive to this – the result is often just as much of a selectively composed aesthetic as previously. This, as we shall see, is inescapable. At least if we are aware of this process taking place, we are in a position to do something about it. Knowledge is power, so they say.

*

As recently as 1750 the population of the UK was just 11 million, of whom the vast majority (80%) lived in rural areas. But the nineteenth century was one of rapid change, and by 1900, the population had nearly quadrupled – to 42 million. By this time, following a period of intense industrialisation and urbanisation, just 30% lived in the countryside. Today, the population is over 64 million. Of which 82% now live in urban areas. Soon, the countryside will be empty.

In this light, the rising fascination with nature writing – and landscape aesthetics more broadly – is hardly surprising. We live in an urbanised society, increasingly cut off from the natural world. The environment is being destroyed; climate change threatens life as we know it. For all their radical potential, the arts have always been fascinated by loss. This is as true of painting as it is of literature. For some years now, the visual arts – painting and photography in particular – have been preoccupied with this landscape aesthetic. It is interesting to note that the word 'landscape'

– originally *landskip*, an anglicisation of the Dutch *landschap* – entered the English language specifically to refer to the genre of painting. That was in 1598. It was only afterwards, with the emergence of the concept of the picturesque and then landscape architecture, that the word began to be applied to the world outside the painting. It was not long before 'landscape' became a verb.

Landscape has therefore always been concerned with framing. It is, in addition, a word that presupposes the presence of a viewer. This viewer may be the painter or the photographer, the lone poet or the hiker. Indeed, the viewer may be a kestrel or a Shetland pony. The issue of animal agency will raise its head later; the point for now is that, however empty a landscape may appear, it requires a subjective presence. Otherwise, by definition, it is not a landscape. What unifies all the different types of nature writers – the deep topographers, the psychogeographers and the literary cartographers that Stephen Daniels names – is this concern for how landscape is constructed as a concept, shaped as an artefact, understood and inhabited. And, vice versa: how we in turn are influenced by the landscape that we have helped to shape. It is an ongoing, cyclical process. This was perhaps the key point in W. G. Hoskins' seminal 1955 book, *The Making of the English Landscape*. History and landscape are intertwined.

Many have trod in Hoskins' wake. Oliver Rackham, for example, observed that 'different meanings tend to cluster around the same sites'. In 'The temporality of landscape', an article published in *World Archaeology* in 1993, anthropologist Tim Ingold wrote: 'To perceive the landscape is ... to carry out an act of remembrance.' But for Ingold, such an act is not one that casts the gaze inwards into our own minds, but outwards into the landscape itself. He continues: 'remembering is not so much a matter of calling up an internal image, stored in the mind, as of engaging perceptually with an environment that is itself pregnant with the past.' Like rings in a tree trunk or furrows in a field, layers of sedimentary rock or the number of species in a hedgerow, nature too has a memory. To attempt to read the landscape is therefore to be alive to these traces of memory.

Such writing emphasises the symbiosis between humans and the environment. It seems strange, therefore, that the landscapes which currently predominate in contemporary art are so often devoid of figures. Orton's photographs in *The New English Landscape*, for example, depict bleakly beautiful East Anglian landscapes – empty and grey under grey skies. Here, the earth is scoured by the tracks of a JCB; there, a greenhouse crumbles before our eyes. A fence collapses. The watery lands stretch out flat into the distance. Arguably, the dominant image in a certain sphere of contemporary art today is that of Modernist architecture in ruins and overgrown. Instead of human life, such works display a preoccupation with the traces of human life: especially architecture. Like Shelley's 'Ozymandias' or Jefferies' *After London*, few things epitomise the futility of human aspirations like architectural grandeur overrun by weeds.

This is evident in the paintings, pastels and drawings of German-born artist Wieland Payer, for example, which depict semi-dilapidated Modernist structures discovered decaying in exotic jungles. Or Suzanne Moxhay's graffitied brick arches, through which we glimpse misted pine woodlands in the middle distance. Or Ged Quinn, whose crumbling contemporary buildings are sited in pseudo-Classical or Romantic landscapes. In 2014, Tate Modern held an exhibition entitled *Ruin Lust*. Works by Paul Nash, Laura Oldfield Ford, Keith Arnatt and Rachel Whiteread confirmed both the lasting appeal of the ruin and its changing significance.

Worpole is right to say that there has been a significant shift away from the quest for sublime purity that underpinned Romanticism and Modernism; he is right to argue that it is an aesthetic that nonetheless continues in the photography of walking magazines and television programmes about the countryside. He is also right to observe that the aesthetic of 'the new English landscape' is a largely empty one. Like the tourist attempting to exclude unsightly crowds from their photographs, much is left out of contemporary art and nature writing. Of course, exclusion is an inevitable part of any act of creation, but we can often learn a lot from what gets left out. This struck me especially while reading Robert Macfarlane's *The Wild Places*. What lingered was what was not talked about – the friends waiting patiently in a boat as the author spent the night alone on an island; the long drives in between these wild, magical places. For many of today's artists and writers, the ethical obligation behind their work it is to reconnect humanity with the environment we inhabit – to explore, multiply, complicate the boundaries. Macfarlane professes to do the same, but his journeys are frequently notable only as an absence. Is he at risk not only of failing to bridge the gap between humans and the environment, but also of instituting over and over the monumentality of a singular division?

Where Macfarlane went in search of the pure, wild experience, and eventually admitted to its impossibility, many other writers and artists have taken that conclusion as a starting point. There is no pristine purity; rather, man's presence is felt by his absence – the traces left when industry has moved on. 'The absent has a geography too,' writes Worpole with characteristic elegance. 'The challenge for artists and others is how to represent it. The challenge for politicians, planners and developers is how to respect it.' But what exactly does it mean to have such an ethical obligation to absence? If absence may be seen to refer both to the past and to the future, might this provide a starting point for a thinking that is both conservative and radical? Or by privileging absence over presence are we at risk of fostering misanthropy?

I stop for a drink of water and look once more through the photographs on my camera. Fields and hedgerows, dew and sunset: all of them are empty. There is not a single person doing anything more than walking into the distance. Footpaths, signposts, litter, churches: humans only exist in what they leave behind.

*

As the light begins to fade on the fourth afternoon I am alone. On the map, Calvert Green in northern Buckinghamshire jars against the patterns of the surrounding countryside. No lazy orange contours meandering leisurely across a plain white background. No church with a spire. No pub. Here is only a large expanse of irregular black-and-white dots and splodges. It is the Ordnance Survey symbol for landfill. According to them, that is all we need to know of this area. Or perhaps it is all we can know: these kinds of waste landscapes change so quickly that mapping them is pointless. As soon as the ink is down on paper, the lines in the landscape have moved on.

The interior may be a mystery, but the borders are clearly delineated. The site takes the form of two oblongs tilted anticlockwise through forty-five degrees or so. The larger is to the north, the smaller to the south: both constrained on one side by the presence of a railway line. Ruler-straight, it divides green fields and evocatively named woods (Sheephouse and Decoypond) from the sandy expanse of silt and scar. Meeting the railway line at just off the perpendicular is a track running from the north-west down south and east, with the same dead-straight linearity that denotes the authority of map over land.

Calvert is not a place of long history; perhaps that's why its land has been treated with such violence. The hamlet was founded in 1900 for the sole purpose of housing workers for the local brickworks. Arthur Werner Itter had chosen the site thanks to the opening of Calvert railway station in 1899 – one stop on the Great Central Railway from Marylebone to Birmingham. Calvert Brickworks was then opened the following year to extract Oxford clay for low-quality bricks known as flettons. At its peak, despite the closure of the station in 1964 following the Beaching Report, Calvert employed 900 people and produced 5.5 million bricks per week. At one stage, nine chimneys would have dominated the landscape here. But as demand gradually ground to a halt, the brickworks were closed in 1991 and the last of the chimneys demolished four years later. Calvert's is a short history of extraction and intrusion.

Today, the vista is changing fast, but it remains just as strange: a working landscape, as Worpole says, with its own distinct aesthetic. Three of the old clay pits have been flooded: two are now vast lakes used for angling and kayaking, and one is a nature reserve for wildfowl. Another is a landfill site. Man has plundered what he can from Calvert and now he is pumping back his rubbish. They've been filling it, I'm told, since the early 1980s: a layer of rubbish, then a layer of clay, a layer of rubbish, then a layer of clay. Now they're building a £275 million incinerator to burn what will no longer be buried, and HS2 Ltd have plans for a depot just north of the village. Despite vociferous opposition from local residents, the incinerator was approved by the council in 2012 after what the Bucks Herald described as a 'marathon' council meeting. Unfortunately, my map is from 2011, which means it predates the incinerator. But it's not until after the walk that I realise this. In the meantime, the pace of industrial change here causes me some serious navigational problems.

I skirt the crest of the hill just south of Finmere Woods on my way north-west from Quainton and congratulate myself on my map-reading today. I'm making steady progress, and I'm on track to make it to Calvert and set up my tent well before night. It's the by-now-familiar post-lunch high. Pride, in this instance, comes before rainfall.

Gently it descends at first. I'm not worried, for I know where I am and this time I'm well-equipped. A bin liner cut with strategic holes serves to keep my rucksack dry and I'm fully waterproofed – head to toe. If anything, the rain lifts my spirits further: here I am, out here alone, facing the elements and surviving. It's the same feeling I have on top of a mountain: ridiculous, but I feel it nonetheless.

Where does it come from, this sense of man against nature, nature as an adversary to be conquered? Colonialism? Romanticism? In her 1992 book, Science as Salvation, philosopher Mary Midgley notes that the language of early modern science characterises nature not as a neutral object (as we might expect of Enlightenment-era rationality) but as:

a seductive but troublesome female, to be unrelentingly pursued, sought out, fought against, chased into her inmost sanctuaries, prevented from escaping, persistently courted, wooed, harried, vexed, tormented, unveiled, unrobed, and 'put to the question' (i.e. interrogated under torture), forced to confess 'all that lay in her most intimate recesses', her 'beautiful bosom' must be laid bare, she must be held down and finally 'penetrated', 'pierced' and 'vanquished' (words which constantly recur).

Reading such lines, I can't help but think back to Ada Cecil Wright's description of force-feeding in Aylesbury prison. A silent but 'troublesome female' is tied down, her mouth forced open, and the 'unspeakable' stomach tube is rammed down her throat.

Could man's perceived superiority over nature be linked to the history of patriarchal domination? Certainly there are parallels between the two, if not necessarily a causal relationship. Is this what underpins my feelings of triumph at the top of a mountain? Or at overcoming the wind and the rain here near Quainton, only a few miles from the scene of Cecil Wright's torture? The more I read and write and walk and think, the more those feelings seem misplaced. But still they linger – and I am exhilarated by them. Maybe they are ingrained in us – not as some kind of essential characteristic, but rather as an opposition repeated over and over again in philosophy and science, in books and on television. Arguably, the whole of Western civilisation is grounded on this opposition to nature. Instinct can be cultural too. Besides, it helps sell hiking boots.

As these ideas drift in and out of my thoughts, it occurs

to me that I might be lost. With no mountain summit to climb (navigation is easy when the only way is up) I seem to have drifted off course. Or at least I think I have. In the near distance the skeleton form of industry rises into the sky: it's the new incinerator that I was told about yesterday. It's not on my map and I'm starting to worry. The incinerator's industrial verticality is a sudden and disconcerting presence in the gently rolling landscape. I instantly begin to doubt the accuracy of my navigation. But it makes for some great photos.

Not only is it huge and hideous, but also somehow thrilling. Like careful parents, a pair of orange cranes tend to their growing young: metal grids and concrete cladding growing from among green fields. One day soon it will fill its nest, and the cranes will go elsewhere and build again afresh. Once it is up and running, the incinerator – or 'energy from waste' facility, as it is known – will produce twenty-two megawatts of electricity, enough to power up to 36,000 homes. The contract is worth £275 million and, according to the council, it will save local taxpayers over £150 million over the thirty-year life of the contract. Those who oppose such schemes are invariably labelled as NIMBYs. But nobody wants the techno-sublime in their backyard.

The incinerator's rising bulk makes a useful navigational marker for the walker who has temporarily mislaid his bearings. At least it does for a time. The rain drives downwards – the surrounding countryside is a washed out wall of slate grey. As I approach from the south-east I expect to come to a footpath, running alongside the disused railway. But I cross over and no such path presents itself. Instead, here is a road – brand new, it seems, unmarked and unfinished. Perhaps I'm not exactly where I thought I was. I decide to follow it north-west as it heads, raw-edged, towards the incinerator's hollow hull.

I hear the rising whine of a dog pack in the distance. Slowly it advances towards me, no quicker than my own walking pace. Gradually, or perhaps all of a sudden, it dawns on me: these are not dogs, but the clanking whir of motorised machinery. Where in god's name am I? I look again and again at my map. The rain eases to a spatter on the plastic casing. There is no road where I'm walking. I'm in the middle of the map; yet I've disappeared off it. And I think my boots are beginning to leak.

I decide to approach the incinerator itself, to give in to the stereotypical fear of the modern man: asking for directions. Surely somebody can help me there? In a toothpick sentry box sits a man in a high-visibility jacket. He watches as I approach. I try to look lost and unthreatening. Why the need to act the truth? This is not a place designed for the casual visitor. He eyes me with suspicion. The gnarled old walking stick surely proclaims my innocence? Perhaps not.

I approach and say hello. The man is short and solid, with three small parallel lines of scarring under each eye. In a twanging Nigerian accent he cannot help me.

'Where are we?' I ask.

'I do not know,' he says.

'Can you show me on this map?'

He takes the map and looks at it for some time. He turns it over, squints, and shakes his head.

'I do not know where this is,' he says, returning the map. I am utterly baffled.

I try at a nearby portacabin, where another man in high-visibility vest is of equal help. Lost in their own lives: how did these people even get here if they don't know where here is? Perhaps they're thinking the same about me. Or perhaps they don't trust me. What secrets are hidden behind these branded walls? 'Waste is our energy,' proclaims one hoarding in jaunty-coloured lettering. Who reads these signs?

As I prepare to leave I spot a third man returning to his lorry.

'Excuse me,' I ask. 'Do *you* know where we are?'

'Yes,' he replies. 'We're just east of the M40.'

'Could you show me on my map?' I ask. It takes a few

minutes but this man succeeds. He's English, although I can't place his accent. There is a single earring through his left lobe. He knows where we are. The road I have been walking on is brand new, he says. I realised that.

'That's why it isn't on the map,' he explains. This had not occurred to me.

'It goes all the way up to Calvert,' he says reassuringly. 'Just follow it along, and you'll be fine.'

I thank him wholeheartedly as he gets up into his lorry. But something in my eyes must tell him something. I'm no explorer. Pity flashes across his face. 'Do you want a lift, mate?'

'Oh no, no, I'll be fine,' I reply. 'Thanks again.'

As I turn to follow the road once more, he drives away. I feel a sudden pang of loss – that, I'm certain, was a missed opportunity. I haven't gone more than ten yards when the Nigerian man rushes out of his sentry box. Finally, his suspicions are justified!

'You cannot go this way,' he says. 'This is only for lorries. Too dangerous for you.'

My heart sinks: I'm sick of walking. Why did I refuse that lift?

The security guard tells me there is a footpath that leads up to Calvert. I will find it easily. Given that ten minutes ago he couldn't even locate us on a map, I don't entirely trust his judgement. But I have little choice.

As I walk on and on, through fields and along hedgerows, it soon becomes apparent that I'm going the wrong way. My brief belief in my own navigational skills has collapsed. But nobody else has been much better. I seem to be circulating the incinerator from all angles. The rain has washed out the light. The sun is setting and I feel the gently unmistakable swell of panic rising slowly through my belly. I know where I am, but I'm completely fucking lost. I change tack, hoping to find a path that will get me back on track. But to no avail. Why are the footpaths so badly demarcated here? My photos from this afternoon show the incinerator from almost every conceivable angle. I'm going round in circles.

Eventually I decide to backtrack completely and start again. This time I see it: hidden in the bushes, a tiny track, hardly a track – a little line of trodden grass, nettle-grown and bramble-crossed. I gaze down upon the railway tracks which run alongside in the V-shaped valley below. To the left is the incinerator; to the right, a sign tells me it's a nature reserve. The rain has cleared to reveal a sky of faded azure. The sun sets saffron behind the clanking of machinery and the two proud cranes. This is the new English landscape, off the map, here, where nobody can find us. I'm warily confident that I'm walking the right way, gently panicking that I may not be. I feel alive.

As the path veers right, I turn left. Inexplicably. This place has sapped all reason and knowledge. I am swiftly back on the road I was warned off. It arrows ahead, dead straight to Calvert, a road with purpose. A small bulldozer passes me by. I wave hello. The men on board wave back. They do not suspect the walker. On the left now is the vast expanse of the landfill site.

From the ground rises a battalion of knee-high valves, like an army of skeleton soldiers rising from the rotting teeth of a thousand toy dragons sown in the ground below. It's a moment of strange discovery for me, but I am not the first: photographer Jake Davis has recently published a book entitled *Gas Pipes, A Typology*. Few things could so exemplify our changing attitudes to landscape aesthetics than Davis's cold grey images. Periodically I can hear a fart from one of the valves – a flatulent release of built-up gas. A layer of rubbish, then a layer of clay, a layer of rubbish, then a layer of clay.

Above the landfill, birds swarm in the mid-distance. Silhouetted kites screech and wheel. What is it with birds and waste? I walk onwards for what seems like hours. A jeep passes, then another. This is no place for pedestrians. I don't seem to be making any progress through this long, straight landscape. Is the very road moving against me? Another line in Honor Gavin's Midland springs to mind. I have it with me in my rucksack: 'We walked for a time that seemed endless through space that seemed edgeless. Either edgeless or nothing but edge.' At least her narrator has a companion. I am here alone.

Truly this is the new English landscape.

I eventually come to the exit of the landfill site. Signposts urge hygiene and regulations. Nearby is an estate of 300 homes built on the site of the old brickworks. To the first-time visitor, Calvert Green itself is a strange, blank nowhere of a place. After the striking landscapes of the landfill and nature reserve, the village is little more than a cluster of identikit houses, built for brochures and profit. Given the track record of the developers, David Wilson Homes and Persimmon Development, it's hardly surprising.

Persimmon Homes was founded in 1972 by Duncan Davidson, the grandson of the 15th Duke of Norfolk. After serving in the British Army, Davidson joined developers George Wimpey (later to become Taylor Wimpey) where he managed construction work in Iran under the country's last shah, Mohammad Reza Pahlavi. Returning from Iran to the UK, Davidson founded Persimmon Homes, which has since become one of the biggest players in the UK housing market. In 2012, they built just under 10,000 homes across the UK – 8.5% of the total.

Time and again, however, their developments have been

opposed by local residents and blocked by local councils, but somehow sneak through on appeal. Persimmon has long been known for shoddy workmanship. In 2013, they were ordered to stop working on a development in Gateshead for breaching planning regulations. A Glasgow development was described as a 'disaster' and a 'nightmare' for residents following repeat flooding. By contrast, Duncan Davidson himself lives in the nineteenth-century Grade II* listed mansion splendour of Lilburn Tower, near Wooler in Northumberland. In 2006, *The Telegraph* reported that he owned some 20,000 acres of land in the surrounding countryside. It's a far cry from Calvert Green.

The first residents moved into Calvert Green in the autumn of 2001. Thirteen years later there is still nothing here, nowhere that a sense of community might be fostered. In 2013, the village hall that Davidson built for prospective residents was damningly described in a village document. There have been complaints of inadequate kitchen facilities, inadequate storage space, lack of flexibility, insufficient toilets and lack of changing facilities. A plan is finally underway to extend it. Such is the destiny of today's rural housing developments. What can't be sold for profit is not worth building. Cold and lonely in the accelerating gloaming, I stop to ask a dog walker if there is a pub in the village.

'Oh no,' she replies, almost laughing.

'Are there any shops or anything in the centre?' I wonder.

'In the centre? There isn't a centre.'

'So what's down there?' I point along a road lined with red houses.

'Well, there's a small green, but that's about as close as it gets to a centre.'

I investigate anyway. She's right. I feel uneasy. There is no warmth here. I cannot stay. I decide to keep walking.

Two miles up the road is the village of Steeple Claydon. They have pubs in Steeple Claydon. Their lights beckon to me through the dark. On the way up the hill towards the village, I'm on the look-out for a suitable field in which to spend the night. It's funny how it changes your view of the countryside when you need to sleep in it. Priorities shift. You need shelter, concealment, an easy escape route. You also need fields that don't have animals in them. Fortunately, I realise this in advance.

After setting up my tent in the dark I walk into Steeple Claydon and the Prince of Wales. It's Friday night – full of life and warmth. I sit at the bar, reading and periodically ordering pints. A man looks at my huge rucksack, propped up against the bar, and approaches out of curiosity. 'The majority of people round here are seriously anti-HS2,' he tells me when I explain the nature of my journey. 'But I'm relatively pro – house prices have fallen or stagnated but they may rise if they have the work depot nearby. There's also the idea of a station between here and Calvert. It could be a real boon for this area.' He's lived here for ten years.

As he walks away I ask the landlady if they're serving food. 'Oh no,' she laughs, as if only a fool would think so. Right beside my head is an advert extolling the virtues of the pub's home-cooked fare. I look at it and then slowly back at the landlady. I decide not to say anything. I head to the chippy instead. Then, fuzz-headed and grease-fingered, I saunter back down the hill, to fumble contentedly with the zip on my tent – pitched too near the road after all – and then to sleep, car-lit and fitful.

VI

A Premature End

Chetwode – Twyford – Finmere – Mixbury
– Evenley – Turweston – Sulgrave –
Thorpe Mandeville

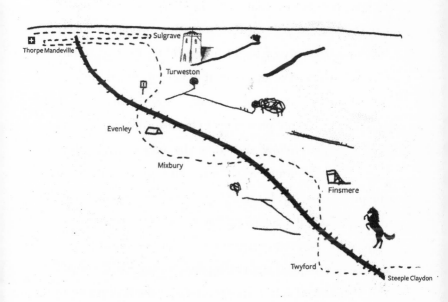

Sitting on a low stone wall outside the parish church of Chetwode, about four miles south-west of Buckingham, I wonder how close I have just come to death. The experience – and an unrelated pain that follows it – will force me to think in depth for the first time about the importance of the human body. Might our bodily vulnerability provide a clue to our relationship with other animals – both our similarities and our differences? Could the body change the way we think about thought itself? Perhaps I'm over-magnifying the afternoon's incident in my mind. But that horse was very big, and very close.

I've always been terrified of horses. Or rather, my fear has become so ingrained that I've forgotten its origins. In fact, now I think about it, it wasn't always this way. I have a hazy childhood memory of happy horse-riding through sunny rural anywhere. We even spent a hot afternoon clearing fields of yellow-flowering ragwort: if dried and mixed in with hay it is highly poisonous to horses. Alive, its flowers glow a golden yellow and drive the bees doolally. That evening, we sat around a campfire and I cut my finger on a ring pull. I have no idea where or when this memory comes from – perhaps it's not even mine.

Since the midnight apparition on the first night, horses have been a frequent sight along this journey. On the fourth day, I passed quickly through a field of them standing in the rain. They gathered after me at the stile as if imploring me to stay and entertain them. I walked on, looking back with regret at my own fear. My wife, Crystal, seems able simply to approach strange horses – she holds out her hand, and pats their neck, and soon they are the best of friends. Perhaps they can sense her affection for them. Perhaps they can smell my fear. On this fifth morning, I passed through another field – this time of smartly liveried ponies, each in its own neat blue jacket. They looked at me with the habitual disdain of the over-pampered, softened only by a momentary flicker of curiosity. They soon turned back to their grass.

The history of the horse in Britain is a long and fascinating one. The oldest known horse remains were found in Pakefield, a suburb of Lowestoft in Suffolk, and date from 700,000 BC. To put that in context, modern humans have only occupied Britain for some 40,000 years. Horses have been in this country nearly eight times longer than us. From objects of the hunt, horses gradually came to be employed as tools of the hunt. Domestication had begun here by 2500 BC, and the horse became the fundamental component of military strategy up until the decline of feudalism and the emergence of the longbow in the fourteenth century. From symbols of status to modes of transport: through the nineteenth century, horses gradually replaced oxen as the animals of the plough.

Although the subsequent industrialisation of agriculture removed many animals from the land, in certain areas horses were still widely used well into the twentieth century. Just to the east of where I'm walking today lies the village of Hardwick (a common Anglo-Saxon place name meaning 'livestock farm'). In 1966, Hardwick was immortalised as Byfield in Richard Hillyer's beautiful memoir *Country Boy*. In the book, Hillyer (whose real name was Charles Stranks) tells of his upbringing in the tiny village. Raised in a world of back-breaking agricultural labour, Hillyer finds himself cut off emotionally and intellectually from the community by his intelligence and by his love of reading. His is a largely private, internal world, characterised by moments of magic in books and nature.

Throughout *Country Boy* animals are a recurring source of fascination. The villagers, for example, are repeatedly compared to animals. 'My father had the patient courage of an animal,' writes Hillyer, in what seems intended as a compliment but nonetheless not an unequivocal one. Hillyer is not alone in describing workers in this way. Several times in *Capital*, Karl Marx does the same. 'The slave-owner buys his labourer as he buys his horse,' he writes. As if in response to Marx, Richard Jefferies wrote in his 1885 essay 'One of the New Voters': 'a man is not a horse' and then again a few lines later, 'Roger the reaper is not a horse'.

In *Country Boy*, the patterns of rural life that surround the young narrator are both comforting and deadening. It is a world marked by 'the heavy stupidity, the animal indifference' of his fellow humans, who exist only to work in the fields. In many ways, the animals are more important than the men, for whom they are supposed to be tools. Hillyer notes, for example, that the working day is 'limited only by what the horses could stand, the men didn't matter'. It's hardly surprising that, in such circumstances, man and animal occasionally come into conflict.

In one especially heart-rending scene, Spicer, the horse-keeper – described as 'a surly beast at the best of times' – resorts to repeated violence against the horses at the plough. He 'dashes at the horse, curses it, beats it, kicks it, his heavy boot coming up with savage impact on the smooth, tight skin of the horse's belly'. The whole episode comes about due to the narrator's own nervousness with such animals – his fear and his lack of that apparently innate ability to understand and guide them. This comes in stark contrast to the dexterity of his brother John, who seems to have a natural way with horses in particular. Hillyer's guilt at his own incompetence is palpable: 'I could have saved [them] from such treatment if only I had known how to handle them.' When I read of John, I can't help thinking of Crystal. It is Hillyer with whom I identify.

And now I'm climbing over a stile, just off the road through Chetwode. I brush aside some branches and enter a large open field. Three adult horses look up at me, bored, and return to their grazing. A fourth sidles over to say hello. Hello, I say in return. As she comes closer I stop and hold out my hand, as I've seen Crystal do so many times. She comes closer.

The last time I had been this close to a horse it had not ended well either. On our honeymoon, Crystal had somehow persuaded me to accompany her riding. It was an idyllic afternoon as we rode along the beach and through the sea. I say 'rode', but I simply sat atop the horse as a friendly local ex-jockey walked along beside with a rope to keep the horse in check. In the home straight, however, the horse decided that he had had enough of this obedient slow progress. Perhaps it was being overtaken on both sides by a pair of cantering males; perhaps it was the proximity of home and dinner – but inside his horsey head a switch flicked discernibly. He threw his head from side to side and the man, who had been in total control up until now, suddenly lost his grip on the rope. In that moment I was alone atop this huge dark beast. As it crested a small mound of sand it reared upwards, throwing its head back. I managed to cling on – but not for long. On the downwards slope it bucked again and I half-slid, half-fell off the side of my high horse. Betraying my inexperience in such matters I thrust out a hand to cushion my landing. This is how wrists are broken: fortunately, the sand was soft and forgiving. Not so the horse. As I landed, I looked up. Above me and towards me, coming hard, the black, kicking hooves right at my head. They say that in such moments your life flashes before you. All that flashed before me was the hot fear of imminent pain. I shut my eyes and ducked, I think, or rolled. Or fell. I felt nothing. I braced for the sudden onrush of agony – pain always waits one tricky moment before launching its full-frontal assault. Still nothing. I got to my feet, swayed a little, and breathed. The man ran towards me – relief and terror writ together across his wide brown eyes. As the horse disappeared into the distance, I laughed a nervous little laugh.

This memory is, if not quite at the forefront of my mind, then certainly somewhere lurking around, as I continue to proffer my palm to the Chetwode grey. She approaches and snuffles at my empty hand. Slowly, with my other hand I reach up to stroke her face. She breathes hot and loud upon my hand. I wander what she is thinking, but her eyes are inscrutable. It is, I think, the same confrontation with ignorance in the face of the other that Helen Macdonald experiences when looking into the eyes of her goshawk. 'What is she thinking?' she asks at one point. 'What is she seeing?'

The process that Macdonald goes through over the course of *H is for Hawk* not only involves learning about the mind and life of the animal other, but also about the limits of that learning. There is, ultimately, only so much we can know. 'I cannot know what she is thinking,' Macdonald admits in prose of simple brilliance towards the end of the book, 'but she is very alive.' It is the same conclusion drawn by Mark Rowlands about his wolf companion in *The Philosopher and the Wolf*, by Jacques Derrida when his cat sees him naked in 'The Animal That Therefore I Am', and by countless others. However deeply science can probe into the brain of an animal, however accurate our simulations of the eyesight of cats or bees or hawks, ultimately there are some things we cannot ever know.

I look up into the big, dark eyes of the grey face in front of me. I have no idea what it might be thinking, or even if 'thought' is the appropriate word. I smile nervously and decide not to push my luck. I say goodbye, withdraw my hand, and turn away to walk slowly onwards. Is this a mistake? If so, I won't know it yet. The grey follows me close behind – just as I've seen a little pony do to a lone lost walker in the Oxfordshire countryside when I was on holiday with my father a year or so before. That pony nipped on to the girl's rucksack and followed her up the hill. She looked terrified, but we smiled and the pony skipped off playfully.

This time I laugh too. But as I walk on, the grey's pacing becomes increasingly erratic. Suddenly she is up alongside me. As I turn, she retreats away. Then back towards me, then once more away – this time rearing up and kicking its rear legs out straight towards me.

'Holy shit!'

Panic floods upwards. I try to keep calm, keep walking slowly onwards. No sudden moves. That's the correct response, right? Again it approaches fast, right up close to me, darts back and kicks. I duck away. How the fuck am I going to get away from this horse? Up ahead the field simply stretches on. No stile or fence or wall. Nothing to separate me from danger. I make my calculations: there's no choice but to turn back.

I wheel around, holding out my stick to try to keep the horse at a distance. (Finally, it seems to have come in useful.) I make my way as quickly as I can back the way I've come – walking, trying not to appear panicked. I'm not entirely sure who I'm trying to fool. I remember once being followed in similar intimidatory fashion by a herd of cattle when out walking with poet and artist Camilla Nelson near her home in Somerset. As I pretended not to be terrified she told me that if you simply ignore them then they won't do you any harm. What time is it, Mr Wolf? The cow as wolf in reverse. Unlike the cattle, however, I don't think this horse is fooled. Certainly its strafing manoeuvres continue – closer and closer, each time I feel the air rush past my face as the hoofs kick through the air. I hasten towards the bushes and finally – after moments that feel like years, that stretch out interminably as I look back now – finally into the branchy protection of the trees at the edge of the field. I scale the stone stile to the safety of the road beyond. My heart is pummelling against my chest.

It's time to take the long way round, again.

*

It's strange how each new encounter with an animal spurs me on – in this case through fear, but mostly through excitement and a kind of happiness, at the evidence of life carrying on regardless of my presence, just passing through. By contrast, when it comes to other people, it's funny how often my enthusiasm for the walk collapses. While catching sight of kites or foxes feels like a little reward for the solitary walker, the company of people exerts a pull that makes me want to stop moving, to remain in one place for longer than an hour or two. What came first – community or our need for community?

Each time the conversation of others, the friendliness, the openness, the simple act of thinking and talking with others, buoys my spirit. But each time I'm alone again, my solitude is brought sharply into relief and I feel that sinking feeling – by now familiar but still somehow new, my stomach hollowed out afresh each time. Perhaps it is the way the loneliness of the countryside is accentuated; perhaps it's the thought of another night alone in a tent. The company of others is a reassurance; to be alone is to be vulnerable.

Earlier in the morning, I'd stopped for breakfast in the village shop at Twyford. The air was white and cold as I walked down a winding muddy path. On the right was the shop, my eye drawn to the warm glow at its windows where I saw a woman washing dishes.

I walk around to the front, where a sign proudly proclaims that the shop is community-owned and volunteer-run. Best of all, they open early seven days a week. I'm even earlier, but a woman inside takes pity on me and lets me in.

The place is like nirvana for the hungry walker. I ask for a cup of tea and survey shelf upon shelf piled high with jams and cheeses, biscuits and fruit. On the counter are breads and cake, croissants, pastries and buns. I order several and sit happily in the corner, soaring high on butter and sugar. It's 7 a.m., I think, and I've been walking for about an hour. Right now, the sweet, nutty crunch of these pecan pastries is probably the most delicious thing on earth.

As I gorge, the woman who was washing the dishes

emerges, carrying a tray of yet another variety of pastry. She recognises me.

'I saw you struggling along the path earlier,' she says.

My pride is momentarily pricked. Struggling? In my mind, I'd been strolling along care-free and full of early morning joy. Evidently that is not what it looked like. I wonder whose impression was the more accurate.

When the conversation turns inevitably towards HS2, the woman with the tray – Debbie – becomes quickly enflamed. She stalks around the shop, her grey bob just visible above shelves of cereal and wine. 'Farms round here will be decimated,' she says. 'The noise testing has been a total sham. It will ruin the reason we actually want to live here, which is because it's peaceful and quiet. The only sounds I can hear from my garden are birds, the dog, and an occasional aeroplane. HS2 will run right behind my back garden.'

In the corner of the store is a selection of artworks by local people – paintings and drawings and the occasional photograph. Propped up on a shelf, one small painting catches my eye. It depicts a man lying asleep on the ground, leaning against a sign. A black hat is tipped over half his face, a spotted knapsack by his side. There are holes in the soles of his hobnail boots. He's like a character out of Hogarth. And on the sign, the words I've seen so often now:

'Stop HS2'.

'It's all to do with the Chinese,' Debbie mutters darkly. I've heard many different theories about the 'real reason' behind HS2, but this is a new one. Her thinking is that because the Chinese bailed out large sections of our economy following the banking crash of 2008, HS2 is their way of recouping the costs by securing long-term contracts for Chinese manufacturers. 'They're calling in their debts,' she says. It's the first I've heard of the theory, but it won't be the last. A bed and breakfast owner further north in Sulgrave says much the same. The following year, in 2015, George Osborne visited Chengdu to urge Chinese businesses to bid for seven HS2 contracts to build tunnels and track beds worth a total of £11.8 billion. According to a BBC report, Osborne cited Treasury figures that suggest some 265,000 jobs in Britain 'only exist because of our links with China'. At the same time, Osborne was also encouraging Chinese businesses to invest in infrastructure in Manchester, Leeds and Sheffield as part of the northern powerhouse plan. 'We are truly entering a golden era of cooperation between our two countries,' he said. Perhaps Debbie has a point after all.

She is one of seventy local volunteers who help to run Twyford's shop, cafe and bakery. All profits go straight back into the community, and the store has raised money for the village's youth club, gardening club and wine club among others. In 2013, they received funding for a new bread oven from Buckingham Local Area Forum, a group which includes representatives from the county, district and parish councils. It is the fruits of this oven that I am feasting upon.

Interest in these kinds of co-operative ventures is rising – on both the left and the right of the political spectrum. Back in 2013, *The Telegraph* reported that approximately 300 such stores had opened across the UK. Many have received support from the Plunkett Foundation, an organisation set up in 1919 by Anglo-Irish aristocrat Sir Horace Plunkett – a Unionist MP and pioneer of agricultural co-operatives. Several have been held up as examples of the success of Conservative economic and social policy. A Plunkett Foundation online forum was launched at one such community store by Tory MP Oliver Letwin.

What is strange is that such initiatives are simultaneously held up both as a return to the radical politics of communitarianism or syndicalism and as the real-life manifestation of David Cameron's much-lampooned Big Society. A document published by the coalition government entitled 'Building the Big Society' declared as follows:

We will support the creation and expansion of mutuals, co-operatives, charities and social enterprises, and support these groups to have much greater involvement in the running of public services.

How this would be done is, unsurprisingly, not touched upon. Nor is the qualitative difference between running a community shop and taking over public services such as education or libraries or even healthcare. In a 2015 article, former adviser to Tony Blair, Julian le Grand argued that, when it comes to healthcare, employee-owned enterprises or 'mutuals' are 'more productive, with higher user satisfaction and with better paid and happier employees'. He continues:

So long as the competitive playing field is level (and here there is indeed room for improvement in the relevant regulations), mutuals and other form of social enterprise can and will win the relevant contracts.

The problem, as le Grand stealthily places in parenthesis, is that the playing field is not level, and the government's emphasis on volunteerism is easily exploitable. Witness large companies like Asda, Boots and Argos enlisting people to work for free as part of the Department for Work and Pensions' Mandatory Work Activity, whereby people must work for their benefits. To volunteer ought to involve freedom of choice. (It originates, after all, from the Latin verb *volo*, meaning I wish, want or intend.) If that choice is all but removed, it is no longer volunteering, but a new kind of workhouse, without location or walls.

Running an enterprise like Twyford Stores may not be comparable to taking over sections of the health service, but for those involved it is a lot of work. The two women have been in the shop about the same length of time that I've been walking this morning. In today's corporate language, it's hard not to wonder how 'sustainable' such initiatives can be. The idea of these kinds of stores is that, being run by the community for the community, there should be a clear understanding of what the community wants. Clearly, on a Sunday morning in November, that is pecan pastries, and lots of them. Unfortunately, they neglected to account for the outsider. By the time I'm finished here – having bought a few extra to take with me for later – there isn't a single pecan pastry left. The place hasn't even opened yet. I feel momentarily guilty. But it soon passes.

*

Above a paddock a kestrel hovers. A pylon looms overhead. I stand and watch as a crow harries a kite across wide open sky and open field, into the bare branches of an ancient oak. The fleeing kite is three times the size of its pursuer. As I walk, I hear a fox squeaking in a copse to my right. I startle another, and it bounces into wooded cover up ahead, the white tip of its fat, dark brush a jolly sight in the morning's struggling sun. I cross another long, straight line of disused railway, overgrown with trees – beech, I think, and alder. I come across the most enormous mushroom I have ever seen in my life. It is three times wider than my booted foot is long. Even now, when I look at the photograph, I can't quite believe it was real. On the boundaries of Northamptonshire, Oxfordshire and Buckinghamshire, all the farm animals have horns. I'm far from London and home, and far from Birmingham too. The countryside is beginning to confuse me.

Outside the Red Lion at Finmere, I get chatting to a middle-aged couple. A sign on the wall says the pub should be open at noon. It's quarter past and all three of us are a little baffled by the lack of action. Once again my backpack is the starting point for conversation. When I explain what I'm doing, it turns out that they're both hugely – if vaguely – in favour of HS2. Or at least, she is. 'Osborne's plan for connecting the northern cities is brilliant,' she says, 'but it wouldn't make sense without HS2. It's progress! I think it's a fantastic thing.' Her husband seems less sure, but happy to have his opinions steered by his wife, on this matter at least.

The rain is starting to fall and there is still no sign of the pub opening. So they drive me to another pub nearby to continue our conversation in the warmth. I worry I'm going to smear mud over the inside of their pristine four-by-four. But they seem genuinely unconcerned. In the car we introduce ourselves: Neil, Claire, Tom. They live in a nearby village in Oxfordshire. They're on their way to pick up their daughter from her singing lesson, they have some time to kill, and they're eager to chat. I'm in no hurry to keep walking. It turns out Neil and Claire are also extremely good company.

The pub we eventually decide to stop at is utterly outlandish. It's Saturday, 8 November, over a week since Halloween. Yet the place is fully decked out in the most all-consuming, seasonally festive decor I could possibly imagine. Pumpkins line the bar. Orange lanterns, silver tinsel, paper witches and ghouls cluster across the ceiling. Every conceivable surface is strung with white, woolly fake cobwebs. In darkened corners, life-sized figures lurk – a witch, a goblin, a fully kitted-out Freddy Krueger.

To me, there's something heroic about the whole thing – a monumental effort to boost visitors, to keep the pub alive. But there's something tragic too. The landlady is all of a rush, as if she and her son can barely keep up with the Saturday lunchtime crowds. We're the only people here. God knows how such places survive – or how long they can last.

We order coffees, sit down and continue our conversation.

We talk about my walk, about the tradition of such undertakings. I don't think I sound especially convinced by my own rationale, so Neil tries to reassure me. 'It's generally accepted that walking a route makes it authentic,' he says. 'It's a chance to really feel the landscape, and to talk to people.' He's right – here I am, talking to people. In a pleasing kind of way, the very fact of him saying so proves him right.

Neil, it turns out, is especially interested in place names. The suffix -worth, I mention, is from the Mercian word *worthing* for ditch, palisade or enclosure. Examples near the HS2 route include Rickmansworth in Buckinghamshire and Kenilworth in Warwickshire. Their names point to a forceful imposition or defence of land ownership. Neil wonders when I'll cross the historic boundary between Anglo-Saxon England and the territories ruled by the Danish from the ninth to the twelfth centuries. I have a feeling I already have. I mention the -by suffix – which stems from *bi*, a short form of *byr*, the Old Norse for a village or settlement. The word survives in English phrases like by-law and by-election as well as hundreds of place names. To the north of here are towns like Badby, Holdenby, Barnby, Thornby and Naseby – evidence that you're entering the domain of the Danelaw.

In addition to the geographical territory, Danelaw also refers to a set of legal terms created following Alfred the

Great's victory over the Danish forces at Edington in West Sussex. A. L. Morton credits Alfred's victory not only to superior military tactics, but also to deeper differences between the two societies. Under Alfred, argues Morton, the transition from a tribal society to a feudal one was under way well before the Norman invasion of 1066. It was under Alfred too that the idea of a state began to emerge, with 'the acquisition of special powers by a minority'. Due to what Morton describes as 'the undeveloped social structure of the Scandinavian peoples', Danish armies tended to split up into smaller groups when confronted with sustained opposition. English feudal ones did not.

Alfred's victory was followed by the building of towns or 'burghs', such as Wallingford, a few miles to the south. As Michael Wood writes in *In Search of the Dark Ages*: 'the recovery of urban life in England in the tenth century was the result of deliberate royal planning rather than organic growth.' After this recovery came the Normans. England was becoming a complex and highly stratified country containing Britons and Jutes, Romans and Jews, Angles, Saxons, Danes and Normans.

Neil argues that, despite these and subsequent waves of immigration, the continuation of the English parish system has helped to maintain a sense of regional integrity. 'Parishes are like pockets of local identity,' he says, 'which they don't have in France for example. It also helps that we were never invaded during the war.'

What interests Neil in particular is the way such a long history of immigration can be detected today – not only in place names but in faces too. 'Look at Lord Patten,' he says, naming a man I've never heard of. 'Now there's the face of a true Anglo-Saxon. Lord Risby, on the other hand: that's a very Norman-looking face. You can go right back to Alfred's battles against the Danes,' Neil continues. 'It's all still there in people's faces.' Claire nods in agreement.

This seems like dubious territory to me. I tell them about an article I read before setting off on this walk. It was published in the *Journal of the Royal Anthropological Institute* in the early 1920s, at the apex of interest in phrenology, the (pseudo)science of skull measurements. The article attempts to account for the 'particularly dark people' who live in the country around the Chiltern Hills. Anthropology of this period was often characterised by attempts to fix racial characteristics. The article begins by referring to the controversial cephalic index (which relates the width of the head to the length of the body) in order to argue that 'the black-haired people are distinctly longer headed than are the average North Chiltern dwellers, and in this respect approach the Mediterranean or Long Barrow more than the Anglo-Saxon type.'

The authors sample approximately three hundred local workers, a number which they admit is 'a small series from which to determine nigrescence'. Much of this 'science' is open to criticism. But one of the more interesting conclusions that the authors draw is that 'about half the working-class rural male people in the North Chiltern area can trace their ancestry back for three generations to some part of the same area.' If this is true, then the kinds of observations that Neil is making also have some validity. Just as in the place names, the history of Britain lingers on into the present – as long as you know how to read it right.

I look again, more closely, at Neil. His polo shirt and jumper are utterly placeless, but his high forehead, receding grey hair and short, straight nose suggest something Nordic about his ancestry. Claire, by contrast, has a small, round nose, dark eyes, dark, curling hair and clear, white skin. 'An English rose,' Neil says.

Before long it's time for Neil and Claire to go and collect their daughter. They drop me back outside the Red Lion in Finmere, which has finally opened, and we say our goodbyes. As we do so, however, there is a pause. For a moment, I think I should ask for their email addresses or phone number. I've genuinely enjoyed their company. For that moment I think they're thinking the same. But that moment passes, and they get back into their car. I turn and walk into the pub as the doors of the four-by-four close crisply and the engine hums smoothly into life.

Inside the Red Lion, I order a pint and sit down, feeling empty and deflated. I sit and drink and eat. Several pairs of my socks are drying on a radiator to my left. My phone is plugged into a socket in the wall. My rucksack lies on the floor. A pink-faced, pink-shirted man who acts as if he runs the place eyes me with dislike as he walks past – I'm not convinced I smell my best.

As I eat, the rain outside gets heavier. My enthusiasm for continuing this walk – already waning – sinks with every droplet of water that slides down the window. If this pub had rooms, I'd book in for the night. I text a friend who lives nearby, hoping he might fancy an afternoon in the pub and then let me stay at his house. It is a Saturday after all. Unfortunately he has prior commitments. I have no choice but to keep going. I take my socks from the radiator, slowly put on my waterproofs, and reluctantly step outside, leaving the warmth of the pub behind me. Fortunately, I don't have far to go.

Before long I pass through the village of Mixbury. Another suffix of Old English derivation (this time -bury from -burgh), but whether this was one of Alfred's initiatives is hard to tell. Beaumont Castle, which once stood here, is long gone. Only the vestiges of a moat and a leafy mound, part-visible through the dark leaves of a snowberry shrub and the spongy white berries from which it takes its name. On my left is All Saints church, one of dozens of square-towered churches built across the region in the decades following the Norman invasion.

Just over the border into Northamptonshire is the village of Evenley, where I'm staying the night. The rain is easing as I push through a gap in a hedgerow and set up tent in the corner of a field, concealed from passing cars by the hedge and trees, just out of sight of a house looking down from an elevated position in the village. It's practically stopped as I enter the pub: the second Red Lion of the day. I feel exhausted and desperate to speak to my wife. My mobile doesn't have any reception so I ask to borrow the pub's landline. Crystal is encouraging, but speaking to her only makes me wish I was at home. We chat briefly and I hand the phone back to the landlady.

'You sound a bit lost, mate?' says one of the men at the bar.

I explain what I'm doing. Almost immediately, I wish I hadn't.

'Don't talk to me about HS2!' says the man.

His friend disobeys: 'It's going straight through Chetwode Priory,' he tells me. 'That place is worth £7–10 million – it's the man's life work. And now he can't sell it at all.' He seems genuinely put out on behalf of the local millionaire.

'We'd be better off investing in canals,' says one man with lustrous silver hair, 'like in Germany.'

'It's the biggest white elephant,' says another.

'There is an election coming up though,' says the first man. 'If Cameron thinks HS2 will lose him an election, then he might just change his mind.'

That has been the view of anti-HS2 campaigners all along the line. Unfortunately, as it turns out, not enough people know or care. I apologise for turning their conversation from amiable and social to heated and political. I go to sit in the corner and read. They continue grumbling about HS2.

I sit and think and drink. I think about my encounter with this morning's horse – already so long ago. I think about community – what it means and why it matters. And I think about the changing attitudes to walkers that I've noticed over the course of this walk so far. From looks of pure bafflement, even suspicion, in London, to interest and sympathy out here in the countryside. That first mumbled hello on Wormwood Scrubs was the watershed. Just then, the silver-haired man approaches, a little flushed.

'I just wanted to check you have a place to sleep?' he asks.

'Oh yes, thank you,' I rebuff him. 'I already have my tent set up down the road.'

I'm not entirely sure why I continually bat people away

over the course of this walk: the workman offering me a lift, not asking for Neil or Claire's email, now this friendly man. As he walks away, I feel all aglow from his apparently genuine concern for the well-being of a perfect stranger. In my present state of emotional yo-yoing, I feel foggily sentimental. I've probably just had too much to drink.

As the evening progresses, it transpires that there is an event taking place. I sit in the corner attempting to look inconspicuous as a surprisingly glamorous party enters its initial phases. Men and women stand and chat. Smartly dressed teenagers hand round things on trays. Before long, I decide it's time to go. I squeeze through one well-dressed group to retrieve my boots from the fireside warmth. I'm becoming increasingly conscious that I smell. I sit in my tent eating the last of my bread and cheese.

*

The sixth morning is exhilarating. It's cold and the air is close and damp. A sourceless light echoes off the mist and fills the air with a pearly whiteness. In the centre of the field is a neat double row of trees, forming a long, straight avenue that runs parallel to the road and up into the village. It must be a vestige of landscape improvements. On my map the names Fish Pool and New Pond suggest similar alterations.

In the mist, the neat line of trees is blurrily beautiful. The morning is punctuated by the yelps of foxes and the nearby cheepings of a robin. This is the best I've slept so far on this trip. Perhaps I'm getting the hang of the whole thing after all. Today I only have to walk as far as Sulgrave, a village on the other side of Bracknell where I've booked to stay in a bed and breakfast. As much as I'm nearly enjoying camping, I could do with a bed, and a wash. Unfortunately, my new-found confidence proves to be misplaced.

The morning remains cold and beautiful. Pheasants scuttle into a copse; a winter flock of yellowhammers flees into the trees. Tied to a gate along a frozen muddy footpath is a 'Stop HS2' sign – its bold black and red lettering already overgrown with a dusting of lichen. The piercing cry of a kite rings out overhead. The signs of industry, past and present, are never far away: great hay bales looming square in the morning mist; a disused railway, arrow-straight and overgrown; a sewage works; and everywhere the detritus of the farm. But in the crisp frost, all is white-edged and beautiful. A flock of noisy meadow pipits gathers by the trees on the edge of the old train line just north of Bracknell. The fields here are getting bigger: vast and empty, they stretch into the distance.

Gradually, however, I can feel a pain beginning in my left knee. Slowly at first: a soft ache, then gradually stretching in narrow bursts up the outside of my thigh towards my hip. I decide to pick up my pace in order to arrive quickly at the bed and breakfast and rest for the remainder of the day. In retrospect, this proves to be an error. I should have just slowed down, and I'm in real pain by the time I arrive in the elegant little village of Sulgrave.

Sulgrave, I discover, has an intriguing history. In the mid-sixteenth century, nearby St Andrew's Priory had its estates seized by Henry VIII during the Dissolution of the Monasteries. As part of the king's efforts to consolidate his power base among the new generation of wealthy wool merchants, he sold three local manors, including Sulgrave, to one Lawrence Washington, formerly Mayor of Northampton.

A. L. Morton writes: 'While the feudal nobles had shown their importance by the size of their armed following, their descendants were judged by their dress and the style of their houses.' Washington, typically, immediately set about building Sulgrave Manor. Constructed from local limestone, the building has been heavily adapted over the centuries and is now open to the public. Above the main door is the Washington coat of arms: two bars (or stripes) and three mullets (or stars) in red on a field of white. Lawrence Washington also expanded the parish church, and the same coat of arms can be seen on a stained-glass window in the south aisle. A measure of the family's wealth and influence is in the number and calibre of places across England marked with their arms: from Selby Abbey to Trinity College, Oxford. This design is significant too. In 1656, John Washington emigrated to Virginia, where he amassed great wealth through tobacco farming and slave labour. His great, great grandson was none other than George Washington, the first President of the United States. It has been argued that the Washington coat of arms was the original inspiration for the Stars and Stripes.

After showering, and lying on the bed for what seems like an eternity, I drag myself up and walk very slowly around the village. The site of a Saxon ringwork castle is now 'Castle Green public open space'. Until the Enclosure Act of 1767, all this would have been common land – traces of traditional ridge and furrow can still be seen to the south-east of the village. Now, it takes 'substantial grants' from the Esmee Fairbairn Foundation and South Northants Council to establish Castle Green as a 'Registered Village Green', managed by a committee on behalf of the parish council. Through the bare branches of a slim, leafless beech, the sun glows across well-tended grass.

I limp the mile and a half from Sulgrave to the Three Conies Inn in Thorpe Mandeville for supper. I walk up to the bar, a girl ambles over from where she sits chatting with her friends, and I order a pint.

'Are you still serving food?' I ask her, rhetorically.

'Sorry, we stopped serving at six,' she says.

I look at the clock on their wall. 'But it's not even five to.'

'Sorry,' she says, with a visible lack of contrition. 'We've stopped serving.'

She returns to her friends by the fire. I limp back to Sulgrave in a quiet and powerless rage.

*

The next morning, after a vast cooked breakfast, I set off once more from Sulgrave, treading carefully. Now, with my backpack on, each step is its own small test. It's like trying out new shoes, or a new limb – gauging the effects as I go, hyper-sensitive to any little sensation that might denote pain or its imminent onset. So far, so good. It's only one and a half miles to Thorpe Mandeville, where I'm meeting a photographer outside the Three Conies, scene of last night's inhospitality. I'm due to write an article about my journey for *Country Walking* magazine and they've sent along Tom Bailey to capture the story: images of me striding along country footpaths, pausing to consult the map, leaning against a picturesque stile – that sort of thing. We're due to spend the best part of the day walking together. I've put on clean cords specially.

After barely five hundred yards, however, I can feel the pain returning to my knee. It's a gradual incursion. At first, I can hear barely a whisper – maybe just an echo of a remembered pain. I stop regularly to stretch the knee: lifting up the toes of my left foot while keeping the heel on the ground and leaning my weight over it to stretch the muscles up the back of the leg. I think this is the right thing to do. But as I continue walking, the pain slowly spreads and sharpens. It starts small – deep within the outside half of my left knee – somewhere around the back. Gradually it unfurls itself – higher and higher up the outside of my leg towards my thigh and up again to my hip. As it does so, the sensation shifts from low ache to sharp, slicing pain – I can feel it tearing like razored forks up from knee to thigh and up around the back of my hip, longer and tighter with every step.

I stop and stretch and carry on. My steps are getting shorter and shorter and slower and slower. I stop more and more often. It's only one and a half miles but I'm going nowhere. I'm not entirely sure how late I am to meet Tom, but by the time I arrive at Thorpe Mandeville I can barely walk.

We say hello, shake hands, and I explain the situation. Tom is exactly what I had expected – tall, calm, competent and well-equipped. He has painkillers. Why didn't I bring painkillers?

Instead of continuing the walk as planned, we drive around in Tom's car, stopping at especially picturesque or historic points in order to take photos. I empty out my rucksack but continue to carry it on my back – for authenticity's sake. After the strong dose of painkillers my knee feels fine. But I continue to limp and even wince from time to time as we climb a slope to get the right shot. I feel increasingly like a fraud.

As we walk and drive, we talk about walking and about the countryside. Tom, of course, has been 'wild camping' several times, but mostly in the Lake District. 'In the Lake District,' Tom tells me, 'it's OK to pitch camp pretty much anywhere as long as you're above a certain altitude.'

He seems impressed that I spent a night in a tent in Perivale. Or maybe he's simply trying to sound encouraging – I think perhaps Tom thinks I'm an idiot. He wouldn't be wrong.

We discuss the pleasures of getting lost, and of not getting lost. I complain about navigation through neglected footpaths. Tom advises the use of binoculars to locate stiles at the far end of long fields. He even tells me how to fold a map: 'You have to be forceful with maps,' he says. 'Don't let them get the better of you.' So far on this walk, I'm afraid the maps have certainly got the better of me.

We stop outside Edgcote House and admire the regularity of the hedgerows. 'You must be doing the HS2 route,' says a local estate hand with uncanny perspicacity. I still don't know how he came to that conclusion so quickly and with so little evidence to go on – we hadn't even said anything.

We stop next to a field in which the battle of Edgehill took place in 1642. It was the first pitched battle of the English Civil War and its lack of clear, decisive victory for either Royalists or Parliamentarians precipitated four subsequent years of intermittent warfare. I stand next to a large sign for the Battlefields Trail and try to look like a walker as Tom takes photographs.

At around noon we arrive in Chipping Warden – the village's warm sandstone buildings glowing rich amber in the November sun. I sit on Chipping Warden steps – a square arrangement of stone stairs that denotes the town's medieval marketplace (the toponym 'Chipping' derives from the Old English cēping meaning 'market') and originally bore a large cross. Tom takes a photograph.

We're here in Chipping Warden to meet Andrew Bodman, another of the anti-HS2 campaigners who replied to my initial email. Andrew is waiting outside The Griffin, wearing a navy blue fleece and clutching a buff-coloured folder, plumply packed with sundry papers and documents

– all relating to HS2. The week before my arrival, Andrew acted as the local guide for the parliamentary select committee who were visiting a series of locations along the route. Andrew gives me the same information that he gave to them. A retired IT project manager, he is another one of these calm, competent men who make me feel so foolish. Deliberate and methodical in his speech patterns, he reminds me a little of a driving instructor I once had. He's precise, logical and extremely well-informed. There's also a sense in which part of Andrew rather relishes this fight against HS2. He doesn't disagree: 'One of the things I like doing is research and analysis,' he says. 'And I've done a lot of research and analysis on HS2.'

The Griffin, it turns out, is not serving food, so Andrew drives me to the Hare and Hounds in the nearby village of Wardington. Tom follows behind. Over the course of the journey and lunch, we discuss HS2. Andrew, who has lived in this area for over thirty years, is a fount of knowledge – both in terms of the national political process by which a project like HS2 is conceived and endorsed, and in terms of the minutiae of local detail that is so often lost in the official maps and documents and press releases. He tells me about a planned maintenance loop between Wormleighton and Boddington and the effects it will have on houses in Lower Thorpe, nearby ancient woodlands, the British eventing team (who practise nearby) and the Banbury Ornithological Society nature reserve. He tells me about the construction site to be based at an old World War II airfield near Chipping Warden, and the hundreds and thousands of HGVs going back and forth on these country roads. Locals are petitioning for a bypass. These 40-tonne HGVs are 2.9 metres wide (including wing mirrors), Andrew says. He takes us to a narrow section of lane near Aston-le-Walls – it's only three metres across. He's measured it.

As well as the local details, Andrew is politely scathing about the entire process of HS2 – from its political conception to the choosing of the route, and its top-down design. 'It started as a political project,' he says, 'not an engineering project. Politicians don't tend to do detail. Now the engineers are tasked with making it work.' He cites work done by John Tomaney, Professor of Urban and Regional Planning at the Bartlett School of Architecture. 'The government argument is based on hope and faith that it will bring money to the Midlands and the north,' he says. 'But the evidence suggests that any gain will be to the capital. The Conservative Party have invested an awful lot of political capital and they would find it very difficult to do a U-turn at this stage. But their arguments don't stand up to scrutiny and are not supported by independent evidence.'

While Osborne and co. have been seduced by the high-speed railways of Germany and China, Andrew emphasises that Britain is not a big country. 'Long-distance rail is not the place to invest,' he says. '86% of rail travel to London is from the south or east. HS2 will pull £8 billion from existing rail services.'

Andrew also tells me about his experience acting as a guide for the select committee. Local campaigners, for example, raised a cherry-picker some sixteen metres in the air to demonstrate the height of the wires at what will be the Edgcote viaduct. That had a discernible impact on the assembled politicians. 'The trouble with HS2,' says Andrew, 'is they are not good listeners. MPs are more ready to listen. The committee's chair, Robert Simms, is trying to get HS2 staff to be more sympathetic. The problem is that the select committee cannot challenge the principle of HS2.' I'll come back to this point later.

As we discuss HS2, I find my mind wandering. I can't help thinking about my leg, wondering if the injury is serious, increasingly convinced that I'm not going to be able to continue the journey. While Andrew's struggle will continue for years, I feel mine is coming to an end. I feel like a fraud: I was supposed to arrive here on foot; here I am, getting in and out of cars and putting a rucksack on for a photographer. As much as Andrew is fascinating, right now I'd rather be left on my own.

We drive to a number of different locations. I get out and walk slowly over the fields where the lost village of Wormleighton is said to lie. As the sun begins to dip, you can just see the gentle undulations in the field where the houses used to be. This is one of a number of abandoned medieval villages in the surrounding area: W. G. Hoskins has estimated that, of some 1,300 across England, 250 may be found in the adjacent counties of Warwickshire, Leicestershire and Northamptonshire. In the case of Wormleighton, Hoskins notes that it was William Cope, Cofferer of the Households to Henry VII, who evicted the occupiers of twelve farms and three cottages in 1498. Some also attribute blame to the Spencer family who owned much of the land here and transferred it from labour-intensive corn-growing to more profitable sheep-grazing. The land had already been taken from the peasants; now the jobs were too. The village was finally abandoned after the English Civil War when the Spencer family home Wormleighton Manor was burned down in 1645. There is here a palpable sense of loss.

As my painkillers wear off, it's becoming increasingly obvious to me that I'm not going to be able to continue the walk. Both Andrew and Tom advise me to stop. 'There's no point in doing yourself permanent damage,' says Tom. Reluctantly, I agree.

It sounds stupid, but this injury is the first time I have

really thought about my body throughout the course of this walk. So much writing emphasises the way in which the experience of walking unites body and mind in a perfect rhythm of natural progression. But this assumes a certain level of fitness – a level, it transpires, that I simply do not have. Body and mind are not one. Why am I only just realising this? As a typical English literature student and then arts professional, much of my theoretical reading is still deeply rooted in the postmodern theories of the 1960s and 1970s. Such writing, as subsequent thinkers have noted, tends to eschew any interest in the body beyond sexual desire. Biology is viewed with suspicion. The result, Terry Eagleton argues, is that 'The very word "natural" provokes a politically correct shudder.'

Postmodernism may have privileged the mind over the body, but it did not institute the division. That is often said to stem from Descartes. His famous dictum *cogito ergo sum* underpinned the argument that it was thought that defined humanity – not only reassuring us that we were indeed real, but also serving to distinguish us from the rest of animal nature which he regarded as mere automata. Ever since Descartes, it has been through consciousness that we have sought to differentiate ourselves from other animals. But as an increasing body of evidence grows that animals too may experience something akin to consciousness, this argument begins to break down. It's also worth pointing out that, as both neuroscience and linguistic theory have shown us, humans are rarely as fully conscious as we like to think. Our brains can make decisions unconsciously that we later attribute to our rational minds. We are never fully in control of the language we use, its effects on others or ourselves. As French philosopher Jacques Derrida has put it:

> One must not be content to mark the fact that what is attributed as 'proper to man' also belongs to other living beings if you look more closely, but also, conversely, that what is attributed as proper to man does not belong to him in all purity and all rigour; and that one must therefore restructure the whole problematic.

This quotation comes from a series of lectures from the early-2000s. Published posthumously as *The Beast and the Sovereign*, the books see Derrida thoroughly unpick numerous attempts – by the likes of Aristotle, Jacques Lacan and Martin Heidegger – to delineate a singular division between human and animal. The lectures are an expansion upon an earlier essay, 'The Animal That Therefore I Am', in which Derrida argued that to insist on a clear divide between 'human' on the one hand and 'animal' on the other is not only foolish but violent. Derrida stresses that he is not seeking to 'efface the limit' between humans and other species. To do so risks the kind of 'biological continuum' that underpinned the Holocaust. Rather his aim is to 'complicate, thicken, delinearize, fold, and divide the line precisely by making it increase and multiply'. He plays on the untranslatability of the French word *bêtise* to suggest that what might be 'proper to man' is not reason or consciousness or language, but stupidity, clumsiness, and an animal-like cruelty.

But perhaps to focus on the mind was a mistake from the beginning. Camilla Nelson once made this point to me when I was extolling my love of Derrida in a pub in south London. At the time, I'm not sure I really knew what she meant, but now I think it is beginning to make sense. As Rebecca Solnit argues: 'Usually the uniqueness of human beings is portrayed as a matter of consciousness. Yet the human body is also unlike anything else on earth, and in some ways has shaped that consciousness.' Solnit is not alone in believing that more philosophical attention ought to be paid to the body. More specifically, Colin Tudge has emphasised the evolutionary importance of the shoulder and the hand. For Mark Rowlands the posterior is what sets us apart from other species. We like to praise our brains or our opposable thumbs, he observes. 'But I think a good case can be made for the arse being the crowning bodily development of human beings.'

Solnit also observes how postmodernism's use of the term 'the body' serves to reduce our biology to the status of mere object. A nagging concern throughout this walk has been the worry that I may be reducing other people to the status of landscape – to be studied and observed like plants or a passing fox. This is the same trope evident in the writings of European botanists on the native peoples of South America. It lingers too in today's nature documentaries: in what other programmes do indigenous people feature? But now it occurs to me that I may have been treating my own body in the same way – as something external from me, to be observed and analysed from a strange, uncanny distance.

However, as this inconvenient – and excruciating – injury is beginning to make clear to me, the body has strict limitations, especially if it is as unathletic as mine. My mind may wander of its own accord but my bodily experiences are very different to those of imagination or memory or dreams. Rowlands has made a similar point about running: 'in the freedom of running distance, the distinction between mind and body is likely to be augmented rather than effaced'. Part of me has always known this, I think, but it is only now that I am beginning to understand how philosophy and the human body might best fit together. There is much more still to come.

Andrew gives me a lift to Banbury station and I take the

train home. Instead of spending another night in a tent, I arrive in Amersham in the early evening, feeling dejected. I call the campaigners I was supposed to meet in the ensuing days and explain what's happened. I intended to walk from London to Birmingham along the route of HS2. I've failed.

VII

Beginning Again

Thorpe Mandeville – Edgcote –
Chipping Warden – Wormleighton – Ladbroke
– Southam – Bascote Heath

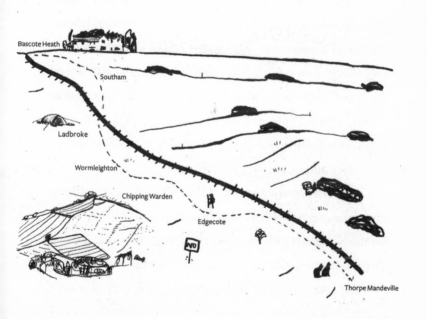

Back in Buckinghamshire, the reality of my failure affects me with a strange force. I should be trekking through fields, meeting campaigners and getting to know the people and places of Northamptonshire and Warwickshire, before arriving, tired but triumphant, into Birmingham city centre. Instead, the next four days proffer themselves as a disconcerting blankness. I'm conscious of being distant and irritable. That the pain in my knee seems to have vanished does not improve my feelings of disappointment.

No sooner have I walked in the front door than I begin to regret cancelling all my meetings with those who live along the route of HS2. I ring several people again to reschedule and, the next day, take the train back up from Marylebone. I want to understand what it is like for so many retired, middle-class men to fight against a system that has served them well for so long. How can the individual fight against the top-down imposition of a project like HS2? And what might that fight reveal about the structure of UK politics – its history and its possible future?

I meet with retired engineer Dan Mitchell, who tells me about the major problems that he anticipates HS2 will cause for the National Grid. He calculates that it will cause serious disruptions to nationwide electricity supplies, to the extent that the line may even require the construction of a new power station. Nobody else seems to have considered it. I meet with Chris Langton, who drives me around the villages of Berkswell and Burton Green in a white, high-powered sports car. He used to work for Land Rover, he tells me. Their headquarters are in Solihull on the outskirts of Birmingham. It's the latest incarnation of the area's long-standing and hugely profitable relationship with transport – canals and rail, bicycles and cars. I meet a retired couple and a worried widow, a church warden and a local builder. The impact for many of these people is upon community: here, HS2 is not an issue of countryside aesthetics or environmental impact, heritage or economics, but of relationships between people – communities divided in two, people cut off from vital local services and from each other. In an age where it seems that everything is merely a click or a tap or a swipe away, it's easy to overlook those for whom physical proximity is a priority and for whom access is not merely a matter of what may be reached, but what can be. These people are Britain's vulnerable, and they have much to lose.

I try to capture some of this in an article for *The Independent*, in which I admit to failing to complete the walk. I also write a separate piece for *Country Walking* magazine, in which I don't. While journalism loves the personal story, walking magazines are rarely fond of failure. I arrange an appointment with a physiotherapist, who prods repeatedly at my knee, kneads it and pushes it. He tells me

I have something called iliotibial band friction syndrome. It's neither rare nor serious. For reasons that I can't quite explain, this saddens me. I probably could have continued after all – if only I'd known, and dosed up on painkillers. Instead of coming as a relief, the triviality of the injury feels like a weakness of will, rather than a weakness of body. That makes me responsible for my own failure. It is my fault.

*

On a muggy morning in July, I start again. It's now seven months since I was forced to cut short my attempt to walk from London to Birmingham. In that time, the Conservatives have swept to a comprehensive victory in the general election. The rise of the fringe parties failed to materialise in the manner that many had expected – in part on account of the UK's first-past-the-post electoral system. The Green Party secured 3.8% of the vote but only succeeded in holding their one existing parliamentary seat. UKIP came in third with 12.9% of the votes, but also only won a solitary seat. In Scotland, Labour were decimated by the SNP. Ed Miliband, Nick Clegg and Nigel Farage all resigned, although a few days later Farage rescinded his resignation and, at the time of the walk, remained the leader of UKIP, although not an MP. Following Miliband's departure, veteran left-wing back-bencher Jeremy Corbyn won the resulting Labour leadership election, much to the surprise and evident consternation of the nation's media. Corbyn had once argued that HS2 'benefited the few rather than the many' and would transform 'our great regional cities into dormitories for London businesses'. Given that David Cameron had previously stated that HS2 would only go ahead with a cross-party consensus, some campaigners began to hope that Corbyn's surprise victory could finally see the project abandoned. Now, with Cameron replaced by Theresa May following the result of the EU referendum, predicting anything in UK politics has become virtually impossible.

All the while, the discussion around immigration became ever more divisive and, until the run-up to the referendum, HS2 was rarely out of the news. In December 2014, HS2 Action Alliance and Hillingdon Council in west London lost their legal challenge in the Court of Appeal. Then in January, the Commons Public Accounts Committee expressed scepticism that the line would deliver value for money. Nigel Farage made UKIP's opposition to HS2 a central pillar of his election campaign. So too did the Green Party. The media kept up their opposition to the project, but anti-HS2 meetings became gradually smaller and less high-profile. A certain feeling of inevitability began to become increasingly evident.

On Tuesday, 14 July, I take the train from London to Banbury and then a bus to Thorpe Mandeville, the village where my walk concluded the previous year. But taking a local bus in Northamptonshire these days is no simple matter. First, I had to register my details – name, address, phone number, email address – on the CountyConnect website. Then I received an automated email, which came, rather bizarrely, from a lincolnshire.gov.uk email address:

Thank you for your registration request to join the Northamptonshire CountyConnect service. We are currently processing the information you have supplied and we will be in contact with you shortly to confirm your membership details. This will normally be within 24 hours.

Sure enough, the next day I received a call from one of the staff at the council, and my registration was completed. I then received a membership number which I was required to use in order to book the bus service. Except I could not book the bus service more than a week in advance, so was required to wait until nearer the time of the journey before making my booking.

Outside Banbury station, I stand bewildered. It has two exits but there is no sign saying where my bus will stop. I ask at the till but the woman has no idea what I'm talking about. A customer overhears and is adamant that I need to walk to the bus station. I'm not convinced, so I call the CountyConnect helpline and am assured that my bus is on its way.

Eventually it arrives – only a few minutes late – and leaves. I'm the only one on it. As the bus heads towards Thorpe Mandeville, we stop periodically to pick up other pre-booked customers. Once I've got over the initial over-complexity of the registration system, this approach to local public transport strikes me as eminently sensible. What need is there of expensive petrol-guzzling buses running up and down the leafy lanes of Northamptonshire if there is nobody actually in them? On the other hand, it's impossible not to think of those who don't have access to the Internet, who don't know how it works, who are unable – for whatever reason – to plan all their journeys in advance, or who are understandably loath to hand over personal details to a public-private partnership with the local council. After all, should it really be necessary to register one's name, address, phone number and email address simply to get on a bus?

In 2014, local newspaper the *Banbury Guardian* published letters complaining about the difficulty of booking by phone. I may have experienced a smooth journey, but this is apparently not always the case. As services have been cut, journeys have been subject to last-minute changes, with one correspondent complaining that 'a 20-minute trip can be doubled or tripled without warning'.

Half-conceived thoughts of privatisation, council cuts and local transport are drifting through my mind as the bus pulls to a halt next to the sign for Thorpe Mandeville. Outside on the verge, I have a drink of water and put on my rucksack. It's considerably lighter than last time around. This leg of the journey should last just four days, so I've only packed a couple of poetry books. No spare shoes or trousers or shirts. No binoculars or Dictaphone, oversized camera or hefty history books. The forecast is set fair for the week – keeping warm is not going to be the problem.

I walk past the Three Conies, muttering to myself about last year's lack of hospitality. I pass the low, squat village church, and set out into the fields: following a straight rust-coloured mud path through fields waist-high with grey-green corn. I'm trying to walk slowly – wary in case my leg recalls this place. But already the landscape feels so different from last time; now, it's full of life and growth and movement. In November, I trudged through endless fields of empty muddiness. Today, flies buzz under skies of low white and grey. The air is hot, but the fields are full of a sense of what is to come.

That sense of homogeneity remains, however. Uniform

fields stretch over gentle hills and out of sight. Lines of woodland, hedgerow, fence and path all seem uncannily regular. These are what W. G. Hoskins calls 'the planned landscapes of Georgian times'. This is what much of the Midlands looks like. A bridleway intersects my path on the perpendicular. Its edges are fringed with longer, sandy-topped grasses. It cuts a long straight line through the green landscape. I remember walking next to this with Tom, the *Country Walking* photographer, back in November. I haven't been walking for long, but it's still a relief to know I'm heading in the right direction. To my left is Danes Moor, the site of two major battles – the first, in 914, between the Danes and the Saxons; and the second, in 1469 during the War of the Roses, in which the Earl of Warwick defeated an alliance of armies loyal to King Edward IV. HS2 is scheduled to run straight through it.

From the tidiness of the landscape, I come finally across mess: Worpole's aesthetics of the working landscape once more. Here are piles of rubble, and bare lengths of grey wood, lines of bright blue piping, plastic bags, and the sad old form of a JCB, its arm looming yellow against the dirty white sky. This patch of waste is a riot of colour: red poppies, purple thistles, white daisies and yellow dandelions cluster among the discarded rocks and brick. Gradually, I become aware of a strange mewling. It sounds like some kind of animal – lost and forlorn, or warning me away. But it can't be. Perhaps it's the wind, sneaking along the rusted tracks of the JCB. Or some kind of creaking: I wonder if one of these piles is on the verge of collapse?

I continue walking around the largest mound of brick and nettles, until I spot a sudden movement – there, near the top, that must be the cause of all that noise. Two tiny kittens: one white with dark grey markings, the other mainly pale ginger, scrabbling among brush and brick. I wonder what they're looking for. Food? Their mother? I wonder what they're doing here – discarded by some callous farmer I hastily assume. My heart fills with sadness and pity. Perhaps I should take them with me? It's only four days of walking, I think to myself. Besides, they're so tiny, they'd easily fit in my rucksack. Don't be ridiculous, I say, almost out loud, and keep walking – with a sense of confusion and regret. What should I do? What should I have done? The soft, sad mewling slowly fades.

For a second time, I find myself among the honeyed stone cottages of Chipping Warden. Again, I meet with Andrew Bodman outside The Griffin. Again, I get into his car and we drive to the Hare and Hounds in the nearby village of Wardington. We order the same sandwiches and sit down to discuss the same subject: HS2. We talk about the progress that the campaigners have made: from vague expressions of sympathy from the parliamentary select committee to concrete guarantees of change, such as the agreement to construct a bypass around Chipping Warden. We discuss the general election – in particular the defeat for Labour MP Ed Balls. 'It's unfortunate,' says Andrew. 'He was our strongest ally in the shadow cabinet.'

I'm most interested in the process that Andrew underwent of giving evidence before the select committee. It sounds like an intimidating experience to me: six MPs sat in a horseshoe formation, with a computer screen on which petitioners showed their presentations. In addition, what Andrew calls a 'flotilla' of HS2 staff was there to provide back-up information to the QC or whoever was speaking on HS2's side. There was also a clerk from the private bill office and an assistant who sat next to the chair to provide technical legal advice. The whole thing was televised so there was also a TV producer in the room. 'HS2 have a big team of people,' says Andrew, 'we're just private individuals.'

It is not just the experience of giving evidence that fascinates me, but the whole labyrinthine process. Petitioners, Andrew tells me, were charged £20 to enter a petition, and were required to deliver it *by hand* or somehow get their MP to do it on their behalf. Sources had to be submitted in advance of the hearing. Travel to and from London was not reimbursed. All of the submissions were then scanned and uploaded in advance of the hearing. It amounts to thousands and thousands of pages printed out, delivered by hand, then scanned and uploaded again: what an extraordinary waste of time, energy and money.

It is through such tortuous processes that the machinery of government comes to serve powerful vested interests over private individuals. Putting together a case against HS2 costs time and money; it requires expertise. That is why so many of those I meet are retired professionals – few others have the energy or the knowledge. The more complex and time-consuming such processes become, the harder it is for ordinary people to have their voice heard, and the less likely they are to have any impact on high-level government decision-making.

As David Pepper has argued, 'the odds are overwhelmingly controlled by and stacked in favour of the industrial/financial complex.' Pepper cites motorway protester John Tyme's assertion that government operates 'not in the national interest but in the interest of one industrial/financial lobby'. But Pepper also goes further, suggesting that the very concept of the 'national interest' is created by vested interests in order to justify their actions to the public: 'what is in the "national interest",' he writes, 'is decided for the many by the few, and in favour of the ideology of a particular class.' Citing US sociologist Dorothy

Nelkin, he argues that technical and scientific expertise frequently function as a means of legitimising the actions of governments and corporations. Government reports into HS2 are a case in point. In 2013, accountants KPMG produced a report 'exclusively for the benefit of HS2 Ltd' which outlined the economic case for high-speed rail. Reports that do not serve the appropriate purpose are routinely redacted or, in the case of a 2011 Whitehall document described by the BBC as a 'warts-and-all analysis of how HS2 was progressing at the time', blocked completely. No wonder Michael Gove felt able to declare in 2016 that 'people in this country have had enough of experts'. The real surprise was hearing this kind of critique co-opted by the Conservative right.

As I noted before, when Andrew evidently relished the research elements of the campaign, there's a clear sense in which he seems to take pleasure from the elaborate performance of the select committee hearing. He is full of praise for Attorney General Jeremy Wright, the MP for Rugby and Kenilworth, who petitioned against HS2. 'He was so impressive,' says Andrew. 'He had the right tone and level of detail.' He is also modestly pleased with his own performances on behalf of South Northamptonshire Action Group (SNAG) and as an expert witness for retired engineer Dan Mitchell who I also met back in November. 'I referred to and provided more than thirty-one sources which supported our arguments. It shows you've done your research.' Andrew tells me that HS2 declined to contest his evidence 'on a point-by-point basis', which he takes as an admission of the validity of his claims: 'If an expert witness is not contested, then it's an acknowledgement that it is right.'

It's hard to know after so much effort what kind of effect all these petitions will have. Individual changes may be made, but it is not within the committee's remit to challenge the basis of HS2 itself. This, as Pepper points out, is standard procedure for such inquiries: rarely do their remits extend deep enough to cancel the project in question, merely to make minor alterations here and there. Nonetheless, Andrew's commitment to the cause is extraordinary, and he is full of ideas about how best to continue the campaign. In the car back to Chipping Warden he mentions in passing that he has cancer. I don't know what to say. I wonder to myself if the anti-HS2 campaign is a way of taking his mind off the disease, or whether mortality acts as a spur to harder work and greater focus. I can only marvel at his energy and selflessness.

I say goodbye to Andrew and set off again, taking the wrong road at first and backtracking after twenty yards or so. I start again, this time heading north along the A361. I've got a lot of ground to cover this afternoon, so I pick up my pace as I turn on to a path alongside a disused airfield. Its edges are alive with an array of wild flowers and billowing, blowsy cabbage white butterflies. I disturb a fat female grouse that crashes away low across a field of corn. I pass a rusting JCB by piles of steaming hay. I ask a man with a dog if I'm going the right way, but I can't understand his accent. I nod and pick up my pace to avoid having to walk together.

I spot a roadside goldfinch in Lower Bodington and an anti-HS2 sign right by a sewage works. There seems a certain irony to this: the countryside, as I've already learnt, is not some zone of pristine purity. We have already altered it beyond belief with our agriculture, our transport, our waste. Defeating HS2 will not bring back what has already been lost. Further along is another sign, saying simply 'No Rail', and lying broken on the ground. Soon the signs themselves will become part of the landscape. Soon they too will have a history.

After Wormleighton stands a red brick house in an undulating sea of yellow-green wheat. But it is not a sea: at sea, the size and form of the waves varies at the surface. This crop is entirely regular; its undulations come only from the contours of the ground underneath. In that way, it is more like a glacier than the sea. Such regularity is the result of centuries of agricultural breeding, but the process has accelerated rapidly since the development and expansion of industrialised farming techniques. Crops are specially bred to respond to chemical treatments for high yield. Uniform growth patterns enable maximum harvesting efficiency. Once we shaped our tools to work the land; now we shape the land to fit our technology.

I cross a stream and into a marshy field. As I find myself trudging through swathes of interminable damp, it occurs to me that my inability to navigate correctly may be self-fulfilling. It's certainly self-defeating. For perhaps the first time on this entire journey, there are no roads or paths running even close to the route. The Banbury Road is too far west; the Oxford Canal too far east. This is agricultural territory. The straight line of orange highlighter across my OS map lances only through the fine dark tracery of hedgerows and polygon fields of empty white. It is exactly this empty whiteness that shows up the limitations of the OS map. As Nick Groom observes in a book review for *The Independent*:

The OS map is effectively the view of the country from the city, in which the landscape is laid out for leisure activities, from walking tours in the 19th century to green-laning and geocacheing in the 21st.

In her seminal book *Wanderlust*, Rebecca Solnit argues that this is an important function of the OS map. It is through these maps that public rights of way through the countryside, hard won from the UK's landowners in the 1930s and 1940s, have been reinforced. In 1949, Clement Attlee's Labour government passed the National Parks and Access to the Countryside Act which instituted in law those paths that every member of the public has a right to access. But it was the process of fixing these routes in map form that, for Solnit, cemented public rights and – just as importantly – public knowledge of those rights. 'Once the paths had been mapped,' writes Solnit, 'they were considered definitive. The burden had shifted to the landowner to prove that a right-of-way didn't exist, rather than to the walker to prove that one did.'

As part of this process, whereby the UK countryside became a place for city workers to escape to in their free time, it came to be viewed less as a working environment than as a space for leisure. As Groom puts it: 'Land featured on these maps is not represented as a working agricultural environment.' The origins of the Ordnance Survey stem not from the egalitarian 1940s, but from some two hundred years earlier: the Jacobite rising that led to the Battle of Culloden in 1746. The first such maps were produced to enable the English army to crush dissent in Scotland. In these first Ordnance Survey maps, ancient means of identification such as field names and the names of parish saints – what

Groom calls the 'co-ordinates' and 'calendar' of local rural lives – were not included. There was no room on the map for myth or mess. Instead the focus came to be upon a shared national history of battlefields and ancient monuments:

> Pre-Roman remains were believed to indicate that the British Isles shared an indigenous, non-classical history, and so these remains were a characteristic way in which 18th-century Britons could imagine that there was an underlying unity to the kingdom defined by the Acts of Union in 1707 and 1801.

Groom's argument is that these Acts, which united Britain with Scotland and then Ireland, were reinforced by a retrospectively historicising justification, in which maps played their part. As the union comes under increasing tension – with fifty-five SNP MPs at Westminster – it will be interesting to see what new maps are made.

In 1999, under New Labour, Ordnance Survey went from being a government agency to a trading fund, which meant that it was required to cover its costs by charging for its products. Then, in 2015, it became a state-owned enterprise, still fully owned by the UK government. The new status of Ordnance Survey also saw a rebrand, with the broad, north-pointing arrow of the War Department dropped in favour of a less militaristic map motif.

More recently, there was talk that George Osborne was looking into privatising it completely. Intriguingly, given what Groom has noted about the nationalistic origins of OS, natural history writer Patrick Barkham criticised the proposed sell-off as 'Britain-hating'. It's worth pointing out that Google Maps, as might be expected, is weak on contours, administrative boundaries and heritage, but strong on anything commercial: pubs, shops and other consumer-facing businesses. Compelled by Google's online supremacy, organisations upload their own information – address, opening hours etc. – so Google doesn't even have to. UGC: user-generated cartography – a neoliberal world map to replace that of the nation state. How closely our ideas of identity are bound to maps.

The irony, Groom concludes by noting, is that it is 'the physical experience of walking' – something encouraged and enabled by the OS maps – which eventually demonstrates their shortcomings. This may be a nice point of intellectual interest, but it hardly helps me find my way. The map may show little of interest for the tourist or the soldier: no shelter, no pub, no ancient ruins, no church with tower or spire. But it's hot here in these fields. The flies are rising from the grasses, midges and mosquitoes waved away. I'm guzzling hay fever tablets. I cross a narrow stream in the certain knowledge that all is about to go wrong. What I ought to do is simply set my compass north-west and walk in a straight line through the fields until I get to Ladbroke, where I had planned to spend the night in some woods just south of the town. It should only take an hour.

And yet, for some reason, I'm unable to do it. I keep walking along the path that runs parallel to the stream. I'm walking due east, knowing, with every step, that I'm going further and further from the line I want to be walking. I know I should turn off, now, turn up, left, north towards Ladbroke. But I don't. I keep to the path, stick to the map, treading down the grass that has been trodden down before, unwilling to step out on my own and trust myself. I follow instead the line on the map, the line worn by farmers or walkers or sheep. The wrong line. Why? Even as I'm doing it, I'm cursing myself and trying to work out some kind of answer. In part, perhaps, it's fear: a lack of confidence in my navigational skills that discourages me from leaving the security of the path. At least on the path I know where I am – even if where I am is wrong. Perhaps it's also simply a fear of the unknown: the blankness of the map, and the featurelessness of the fields as they rise up gently in front of me. Perhaps it's the fear of trespass: I'm allowed here on these paths; the fields belong to the farmers. As has become a pattern on this walk, the weather echoes my map-reading.

It starts to rain.

At least the rain provides refuge from the midges, which now shelter low in the grasses. But inside my waterproof it's hot and soggy. My skin is sticking to itself.

There is some kind of magnet drawing me towards the canal. I attempt to turn north eventually, but I know – or think I know – that really it's too late. The path tails out before it's supposed to. I backtrack once, then twice, and I lose my place on the map. Before long I admit defeat – perhaps I already had. I descend to the canal with a strange combination of anger and relief. I'm angry at the rain and the humidity and the midges, but mostly at myself for having to take this ridiculous detour. But I'm also relieved no longer to be responsible for navigation. Now I need only follow the canal.

Walking alongside the water, I half-consciously spot a small brown mound on the towpath. It crumples underfoot. I look back: it was a vole, its insides popped out like a pile of pomegranate seeds from a velvet pouch of chocolate brown. I can only assume it must already have been dead.

The Grand Union Canal has been managed by the Canal and River Trust since ownership was transferred from the cash-strapped British Waterways (BW) in 2012, following the coalition government's much-publicised 'bonfire of the quangos'. The Trust has quickly made a name for itself as a champion of culture. It has collaborated with Arts Council Wales to run an artist-in-residence programme, teamed up with the Poetry Society to appoint a 'Canal Laureate', and worked with the Landmark Trust to commission a new sculpture by Antony Gormley on the Stratford Canal.

But when it comes to the day-to-day running of their canals, the Canal & River Trust has come in for severe criticism from a wide variety of sources. *Private Eye*, for example, has detailed several instances of the Trust's 'enthusiastic legal team' going after boaters and local businesses, and the *Gloucester Citizen* has reported on live-aboard boaters being 'routinely hassled' by the Trust. A petition on *38 Degrees* lists a number of examples of evictions carried out by the Trust upon the disabled, elderly and mentally ill.

In 2012, *The Telegraph* commented on the salary of then BW chief Robin Evans (£284,000 in 2009) while pointing out that the same management team were transferred from BW to the newly formed Trust. At the time of its formation, there was an estimated £300 million backlog of maintenance work. The aggressive approach of bailiffs and lawyers has been justified in the name of efficiency; but the salaries of those at the top have only continued to grow. The UK's canals are no longer simply safe havens of tranquillity; perhaps they never were.

I look again at my map and see the source of the magnet

drawing me onwards. It is not, after all, the canal, but there, just next to it, far away from my route. By three different places all named Napton Holt is a triangular blue beacon of respite: the symbol for a campsite. For, in truth, perhaps I simply can't face a night in the tent, alone, afraid and in the middle of nowhere. On the first leg of this walk, by the third night, I felt I had nearly come to terms with the process of 'wild camping' – finding a concealed spot, staying out of sight, eating in a pub and retreating under cover of darkness. But now I'm starting again and baulking at the prospect. Besides, it's not so easy to hide in the lightness of a summer evening.

I call my wife. She tells me the campsite is open. She's right.

After setting up my tent in gentle rain, I take a walk around the site. A portacabin has been designated 'Site Warden's'. There is a gravel seating area at the front, with two wrought-iron benches painted green and two matching chairs – their wooden slats stained red-brown. Five planters have been arranged symmetrically where the gravel meets the lawn. I sit on the bench eating bread and cheese, chatting to a black and white dog who hopes I will share my feast. Swifts zip back and forth. Three pigeons snooze on a phone line above.

It's amazing how different this feels to my first night in

Perivale. It feels lovely simply to sit outside – instead of being stuck inside a tent, hiding from the weather and the world. The rain has abated. It's almost pleasant now. The dog is licking stones at my feet. I feel strangely relaxed and safe. It must be something psychological – within me. But then I'm not the only one: one hedge is lined with motorhomes; another with caravan trailers – each extended by the addition of a tent, from small mustard-coloured atrium to mini-marquee. A gas cylinder stands out the front of each. *Do these people live here?* I think to myself, before realising that it's the caravans that live here – the people come and go. I used to sneer at such people – why would you come here when there is the whole of the countryside to park in? But now I understand. Perhaps it's the fear of the illicit. Perhaps it's the fear of other people. The irony is that, here, on this side of the fence, it is the presence of other people that makes me feel secure.

A few yards away, a woman in red wellies chats to a man in shorts doing his washing up. She asks about his holidays. They seem to have known each other for some time. Maybe people do live here after all? The dog, forlorn, presents me with one of the stones he's been licking. I relent and hand him a lump of cheese.

Above, two of the pigeons half-heartedly attempt some sex, and stop. The third looks away – considerate, perhaps, or resentful. Soon all three are silent once more, spaced out from each other at exactly equal distances. A plane sounds like a hairdryer overhead.

On the other side of the hedge, a pair of cows nose by.

The sky starts to pinken. The rain begins again.

*

The next morning, I walk from Napton Holt to Southam along the Welsh Road, the old drovers' road for taking sheep and cattle from north Wales to the markets of London and south-east England. On each side are wide verges and concealed gulleys. I can't help but imagine these as sites of ambush or places of concealment for those on the wrong side of the law. Along the way I pass hilltop wind turbines, prefabricated houses and a nascent business park. I stop for tea and an apple pastry in Jackie's Tea Room in Southam. A mother drops off her daughter at Southam College. Crows have gathered in clusters upon the playing fields. A kestrel hovers, stops, and stoops behind a hedge.

On the far side of Southam, a tractor labours along the road, with a verge-trimming extension attached. I wonder who is responsible for keeping the edges of the road clear. The local council? The landowner? Herefordshire Council's website declares that: 'Trees and hedges are the responsibility of the owner of the land they are situated on.' Hampshire Council, meanwhile, have claimed responsibility for 'maintenance (cutting) of grass, shrubs and trees within highway boundaries.' Here in Warwickshire, the county council states that: 'Our policy is to carry out mowing on a safety basis only, by cutting a one-metre width swathe plus additional areas at junctions and on bends, for visibility purposes, three times a year.' In 1946 there were an estimated 500,000 miles of hedgerow in England. By 1993, this had fallen to just 236,000. W. G. Hoskins praises the diversity of England's hedgerows: 'English hedges are of all dates,' he writes, 'Celtic, Saxon and Danish, medieval, Tudor, Stuart, Georgian, even Victorian in places.' But now they are treated the same by the same machines. Today, according to the People's Trust for Endangered Species, 'neglect and incorrect management, such as too-frequent trimming, are responsible for more hedgerow loss than outright removal.' The kind of mechanised trimming espoused by local councils is in part to blame: 'repeated cutting at the same height can gradually cause whole hedges to die off.' The subsequent loss of species – plants, trees, butterflies and other animals – has been devastating.

At Bascote Heath the grass verges are privately owned and spirit-level even. But the houses are nearly all for sale. Along the B4452, the properties are a 1980s pastiche of semi-suburban prosperity. They were all built by the same man, who – in time-honoured fashion – retained the grandest for himself. Via Google satellite the image is of flat green lawns and a pair of swimming pools. From the road, the view is obscured by a long wall, its gates arched like early Gothic windows. The main house is replete with all the accoutrements of period style: tall square chimneys, brick cornices under a curving roof, gables, oriels, bricked-up Gothic arches and even an eyebrow window. Exactly what period this style purports to represent is hard to say – there's a smidge of the medieval and a healthy dose of Victoriana. More than either, however, in its joyful exuberance, it feels like a product of its era. Prior to the announcement of HS2, this house was valued at £1.3–1.5 million. It was recently sold for £830,000.

I'm in Bascote Heath to meet with Pauline and John, who live a little further along the road. Back in November, when I failed to finish the walk, I'd come here to meet Pauline with Dan Mitchell. John had been away. The couple had recently given an interview on local BBC television in which Pauline admitted that worries over HS2 had driven her to seriously contemplate suicide. It was the first that her husband had heard about the extent of her feelings. At the time he confessed to feeling the same. Unsurprisingly, with such private emotions exposed in public, the interview made for extremely painful viewing. When I'd met her, Pauline had been understandably raw – despair and a tightly-held fist of anger clenched beneath her obvious decency and kindness.

This time, her eyes still glint with pugnacity, but she also seems more relaxed and content. I sense the worst of their ordeal may be over.

'HS2 have agreed to buy the house,' John tells me. 'It's a great relief.'

'We've been fighting for five years,' says Pauline, 'and we haven't let up, and it took its toll.'

The line of HS2 here at Bascote Heath will eventually run underground, through what is known as a cut-and-cover tunnel. A trench is cut into the ground and then covered over afterwards so that it is not visible from the surface. While this may minimise the aesthetic impact, the Woodland Trust points out that the process involves more spoil than bored tunnels. All properties directly on the route must be purchased before being demolished to make way for the line. But for residents who live near to but not actually on the line, it's a different story: HS2 Ltd, I'm told, are only required to purchase such properties in 'extreme circumstances'.

In the case of John and Pauline, John's poor health and that of their son provide the necessity extremity for compensation. The decision comes after a protracted battle, and both Pauline and John credit the parliamentary select committee, and especially the understanding shown by Conservative MP Peter Bottomley. In 2014, Pauline and John appeared in front of the committee at Westminster. As Andrew Bodman told me earlier, this can be an intimidating environment: up in front of six MPs, as well as armies of lawyers and what Andrew described as a 'flotilla' of HS2 staff. As we've seen, this is how the government machine functions to intimidate the individuals that find themselves in opposition. 'It's a daunting prospect to go up there in front of these people and argue your case,' admits John. Many couldn't even face it. Pauline cites examples of local residents – the elderly, the sick – who were simply too intimidated to make the journey to London to argue their case. 'People assume you just get the compensation,' she says. 'But you have to fight for it.' John agrees: 'The onus is on the individual,' he says. 'For people who can't articulate, it is a horrible experience. The committee were very nice to us, but they gave Dan Mitchell a hard time.'

With this one decision having gone John and Pauline's way, now begins the next phase of the battle. The value of their house must be ascertained, along with the price that HS2 Ltd will be willing to pay for it. Needless to say, this is highly convoluted too: Pauline and John tell me that from a group of five different surveying companies (paid for by

HS2, not local to the area in question) they will choose one, HS2 will choose another. If the two valuations are sufficiently similar, then a midway value is offered. If they are not, then more surveyors are called in and the process begins again. Supposedly, says John, this is to give the 'true value' as opposed to the 'artificial' market value of the property – as if there is such a thing as a 'true' value of a property that could be in some way separated from the market in which it is sold.

As John and Pauline explain this labyrinthine process, I look around their living room. It is scrupulously tidy. Gilt-framed landscapes line the walls. A ginger cat snoozes on the back of a florally upholstered armchair. Some people would find this kind of home stiff or formal, but it reminds me of my parents' house and, despite my mud-flecked trousers and sweaty T-shirt, I feel relaxed.

Over lunch, the subject of politics is never far away. The third runway at Heathrow is another major infrastructure project in the news. Pauline notes how the only Conservative MPs to oppose the scheme are those whose constituencies stand to be directly affected: Justine Greening, Philip Hammond and Boris Johnson. Pauline mentions the 'shepherd's crook', a kink in the route of HS2's proposed second phase which takes it conveniently around the limits of George Osborne's constituency of Tatton, to the north-west of Macclesfield. 'Initially he was given credit for that part of the route,' says Pauline, 'but that was swiftly retracted.'

I mention something I've been thinking of over the past couple of days – that such occurrences are an unavoidable aspect of a democracy based upon geography. A politician's duty, in theory at least, is to his local constituency. If HS2 had been scheduled to run straight through the wealthy village of Alderley Edge, for example, then Osborne would have been lambasted for failing to use his influence as a Member of Parliament on behalf of his constituents. That it doesn't is used as evidence of his meddling by those wishing to have other sections of the line relocated.

This system of constituencies reflects the origins of the English parliament. It was William the Conqueror who first established a council of landowners, from whom he sought advice before making new laws. According to historian A. L. Morton, 'Parliament was developed as a tax-collecting apparatus.' But it was these landowners who later pressured King John into signing Magna Carta in 1215 in order to limit the taxes that they were required to pay to the king. In 1265, rebel baron Simon de Montfort summoned his own parliament, which included not only feudal barons but also an emerging class of new knights, growing rich off the wool trade. Although de Montfort was defeated, Edward I maintained several aspects of this new parliament. With the continuing rise of the wool merchants and the sheep-grazing squires, the power of parliament grew. By the thirteenth century, the division between the newly wealthy and the old feudal barons was cemented in the structure of parliament itself: the House of Commons and the House of Lords.

Distinct political parties only emerged after the Civil War had pitted Parliament against monarchy. As Morton puts it:

> Parliament, which had begun as a check on the theoretically absolute power of the feudal king to dispose of the property of his subjects had become in time the guardian of the absolute right of the individual to the enjoyment of his private property.

Feudalism was on the way out: private property emerged victorious. After the restoration of Charles II, there emerged the division between the Tories (rural, royalist, Anglican squires) and the Whigs (merchants, financiers, some landed aristocracy, and the Puritan lower middle classes). These two parties ruled English politics until the collapse of the Whigs in the mid-nineteenth century.

Today, the franchise has been extended far beyond the limits of land ownership, and, with the emergence of democratically elected local mayors and local police and crime commissioners (PCC) as well as local council by-elections, there are more elections than ever before. It calls to mind Saki's short story, 'Hermann the Irascible', in which King Hermann seeks to counter the votes-for-women movement by drafting a Bill 'enacting that women shall vote at all future elections'. Hermann continues:

Shall vote, you observe; or, to put it plainer, must. Voting will remain optional, as before, for male electors; but every woman between the ages of twenty-one and seventy will be obliged to vote, not only at elections for Parliament, county councils, district boards, parish-councils, and municipalities, but for coroners, school inspectors, churchwardens, curators of museums, sanitary authorities, police-court interpreters, swimming-bath instructors, contractors, choir-masters, market superintendents, art-school teachers, cathedral vergers, and other local functionaries whose names I will add as they occur to me.

Hermann's idea is that if the electorate can be swamped with a multitude of elections, they will swiftly lose the desire to be involved in the democratic process. It's interesting to compare this to what happened in Paris in 1871. 'For a few tumultuous months,' writes Terry Eagleton, 'the working people of the French capital took command of their own destiny.' Votes were held for a wide range of public roles, including magistrates, judges and public servants. These positions, Eagleton continues, 'were to be elective, responsible to the people and recallable by them'. It is these last two phrases which distinguish true democracy from the sham instituted in Saki's short story. Elections without meaningful accountability mean little.

It is hardly surprising, then, that in recent years the rise of elections for positions of limited authority or significance has coincided with the continuing fall in voter turnout. Only 37.4% of the possible electorate voted in the 2012 election that saw Boris Johnson hold his position as Mayor of London. The average by-election turnout in the same year was 21.9%. The PCC turnout was just 15%. By contrast, the turnout for 2016's EU referendum was 72%. General elections remain more stable: the turnout across the UK in 2015 was 66.1%, up on previous years but still down on the high point of 1950 when 83.9% of the electorate turned out to vote in Clement Attlee.

The role of the politician has long been split between the interests of the local constituency and the demands of the party. With increasing numbers of MPs now parachuted into constituencies about which they know very little, the division between Westminster and the rest of the UK has intensified. It is in recognition of this bubble that recent governments have championed city mayors, 'devo max' or the 'northern powerhouse'. But, as Saki's story suggests, more occasions for voting does not equate to a healthier democracy. Brexit was sold, at least in part, as a middle finger to this Westminster elite. Perhaps it's now time to stop pretending that MPs represent local interests. Or perhaps, instead, it's time to make sure that they actually do.

Pauline cites a member of the select committee who told her: 'house prices won't be affected once HS2 is built. I live in London. Trains go under my house all the time.' Such an attitude, as Pauline is swift to point out, betrays significant ignorance of the reason why many people actually choose to live in the country: 'peace and quiet' are the words that crop up again and again along the route. A house-buyer in London will accept noise as part and parcel of city living; one in the countryside may not. 'The people making the decisions are London people,' says Pauline. 'They think that what happens in London can simply be transferred to the countryside. But it doesn't work like that.'

As we eat, conversation thankfully veers away from HS2. We discuss John's physics research – a once potentially pioneering idea to detect stars through their emission of X-rays, that turned out, he cheerfully admits, to be completely useless. Pauline tells me of a film about Gustav

Klimt and of Edmund de Waal's *The Hare with Amber Eyes*. We talk about bankers and art, ownership and loss.

After only a day and a half of walking – but in an area of the country that I do not know at all – it's hard to describe the pleasure of a long, leisurely, civilised lunch. I have seconds, and pudding. We have coffee on their patio overlooking the fields of the Stoneythorpe Estate. John makes repeated offers to give me a lift to wherever I need to get to. They invite me to stay the night. I'm sorely tempted, but I must refuse. I've already given up this walk once. This time I have to finish it. Outside the front door I put my boots back on, strap on my rucksack, and say my goodbyes. At least it's sunny, I think, as I set off once more – reluctant but content.

VIII

Countryside Matters

*Offchurch – Bubbenhall – Stoneleigh –
Kenilworth – Burton Green – Borsall Common
– Berkswell*

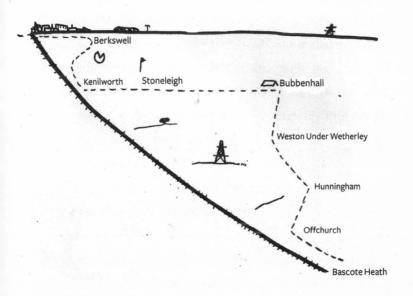

The afternoon stretches out gently before me. Up ahead once again is the Grand Union Canal. After leaving Pauline and John, I continue along the Welsh Road a short distance and pause to look at my map. Just after Bascote Heath, before it crosses the canal, the Welsh Road dog-legs noticeably. Nobody knows how old this road is, but it is likely to be pre-Roman. For such an ancient thoroughfare, this sudden change of direction seems strange. I wonder how recently it has been diverted, and why: was it due to the construction of the canal? Or something to do with a change in land ownership? I try to research who owns the land in this area. I find it impossible to find out.

So far the idea of rural labour has presented itself to me largely as an aesthetic concern. I've seen how labour has been systematically excluded from depictions of the picturesque. I've seen how some among today's environmental thinkers seek to reposition work as the driving force behind humanity's relationship with the landscape. It is through labour, after all, that we shape the landscape that shapes us. But how does this function in reality? In Warwickshire I meet not with retirees, but with those in work – a dairy farmer and a bed and breakfast owner. How will they be impacted by HS2? And, if the project is indeed inevitable – as so many seem increasingly to think – then how can we know when to fight against the future, and when to accept that we cannot control the world – as individuals or as a species?

North of Bascote Heath, I come to Millennium Way – a hundred-mile walking route founded for the year 2000 by the Solihull branch of a network of businessmen known as the 41 Club. The route's eastern half runs from Middleton Cheney through Chipping Warden, Priors Marston, Cubbington, Kenilworth and up to Meriden, a village between Solihull and Coventry. This half of the route runs very close to HS2. To the east of Offchurch, it merges with Ridgeway Lane. Under cover, it is hot and midgy, close with foliage and flies. I disturb a heron, who rises slow and dark from a still and stagnant pond. South of Hunningham, I cross a disused railway slicing through the landscape, now filled with trees. There are butterflies everywhere this afternoon: tan and ivory and bleached bone white, blood red and fiery orange. A pair of buzzards fly low over the sign for Fosse Way. I disturb two more in a field by Hunningham Coppice.

At Weston-under-Wetherley there is not a single shop or pub; only the crumbling red sandstone of St Michael's parish church. It is the same stone now mined in a quarry just south of Coventry: New Red Sandstone. It looms like a red wound ahead of me in the near-distance. This is part of the wider geological strata of the Keuper Marls which consists of mudstones and shales that produce fine red clay. While this is no good for stone building – fine stone must therefore be imported from Meriden or Kenilworth – the clay is ideal for producing high-quality bricks and tiles. These bright red bricks are what give the buildings of Birmingham, and surrounding villages such as Hampton-in-Arden, their distinctively rich ruddy hue. The still quiet of the countryside is rapidly receding. Another plane flies overhead.

In early evening sunshine I arrive in the village of Bubbenhall. I order fish and chips and a pint at the Malt Shovel and ask the landlady if I can put up my tent in the pub's back garden. Much to my relief, she says yes. I order another pint and get chatting to the teenage girl behind the bar.

'People say it's posh round here,' she says. 'Everyone says it's posh.' She's wearing a black T-shirt and black jeans and has an elaborately pierced left ear. It's clear she's not convinced. 'So when you going to get to Birmingham?' she asks.

'Friday, hopefully.'

'Friday?' she sounds incredulous. 'I always think it's slow enough getting the train.'

It's funny: to me, after two days of walking (and an overall total of ten days), Friday feels near enough to touch. It's obvious to say, but time changes when you're walking.

I aim to get to a certain point each evening, and I've had prearranged meetings along the way, but I've rarely been in a rush: never angry at the slowness of others or the delay to a train or running late or missing out. This second leg of the walk, in particular, has been slow and sedate. The days are longer. My destination is never far away. The girl's astonishment reminds me of lines from a poem by Matthew Clegg:

> Air-ways and railways and motorways pay
> Faster than waterways, draining away,
> Slow days are gone days,
> These days.

The poem, entitled 'Slow Days Are Gone Days', possesses a similar kind of rhythm to W. H. Auden's famous 1936 poem 'Night Mail', written to accompany a documentary film of the same name. Both employ what I think are trochaic pentameters: lines of five feet, where the stress falls on the first syllable of each foot. In both cases, the bouncing rhythm lends a sense of inexorable progress. But where Auden seems to celebrate the energies of the machine age, Clegg is much more conscious of what is being lost. The 'slow days' of travelling the canals and feeding the swans are now 'gone days'. But so too are the 'slog days' of loading and unloading boats with hauls of coal or sugar or grain; the 'great days' of the River Don; and the 'boat days' of the '*Valiant, Victory, Progress* and *Sheaf*'. Not all that is gone is to be mourned.

But the slow days certainly are. After the opening couplet, the third line of each stanza shortens to a dactyl and a spondee. Then comes the final line, consisting of a single spondee. Where Auden creates a sense of inevitable progress, Clegg's rhythms are regularly halted. In the majority of the backward-looking stanzas, the feeling in these closing lines is one of celebration or nostalgia. But in the eighth, quoted above, the feeling is suddenly mournful. Only in this stanza does every line rhyme: there is a resignation to a present about which nothing can be done. Planes and trains and cars serve the profit motive; the canals are hardly used. The everyday pleasures of a slow journey through a landscape have gradually been lost. Now it is over to the poets to pen their eulogies. Slow days are gone days. These days.

I've brought a number of books with me on this walk, one of which is a collection of poetry influenced by walking called *The Footing*. By coincidence, I think, it is published by the same publishers as Clegg's work: Sheffield-based Longbarrow Press. I take a seat in the corner of the Malt Shovel and start reading. I read Chris Jones's tales from the Reformation, in which two agents traverse the countryside, sleeping in barns and destroying church artefacts. I read

James Caruth on the links between ownership and limits, land and language. I read Fay Musselwhite on the chance encounter with a dead animal – 'dog-eared rug-matted black' – and I think of the dead vole I trod on by yesterday's canal. In the introduction, Longbarrow's publisher Brian Lewis cites a line from Solnit's *Wanderlust*: 'Every walker is a guard on patrol to protect the ineffable.' I wonder what it is that I'm trying to protect. And whether or not I'm succeeding.

Meanwhile, the pub is lively and filling up fast. All the conversations seem to centre on the girl in black.

'How was Belgium?' asks a man about my age.

'Yeah it was alright.'

'Where'd you go? Bruges?'

'Yeah. It's full of canals. Once you've seen one, you've seen 'em all. But it's nice.'

It seems her boyfriend is bidding on a caravan on eBay. His progress comes to me in fragments:

'Dale! I said no more than two hundred and fifty quid.'

'Twenty-two minutes.'

'Where is it again?'

'Somerset? Oh my days.'

I'm exhausted and I want to go to sleep. But I find myself strangely hooked – I need to find out how much the caravan sells for. Will they buy it?

'Two eight five now.'

'No, I'm not paying two eight five,' she says. 'Why don't we get a nice one, with a shower in it?'

'Three four five now. Two minutes left.'

Silence. They're out.

In one corner, a married couple are discussing the pros and cons of the ribeye steak. In another, a group of pensioners debate the merits of Bombardier against Doom Bar. I overhear snippets of their conversation:

'There's no bad beer,' says an old man in a red jumper. 'It's just that some are better than others.'

Then, a little later, a woman's voice: 'I said we ought to have a prize for who had the least oil left in their oil lamps.'

I have no idea what she could possibly be talking about. A group of men in football shirts arrive for a birthday party. I head outside to my tent. I never do find out what that caravan sells for.

*

At around six in the morning, I'm woken by the calls of a pair of pigeons.

'Short, long, short,' coos the one on the telephone wire.

'Short, long, short short short,' replies the other from a nearby rooftop.

I walk past Stoneleigh Deer Park golf course. 'Warning,' reads a sign, 'these premises are patrolled by Oakwood.' A bus is holding up traffic at Stoneleigh Bridge. On the adjacent path lie two charred banana skins. I pass a sign for Birmingham Road. I'm getting closer

*

On a lay-by south of the A444, a car carrier stops to swap a blue Honda for a black BMW. If I was a criminal looking to swap my getaway car, I think to myself, this is exactly what I'd do too.

On Kenilworth golf course, I stop and wait for three old men to take their drives. Two lusty squirrels decline to stand on golfing etiquette. One of the men shanks into the trees not far from where I'm standing. Further on, a small army of staff are tending to a green with a host of complex contraptions. I sit on a bench to eat an apple and some bread.

In the well-ordered suburbs of Kenilworth a man buffs his silver car outside his brand new brick house. I descend to the Kenilworth Greenway, formerly a railway branch line and, after National Lottery funding, recently reopened as a pathway for cyclists, horse riders and walkers. Blue signs designate this a 'Multiuser Route'. It is long, flat, straight and dull. Last time I was here, I was told by local campaigner Chris Langton that the Greenway is under threat by HS2. During construction, a section near Burton Green will be temporarily rerouted, and will subsequently run right alongside the tracks. The worry is not only that the peace and quiet of the Greenway will be destroyed by the proximity of HS2, but also that such changes will open the door for development in the green belt between Coventry and Birmingham.

As I walk along the Greenway, I notice sporadic signs of its former use: old wooden platform steps and trackside gradient markers. There is a certain irony about this pathway – that it replaced one railway and is now threatened by the construction of another.

Perhaps this walk has gradually recalibrated my approach to landscape aesthetics, or perhaps I'm simply being perverse, but the most interesting sight along the Greenway is a massive National Grid electricity station. It is set not far back from the line of the path, but is semi-concealed from eyes attuned only to the picturesque by trees and fences and nettles. I squeeze through puddles and past branches to take a look. Past scrub and grass, row upon row of metal structures stretch across an expanse of concrete. Wires stretch up into the sky; pylons stalk across the landscape into the distance. I have no idea what any of these things are doing, but I know they are doing something. Like the incinerator at Calvert Green, the combination of scale and opaque functionality lends these structures a sublime magnificence. Lurid 'Danger of Death' signs remind me again of that line from Ken Worpole: 'people only respect landscapes which contain a significant element of danger.' Here, they only add to the fearful allure.

*

Berkswell is a beautiful little village. I'm told much of it is owned by the parish church: there's certainly a feeling of benevolent planning and management about the cluster of little houses and the shop on Church Lane. The name itself comes from Berks Well, a stone-walled water well located just outside the churchyard. Today, the well is fenced off and a public notice warns that it is a punishable offence to throw litter into the water.

When I was here in November with Chris Langton, we spoke to two old men outside the church. 'I think that those who want HS2 should pay for it themselves,' said the man in the tweed blazer, 'especially given the state that the countryside is in.' The other was more equivocal: 'Steam trains, viaducts – they're part of the landscape now, aren't they.'

Chris drove me to meet with one of the local

churchwardens, Chris Philp, who has lived in the area for over forty years. We visited her in her house in Berkswell. I sat on a mauve sofa and admired the immaculate mossy-turquoise carpet. She explained how, despite their names and certain administrative differences, Borsall Common and Berkswell in effect form a single village and a single community. 'It's a delightful community,' she told us. 'We care about each other and support each other. Every single person says this is the best place they've ever lived. I've never known a community like it.'

The problem is that, while many people live in Berkswell, all the services – doctors, shops etc. – are in Borsall Common. HS2 will run right through the middle. 'It will collapse a vibrant community,' Chris told us sadly. 'And what is Britain about if not community?' Schools will be blocked, country lanes choked with HGVs. Chris's route to the church will be closed off for four years. The line will pass just 400 metres from her house. 'I don't want to sell,' she said. 'Where would I go?'

Also in Borsall Common is Berkswell station. This was once the junction of the line that ran to Kenilworth; it is now the Greenway that I have been walking along this morning. Today, Berkswell runs services to Birmingham and London, as well as Coventry and Northampton. The Kenilworth line was closed as part of Dr Beeching's cuts to local rail services in the 1960s. Beeching himself lived in Berkswell. Perhaps it is just coincidence that his local station survived when so many others were closed. But it seems more than a little unlikely.

A short walk up the hill from Berkswell station is Ram Hall Farm, home to one of the most delicious cheeses produced in England: Berkswell. I've got time on my hands so I call a number I find online and head up a narrow country lane to meet with farmer Stephen Fletcher. I ring the doorbell and introduce myself. I follow Stephen around the back of the farmhouse to a small garden area, where we sit and chat. The house is late-Elizabethan, but 'nobody knows who built the house,' says Stephen, 'or exactly when.'

Looming above us, the house combines formal elegance with a certain grim defiance. It's made from ruddy-grey ironstone with oblong, Tudor window frames, leaded panes and a large, heavy lintel above an old, studded wooden front door. A stone path leads straight to the door – no time to waste with the curves and detours of the picturesque. A large single chimney stack juts out of the roof directly in line. This simple symmetry gives the building a directness, and a forceful presence that is the exact antithesis of the hectic eclecticism on show at Bascote Heath. The house has been softened over the years, however: to the right is a small extension, which also looks Tudor to me. To the left, an apple tree breaks the severity of the symmetry. The building may have presence, but it also serves its purposes: one of the chimneys, I learn from Stephen, was previously employed as a bacon smoker; the extension used to house a brewery; and one of the bedrooms was once used for storing cheese. Outside the front door stands a radiator. A rugby ball and a green kicking cone lie on the path.

It's hard for me not to portray Stephen as a caricature of a rural farmer. He certainly looks the part – clad in sturdy work boots, over-trousers and a short-sleeved shirt with blue and white stripes. His face is framed by a greying beard; across his cheeks, the blood branches russet in his veins. He looks strong, but weathered, like a character in a Thomas Hardy novel, or like the house in which his family has lived for over 130 years.Time and again Stephen describes himself as straight-talking. 'I speak as I find,' he says. Is this a challenge to my soft southern sensibilities? It reminds me of something similar written by poet Roy Fisher, himself born just a few miles away in Birmingham. In *Standard Midland*, he writes of that 'plain way of talking we people of central England like to believe we have'.

In many ways, Stephen's story is a typical one. He is a fifth-generation tenant farmer. The family moved here in 1881 and have always been dairy farmers. In that time, they have marked the changes to the local area as well as what has stayed the same: Stephen tells me that his grandfather used to know rain was coming if he could hear the train doors clicking at the station. Now, rain is signified by the sound of the tannoy. It's not just the countryside, but the animals in it. Stephen tells me about a breed of sheep called the Poll Dorset, which has a light-sensitive pituitary gland. This means that it goes on heat as the days get shorter. By crossing the Poll Dorset with East Friesians, Stephen has been able to produce sheep that lamb outside of the conventional season. 'We make cheese all year round now,' he says.

Stephen's parents still own the business, and his son is at agricultural college. The evident desire is that one day he will take over the running of the farm. Such a family ancestry is a source of pride for Stephen. 'Farmers see themselves as custodians of the land,' he says. It reminds me of what Stewart Pomeroy told me back in the Colne Valley on the second day of the walk – that farmers 'keep the green belt green'. Here, on the outskirts of Birmingham, the role of the farmer is equally significant – both in resistance to change and as agents of that change. 'The British countryside is unique,' Stephen explains. 'It has been produced through generations of farming – different people, different crops, and different techniques.'

Fellow-Midlander Roy Fisher expands upon the point in his poem 'The Dow Low Drop'. 'Take out the Commissioners' roads,' he writes in reference to those routes carved through the Midlands by the agents of enclosure. Take out too 'the lead-rakes, poison-copses, cattle-meres, water-tables'. Then 'pick off the farmsteads and the long / cowshit slips on the tarmac'. Take it all away, Fisher urges. Then: 'Shift it / around. Put it all back, naturally.' The comma before that final word – 'naturally' – drawing our attention to the impossibility of such a task. About whether it might even be desirable, Fisher remains hard to read.

The effect upon Stephen of his family's long history is also ambivalent, albeit in a different way. It is not only a source of pride; it is also a responsibility and a burden. 'You don't want to be the one who screws it up and throws away all their hard work,' he tells me. It is this sense of duty which must spur on Stephen and others like him. Because life for Britain's dairy farmers is notoriously tough. According to the Campaign to Protect Rural England, there were nearly 200,000 UK dairy farmers in the 1950s. In 1995, there were 35,741; in 2015, just 9,654. 'The number of dairy herds gone out of business is mind-blowing,' says Stephen. 'It was the backbone of British agriculture after the war, but it's been decimated.'

The story of what has happened to the UK dairy industry has been told many times. Stephen himself attributes responsibility to the combined effects of globalisation and Thatcherism – in particular, the abolition of the Milk Marketing Board in the early 1990s. The Board had been founded in 1933 in order to guarantee a minimum price for milk. 'It took the uncertainty out of the market and allowed farmers to plan,' wrote former dairy farmer Anthony Bradley in *The Guardian*. 'This was vital,' he wrote, 'as a cow cannot be switched off when your milk buyer changes their mind. The MMB pooled all the milk and then marketed it together.'

Under Thatcher, however, the responsibilities of the Milk Marketing Board were removed following the Agriculture Act of 1993. The aim, in theory, was to open up the dairy market and allow farmers to sell to any buyer. The result instead was a rapid growth in the power of the supermarket. 'Supermarkets dictate prices,' says Stephen, 'and prices continue to go down. The cost is now below the price of production.' According to a 2015 *Guardian* editorial, the cost of production is about 32p a litre. Some farmers are getting little more than 20p. According to the non-profit AHDB dairy, the average milk price for August 2015 stood at 23.95p per litre (ppl), a decrease of 7.43ppl (23.7%) compared with the previous year. By comparison, a two-pint bottle of milk costs 75p from Tesco online. That's 66p per litre, or 2.75 times the price that farmers are being paid. This may seem like great news for consumers, but it has destroyed dairy farming in this country.

In his 1776 book *Wealth of Nations*, Adam Smith famously wrote that:

> To found a great empire for the sole purpose of raising up a people of customers, may at first sight, appear a project fit only for a nation of shopkeepers. It is, however, a project altogether unfit for a nation of shopkeepers, but extremely fit for a nation whose government is influenced by shopkeepers.

Thatcher was, after all, the daughter of a shopkeeper. Archie Norman was simultaneously chairman of Asda and Tory MP for Tunbridge Wells. Lord Sainsbury was one of the Labour Party's biggest donors. So it's hardly surprising to see successive governments destroying industry in favour of trade and consumption.

In recent years, discussion has grown around the idea of the so-called 'mega-dairy'. These are already in operation in the United States, where up to 30,000 cows live out their lives indoors. Fair Oaks, Indiana, for example, produces 2 million pints of milk per day. According to the BBC, at Fair Oaks 'milking never stops': 'Each cow eats 100 pounds of food and drinks 30 gallons of water to produce 80 pints of milk in a single day.' Fair Oaks is also a popular tourist attraction, with its own amusement centre. It is hard to be anything but disgusted by images of tourists walking by line upon line of living animals plugged into machines for their entire existence. While China has announced plans for its own mega-farm of up to 100,000 cows, here in the UK the concept has been slower to catch on. Plans by Nocton Dairies to build a 3,770 'cow factory unit' south of Lincoln were scrapped back in 2011. While many opposed the scheme on the grounds of animal cruelty, it is worth pointing out that such industrialised agricultural methods are already employed in the UK for pig meat and chicken and egg production.

Despite the odds stacked against them, the resulting depression and the suicides, traditional dairy farmers have struggled on. 'Farmers aren't quitters,' says Stephen. 'They will find a way to keep going.' Those that have survived are either large-scale mechanised operations or have diversified into other products. Indeed, Ram Hall is still going thanks to a series of decisions made by Stephen and his family during the years of the Thatcher government. In 1989 he decided to diversify the business by introducing sheep to the farm as well as cows. That same year, the family made the first Berkswell cheese. In 1995, they left cows altogether.

The early days of Berkswell cheese sound like a combination of the visionary and the haphazard. 'Specialist cheese was just getting going in the late 1980s,' Stephen tells me. 'I didn't know anything about cheese. We employed the daughter of a neighbouring farmer – she had done some cheese-making at college, then made some at home. That was the catalyst really.'

Stephen's mother Sheila then enrolled at Otley College in East Anglia to learn the technique that they still use, more or less, today. On that first morning there were just 35 sheep at Ram Hall; now over 800 go through the farm over the course of a year. From twelve cheeses a day, they now make seventy. Berkswell has undoubtedly been a success: the cheese has won a number of awards and is now sold throughout the UK as well as in North America and Europe. 'I get a lot of pleasure seeing the product and hearing from people who say that they like it,' says Stephen. 'Diversifying into cheese kept us on the farm.' I get the impression that the pleasures of cheese eaters come a distant second to the ability to keep the family farm alive for one more generation.

Before too long, of course, the conversation turns to HS2. Stephen's response is perhaps the most complex of anyone that I've met so far. He is neither simply in favour nor in opposition. In fact, the rights and wrongs of HS2 don't seem to interest him at all; rather, his primary concern is how the farm will be able to respond to its impact. As a farmer, Stephen has clearly learnt to adapt in order to survive in the face of change – be that the inevitable cycle of the seasons or more sudden, unpredictable developments brought about by economic downturns or political decision-making. Stephen is not interested in fighting HS2: 'I'm not a NIMBY,' he says. 'If it's needed and it benefits the country, then it has to go somewhere. You can wave all the placards you like. If it's going to happen, it's going to happen.'

On the one hand, I can't help but admire this stoic pragmatism. It's a stance underpinned by the desire to control only that which can be controlled, to let fate take its course and respond as well as possible to whatever happens. On the other hand, there is a kind of wilful self-blinkering to this approach – a refusal even to attempt to understand the situation from another point of view, to work with others, to envision a different outcome. The outside world is conceived merely as the creator of obstacles. Campaigners, governments, trade unions: everyone is lumped together in a vague mass of hypocrisy and self-interest. The farmer's age-old task is to keep the farm alive amid the madness.

Stephen mentions a plan in the 1980s to dig a huge new coal pit on the site of the old Massey Ferguson factory in Coventry. Local opposition was driven, as ever, by the threat to house prices. But the real influence, says Stephen, was Arthur Scargill, at the time president of the National Union of Mineworkers (NUM), who opposed the mine apparently on the grounds that it was to be run by a rival union, the Union of Democratic Mineworkers (UDM). 'I was keen to make a bit of money out of subcontracting,' says Stephen with a sense of disappointment. His attitude to today's anti-HS2 campaigners seems tinged with a similar cynicism. 'It's right for people to have the opportunity to voice their opinions,' he says, 'and to seek compensation. But I can't get worked up about it – I've got to manage around it. The people who shout the loudest have the least amount to lose sometimes.'

Stephen has plenty to lose: Ram Hall stands to be seriously impacted by HS2. Although the majority of the farm is rented from the Berkswell Estate, the family does own a small rectangle of land just to the west of where we're sitting. HS2 is scheduled to run straight through it. On the one hand, this is lucky: as landowners, Stephen's family are in a much better position in terms of receiving compensation than if they were simply tenant farmers. Unlike Pauline and John, the Fletchers have an agent working on their behalf. On the other hand, unlike a residential property, a dairy farm is in a much more complex economic relationship with the site that it occupies.

The Fletchers stand to lose significant amounts of grazing land, and have therefore been compelled to restructure their entire farming system. This is no easy task – and it's not helped by the lack of clarity around HS2. 'We plan our cropping two years ahead,' Stephen explains, 'so we're trying to anticipate when it will actually be built.' Perhaps this explains his antipathy towards anti-HS2 campaigners – for they are only adding to the uncertainty over when (indeed, if) building work will finally commence.

'The quality of our milk is due to geography,' says Stephen. That means the family could not simply relocate the business elsewhere: 'we might not be able to recreate what we have here in terms of climate, soil type, aspect, and the people that make the cheese.' Berkswell cheese is therefore aptly named, for it is closely bound to the people and this place. It occurs to me that, in some ways, the same could be said for the people who are being forced out of their homes – if a person is, at least in part, a product of their environmental influences, and if a community is a knitting together of people and place, then it is no simple matter to relocate from one place to another. Communities are like cheese, it seems, and like the ancient woodlands of the Chilterns: complex networks of relations that do not travel well.

After leaving Stephen to his work, I head back down the road to the pub by the station. Inside are four retired captains of industry clad in polo shirts, discussing former colleagues and house prices, golf and hip replacements.

'Why are home-grown vegetables so much better than the ones you buy in the supermarket?'

'Well, they're from abroad, aren't they.'

One of their phones rings: it's the James Bond theme tune.

At the bar stands the landlady, in leopard-print top and copious eyeliner. 'Did you hear about his electronic cigarette?' she asks one of the two men nursing lagers at the bar. 'It burst into flames!'

I order a cheese roll and some chips.

*

After lunch, I stroll back into the village of Berkswell and through the estates of Berkswell Hall. Gently rolling expanses of sheep-mown grassland, patches of woodland, a lake and an elegantly curving stream tell of landscape improvements akin to those made by Humphrey Repton at Shardeloes back along the route in Amersham. This land was given to Thomas Marow of Hoxton by Queen Mary I in 1556 and parts of it have remained in the family ever since. Today, sheep still graze under carefully sited oaks. A path wends through pines out into a field of what look like strange pink-green beans. I don't know what this crop is. A laminated notice warns that the footpath may be diverted or blocked due to HS2. It is full of 'herebys' and 'therewiths' and other such near-impenetrable parliamentary legalese. The house itself has been altered and rebuilt a number of times. The current Grade II* listed building dates from the early nineteenth century. The exterior is plain but the position is excellent. Like Shardeloes, Berkswell Hall has also been converted into flats. A three-bedroom flat in the main house was recently on the market for offers over £500,000.

On the A452 is the bed and breakfast where I'm staying for my final night before walking into Birmingham in the morning. Jamie, the owner, tells me about his experiences with HS2: his mother sold her nearby property to HS2 Ltd at a good rate, he says, but only after eighteen months of battle. He tells me about environmental inspectors counting bats up and down the line, and about a neighbour who invented a family of rare newts to try and stop the entire project. The roundabout a little further along the road was only built three years ago, but is due to be turned into a storage depot for HS2. Jamie, who has lived in the area for twelve years, stands to make a tidy profit during the years of construction. He says that he has already received two payments of £1,000 for permission to bore holes on his land. Now he plans to build chalets in the back garden in order to house those working on the project. I step outside to take a look as a train rushes by behind a thin wooden fence. Sandwiched between the main road and the train line, this would be a noisy place to live; as a place to house the itinerant, however, it's perfect.

I decide I'm in need of a shower and start to remove my clothes. From my trouser turn-ups I turn out sundry seeds into the bathtub. The burrs of sticky willy cling to my socks. In the mirror, I notice a tan line round my neck from the strings of my map-carrier: a temporary memento of this walk. It won't last long.

I end my evening in a Beefeater on a roundabout on the A452. As I sit in the corner eating a tofu burger, Morrissey sings over the speakers: 'Every day is like Sunday.' I walk back to my bed and breakfast as car lights rush by in the early grey dark.

The rain begins again.

IX

Birmingham:
Second City

*Hampton-in-Arden – Bickenhill –
Birmingham International – Marston Green –
Kitt's Green – Lea Hall – Bordesley Green –
Birmingham city centre*

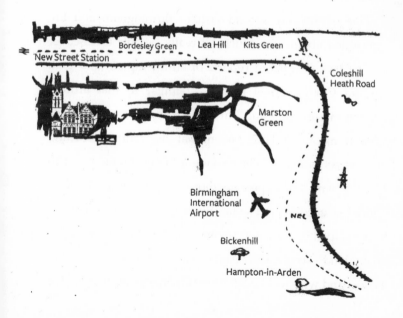

Today, at last, is the final day of this walk. Over the course of ten previous days, divided in two across seven months, I've walked from Euston station out into the London suburbs, over golf courses and farm land, through nature reserves and landfill sites. I've met with concerned conservationists, angry campaigners, stubborn farmers and suicidal retirees. I've stopped for shelter in pubs and cafes and under trees. I've been treated with warmth, suspicion, confusion, pity and amusement. I've got lost in fields and woods, been chased by a horse and been forced to abandon the whole thing due to an almost unbearable pain shooting through my knee. And now, finally, my destination is in sight. I need only walk into the centre of Birmingham and the journey is done.

This is only my second visit to Birmingham and I'm concerned about how much I'll really be able to discover in one day. I've heard reports of an attempted land grab around Curzon Street station – similar to that around Euston in London – and I'm keen to find out what people here think about HS2. Given that the rationale behind the project is that it will provide a big economic boost to Birmingham, I'm expecting more positive attitudes than those I've encountered so far. Birmingham is a city that has been shaped by transport – what will high-speed rail bring to England's second city? And just as importantly, what will be lost and who will be left out? Why does building for the future so often involve destroying the past?

I shower and dress and tuck in to a large cooked breakfast. On the television, Sky News reports that the Botanical Society of Great Britain and Ireland have issued a 'hogweed warning'. The organisation – which became a registered charity in 2012 – is concerned about giant hogweed (*Heracleum mantegazzianum*), a species that, like so many others, was introduced into Britain in the nineteenth century. According to the Royal Horticultural Society, 'the earliest documented reference to their introduction into Britain that has been traced is from the Royal Botanic Gardens Kew Seed List of 1817.' Giant hogweed can grow to over three metres tall and its sap can cause serious skin burns.

In 2015, the Botanical Society started something of a war against the species. They have produced maps charting its spread across the country, and had them republished in newspapers like *The Express* and *Daily Star*. The latter's headline was characteristically understated: 'UK's hogweed hellholes revealed: Are your kids at risk from toxic plant?' On Sky News the Botanical Society's Dr Mark Spencer advocates 'bio-control' – i.e. the introduction of an insect or other organism that preys upon the hogweed: one introduced species to counter another.

Ecologist and writer Hugh Warwick has described his

own accidental, and extremely painful, encounter with giant hogweed: 'They are majestic plants; five metres tall with beautiful umbels. But they have a sap that causes phytophotodermatitis and I must have unwittingly brushed against a plant along the river and ended up with massive localised sunburn. I still have the scars.'

Warwick points out that 'Britain has 1,400 native plant species, but thanks to the accidental and deliberate movement of plants, we now have 1,500 non-native species as well.' Such comparative newcomers – introduced either deliberately by Victorian botanists or accidentally as a result of increasing overseas trade and travel – are, says Warwick, 'alarming to anyone wanting to preserve our island in floral aspic'. But, he asks, 'What would our land look like without these alien species?' He continues: 'We can't go back to the floristic diversity of 10,000 years ago. So where is the line to be drawn?'

Some introduced species are dangerous – not just to humans but to the surrounding ecosystems. Most, however, are benign. Warwick's conclusion is that each species needs to be looked at on a case-by-case basis. It is a very similar conclusion to that drawn by Oliver Rackham about how best to manage our ancient woodlands. There are no hard-and-fast rules that can be applied wholesale. Those responsible for making decisions must be sensitive to the specifics of the case in hand. It is the characteristic response of a knowledgeable ecologist, and it frustrates those – such as politicians or theorists, or even environmental activists – who seek to see the world in terms of black and white. 'There is no original, untouched, British Flora,' continues Warwick. 'Whatever the future holds it will not be the same as now … In the end, there will be plants after we have gone.'

Under the 1981 Wildlife and Countryside Act, it is illegal to plant giant hogweed or encourage it to grow, and landowners are required to have it removed. Sky News notes that many of the recent spate of injuries have occurred on public land. Sky News, of course, is privately owned. On the television, David Attenborough urges caution: 'I don't think we should go mad about it,' he says. Appearing live to promote a new butterfly initiative, he is asked about the concerns around a species that has got 'out of control'. 'Well, you don't particularly want anything out of control,' he replies.

I'm sure he didn't mean this 'anything' literally. Or maybe he did. The wild, by definition, is that which is out of control. The wild, however, is often only acceptable so long as it is over there – held at a safe distance from everyday life, accessible only to tourists on safari or behind glass or via the television screen. Heaven forbid that 'the wild' should come over here, to an English suburb, with children about. Again I think of the point made by Worpole in *The New English Landscape*, that 'people only respect landscapes which contain a significant element of danger.' Today, we live in ignorance of danger, and, instead of learning about it, we expect it to be removed from our pathways before we even walk them.

As we saw in Chapters III and IV, such explorations of 'the wild' are of increasing interest to today's nature writers, conservationists and environmental theorists. We've already discussed the resurgence of rewilding, its charms and its dangers. As an introduced species that has thrived at the expense of others, hogweed is now deemed 'invasive' – that is, out of control. But it is not 'wild' in the sense privileged by the rewilders – native, original, and able to exist in a harmonious state within an existing ecosystem.

But there are other kinds of wildness too. And, arguably, it is in areas like those I will cover today that such wildness may most thrive: the outskirts, the edgelands, the unmanaged and the overlooked. The waste lands. Today may be the end of my journey – a straightforward walk to a clear destination – but in some ways this is my strangest day yet.

Soon after turning off the A452, I come to a pond, set down below the level of the lane. A man in a pine-green fleece is fishing among the reeds, right on the boundary with West Midlands Golf Club. I wonder whether he would be allowed to fish on the other side of the line. As I walk past, a man in an Aston Martin eases across the bridge over the River Blythe and up towards the clubhouse.

On the other side of the golf course are the twenty-five acres of Barston Lake, lined with a number of wooden fishing platforms. There is a black rubbish bin every twenty paces. Gulls squabble overhead and an aeroplane slides by, low above them. I can't help but be reminded of Colne Valley, on the outskirts of London. There are certainly similarities: both are thriving landscapes in close proximity to a city, an airport and a motorway. Neither is simply agricultural or residential or wild. But there are significant differences too. Colne Valley is a regional park established by agreement between local authorities and run in partnership with multiple local organisations. It is a hybrid landscape, with diverse uses.

Barston Lake, however, is a privately operated enterprise run by Nigel Harrhy for the sole purpose of fishing. The lake was created in the 1990s and was stocked with introduced carp from the Naseby reservoir on the other side of Coventry. The Barston Lake website is full of information about the size and quantity of its fish: 'Barston holds the record for a British Carp Angling Championship (BCAC) match venue, producing 1,296lb of fish in a 48 hour match.' But the biggest fish were not born in Barston Lake; nor did they grow here.

In early 2014, two fish were brought in from Kent: 'at the time of introduction they weighed 30lb and 37lb and have both been caught several times'. I had always thought that fishing involved catching 'wild' fish. It turns out I was wrong.

Nonetheless, despite the singularity of its purpose, Barston Lake is a pleasant environment to walk through. The landscape here serves not only clearly demarcated functions but also allows space for secrets – hidden corners where the unintended or unanticipated may take place. From a small pond on my right a fearful racket emanates: two swans and their cygnets are filter-feeding among the rushes. The next pond is hushed and still, its stagnant surface a carpet of feathers. This place has seen violence. Is this what we mean by wild now?

A narrow path takes me out into cornfields. To my right, a train rushes by – semi-concealed by a line of young trees. Across the field I can just see the first red gables of Hampton-in-Arden, a wealthy Birmingham suburb. The wind is picking up. I cross the field, walk down a narrow footpath between two back-garden fences, and emerge on to a cul-de-sac. In front of me is a small van bearing the name 'The Mole Man'. 'Traditional molecatcher,' it says underneath – none of your radical, modern molecatchers round here, thank you very much. I look up the company's website: it turns out Alan Mathie is Warwickshire's only 'master mole-catcher'. Amazingly, there seems to be a Guild of British Molecatchers, that exists to promote the industry. It is they who issue the accreditation for 'master molecatchers'. The qualification requires the payment of a membership fee and the completion of three online questionnaires. The organisation even has a Latin motto: *Existo pia pium exorno veneratio*, which they have translated as 'Be honest, provide respect'. On Mathie's van is a jaunty image of a mole and the similar slogan, 'Where man and mole respect each other'. I've never understood the desire to depict the animal being slaughtered as a cheerful illustrated character. It's the same with chicken shops. And the idea that the murdered moles would somehow respect their killer makes me quietly furious. Surely a garden alive with moles should be more attractive than a flat expanse of precision-striped lawn?

Hampton-in-Arden is a striking place. With thirty-four listed buildings, the village possesses an impressive medieval centre, now protected as part of the conservation area. There are also many elaborate nineteenth- and twentieth-century architectural additions, reflecting the town's rise to commuter-ville prominence after the building of a train station in 1838. As a result, Hampton-in-Arden is a rich architectural mishmash of medieval, imitation-medieval and downright pastiche. The unifying factor across the later centuries is the bright red brick – a product of the local New Red Sandstone that I glimpsed from a distance in that quarry south of Coventry.

Strangely, my favourite buildings here are some of the more recent. There are elaborate suburban villas with turrets and stained glass and herringbone brick patterning. There are high hedges and gates, columns, pillars, mock-Tudor jetties and wooden facades just for show. There's one lovely moment walking through the town on the B4102. To my left is what looks like a Victorian faux-medieval pile – complete with eaves and overhangs. On the other side of the road, directly facing it, is a row of fairly nondescript mid-twentieth-century low-rise housing. What I notice, however, is that the tile typology is almost exactly the same on both facades – lines of little semi-circles, like fish scales or crimping. The new is like the obverse cut out from the old. Placed together, I think they'd tessellate. I wonder where the original design came from. A little further along, I notice it again: on Shadowbrook Lane is a row of five small bungalows, set back at a rakish angle from the road. The tiles are chocolate rather than reddish-brown this time, a nice contrast to the vivid scarlet bricks. The bungalows are lined by lawns and flowers. No moles here. They're twee as anything, but I'm strangely charmed. It's the cumulative effect of one generation of architects responding to the work of their predecessors. It's quite a contrast to the planned towns of Waddesdon or Taylor Wimpey and, even more so, to the destroy-and-build approach adopted by Birmingham town planners throughout the twentieth and twenty-first centuries. Besides, there is a sense of exuberance about the architecture of Hampton-in-Arden that I can't help but enjoy. Birmingham is famous for the brashness of its red brick buildings. Hampton-in-Arden sensitively sets the tone.

Thereafter, Birmingham arrives slowly and suddenly. From Hampton-in-Arden, I cross the M42. Above me is the crackle of pylons; below, the surging traffic. In the mid-distance, the white bulk of the National Exhibition Centre (NEC). Between me and it, horses graze in neatly-fenced fields. In the village of Bickenhill is a handsome church with a spire and external sundial. Outside is the vast oblong tomb of Charles Thornley. On a hill above it, I stop to take off my bag for a moment. The shirt on my back is hot and sodden, but now blown by an ice-cold wind coming from the direction of the NEC. Burnt umber lichen encrusts a nearby concrete post. A plane flies overhead. The sky is grey and low.

The M42 was first announced in 1972 and the first phase was completed by 1976. Today, it stretches from Bromsgrove in Worcestershire to Ashby-de-la-Zouch in Leicestershire. It curves round to the south and east of Birmingham, linking up with the M5 and M6 to form the city's outer ring. HS2 is scheduled to run over and under the motorway between Stonebridge and Bodymoor Heath, before a section of the line breaks off west to head in to Birmingham Moor Street. The other section continues north up past Lichfield.

In *Heart By-Pass*, his 1998 film about Birmingham, Jonathan Meades declares the following: 'Roads create both immediately adjacent wastelands and a hinterland of potential dereliction.' In recent years, these wastelands and hinterlands have proved increasingly fertile ground for art and for literature. Iain Sinclair's *London Orbital* and several short stories by J. G. Ballard arguably kick-started this new interest. More recently, in 2012, poet Alan Corkish edited a collection of photography, poetry, essays and short stories entitled *In the Company of Ghosts – The Poetics of the Motorway*. The collection sought not only to address the history, symbolism and social, political or environmental effects of our motorway networks, but also to explore, as contributor David Lawrence put it, these 'nameless places' in their own right.

In his essay, 'The Autoroute and the Picturesque', Malcolm Andrews describes the way in which driving along motorways serves both to frame the surrounding landscape and to keep it at arm's length. 'You don't enter it,' he writes, 'you keep it an appropriate distance, and in so doing you alienate the landscape as spectacle.' It is arguably as a response to this process of alienation that walking has risen to such prominence as a literary pursuit. In the same book, Stephen Daniels describes such rejections of modernity as a 'byway sensibility' or 'branchline pastoral'.

Later in the article, Andrews explains the difference between the motorway and the ancient lane:

Old roads took their time: they deferred to the smaller-scale culture of travel, and to the physical environment they were negotiating. Motorways by comparison are independent of the natural landscape and unresponsive to it.

Some sixty years earlier, W. G. Hoskins had made much the same point about the difference between roads of prescribed width ('regardless of all considerations but that of directness') and roads that 'had made their own width'. What these new writers have expanded upon is the way in which the motorway not only imposes itself upon the landscape, but actually forces the landscape to respond to it. In another essay in the same collection, Edward Chell goes into detail about the exact way in which motorways do this. He tells us that the M1's first chief architect was concerned about the 'soporific' effects of endless straight roads through the landscape. To counter this, he introduced long, gradual bends in the roads – known as 'Clothoid' curves. Chell describes this type of curve as 'a gently accelerating arc that gradually slows momentum as well as sustaining the driver's attention'. Motorways curve through a landscape that has become merely a means to keep us awake. HS2, poker-straight and shielded from its surroundings by tunnels and cuttings, or lines of trees, has no such concerns. I can't help but think back to Eric Gill's concept of the 'handmade world' or the poetry of Matthew Clegg: 'Slow days are gone days, / These days.'

Birmingham, of course, is famously the UK's motor city. Between 1932 and 1955, the UK was Europe's largest car manufacturer. Its epicentre was in Birmingham and the surrounding cities – Coventry in particular – thanks to companies such as Wolsley Motors, Humber, Rover, Sunbeam, Singer, Riley and Standard in the first half of the twentieth century.

By this point in the city's history, Birmingham was well-established as the heart of Britain's transport industry. In his 1929 book, *The Industrial Development of Birmingham*, G. C. Allen describes the city as 'the leading centre of rolling stock production from the beginning of the railway age'. According to Allen, by 1914 at least 75% of the production value of the area's rolling stock firms was sent abroad: the building of vast railways through the colonies not only served to increase the pace at which raw materials could be extracted but also, by creating and controlling demand, stimulated the success of Britain's home industries.

From trains to bicycles and cars: 1869 saw the first bicycle company launch in Birmingham. In the 1890s, bicycles became lighter, cheaper and more comfortable, and the industry expanded rapidly. Several historians have argued that access to bicycles was an important catalyst in the campaign for women's suffrage. Certainly, as we saw in Chapter IV, the relationship between transport and activism is a close one. As bicycles boomed, cars too began to emerge. In 1896, the Light Locomotives on the Highways Act was passed, allowing cars on roads and stimulating the rise of the motor industries. Associated trades prospered too, as demand rose for springs and weldless steel tubes. From 1900, Birmingham was home to the main centre of Dunlop tyres. From 1912, Dunlop diversified into golf balls.

What is interesting is the way Birmingham's industrial evolution precipitated a kind of feedback loop. The emergence of these new transport industries not only necessitated the building of new factories, but the new modes of transport also enabled new developments in scale and location. The cycle and motor industries began to congregate not in the centre of the city, but in its eastern suburbs. Workers travelled there on the very bikes that they themselves were making. As Allen notes: 'by 1914 there was a marked contrast between the large up-to-date factories of the suburbs and the small, dark shops in the older parts of Birmingham.'

This was just the start of the way in which Birmingham came to be dramatically shaped by its own motor industry. From the mid-1930s well into the 1960s, Birmingham underwent a process of rapid development that included slum clearances, the destruction of historic buildings, and the construction of Brutalist public buildings in the centre and new tower blocks on the peripheries. The man responsible for these radical – if controversial – policies was Herbert Manzoni.

In Honor Gavin's experimental 2014 novel *Midland*, Manzoni is presented as fastidious, driven, inscrutable. He is elegant and authoritative, giving instructions without ever seeming to say anything. Referred to throughout as Humphrey B. Manzino, he stands apart from the other characters in the book and is never entirely a part of the city that he is so radically reshaping. Perhaps it's because he was not a local: Manzoni was born to a Milanese sculptor in Birkenhead in 1899. He moved to Birmingham in 1923 and took over the position of City Surveyor in 1935, aged just 36. 'Humphrey B. Manzino is blue-eyed and gentle. He sleeps in his office, some nights.'

While many of the buildings commissioned under Manzoni have since come and gone, Birmingham's roads remain hugely prominent throughout the city. In his 1975 book *Goodbye, Britain?* journalist Tony Aldous described the city's twentieth century redevelopments as 'purpose-built for the motor-car – on which Birmingham's prosperity hinged and to which its citizens are devoted'. Similarly, Jonathan Meades has described the city's residents as car-obsessed. The adverb 'anyroad' ('anyway') is liberally sprinkled through the conversation of Gavin's *Midland* characters. It crops up too in novels about Birmingham by both David Lodge and Henry Green. The road may have ridden rough-shod through the surrounding landscapes but, for better or for worse, the road is now a part of the local vernacular.

*

I cross a field of low mauve flowers and climb a flight of steps towards the sound of roads. The green dotted line I've been following on the map stops here. This is the final footpath. Under a low-echoing bridge, four cars are parked up by the side of the road, their drivers within in various stages of sleep.

The airport is ahead; my OS map is no use now. I take out the Birmingham *A-Z*. Like leaving London, this is another watershed: I'm still far from the city, but this is no longer countryside. Here, in a world of conference centres and airports, industrial estates and motorway verges, the land has a short memory. History must be sniffed out slowly. Few, in truth, have the energy.

A man in an 'Amey plc' high-vis jacket is strimming the grass on the roundabout, keeping it shipshape for passing traffic, maintaining control. A pied wagtail skips across the concrete pavement in front of me. Around me are car parks old and new – damp concrete blocks from the 1960s opposite white-columned 1990s grids. On my right is Birmingham International, clad with asymmetric shards of shiny grey and an incongruous tower of bright yellow. It matches the bollards and the markings on the road. Outside an industrial estate, a fountain of water shoots five feet into the air before splattering back down into a tree- and reed-lined pond. In white capitals on an adjacent red sign is witten the warning: 'DANGER DEEP WATER'.

Further along, as the cars mutter by, a man approaches. Pedestrians are not common here. What could he want? He sways slightly as he makes his way towards me. He stops right in front of me and, in a strong Spanish accent, asks the way to the airport. He has a bloodied chin and clutches an old bus ticket. I point him in what I think is the right direction. An air steward in polyester waistcoat, towing a small wheeled suitcase across the road, looks back at us repeatedly.

On Coleshill Heath Road lies a pair of sunglasses. One lens has skipped a few yards onwards.

Soon suburbia beckons to me once more. Somebody has inserted a door, with handle, letter box and the number 13, on the divided trunk of an ash tree by the side of the road. I receive the first looks of displeasure and confusion since London: a pair of young men waiting in their car at a T-junction. On the corner of Chelmsley Road stands a woman in a floor-length red maxi-dress. I'm not the only one dressed a little strangely this morning.

In Chelmsley Wood, I'm entering residential territory. Property begins to be more clearly demarcated: a front yard is delineated from the pavement by a narrow line of white gravel, then a line of woodchip, and then a strip of lawn. I pass columns and rows of two-up two-down properties, each with its own square of lawn and low wooden fence. In adjacent front drives are a navy Jaguar and a tattered England flag. 'Heya!' laugh two nurses from their car.

Once upon a time, this area, like all that surround it, was part of the ancient Forest of Arden. Hence the name of so many nearby villages: Hampton-in-Arden, Tanworth-in-

Arden, Henley-in-Arden and the like. But the forest was destroyed to feed the fires of Birmingham's industries. Then, in the late 1960s and early 1970s, Birmingham's inner-city housing was designated as slums, cleared, and the Chelmsley Wood estate was built. Special permission was granted to build on what was then green belt land by Labour's Minister of Housing and Local Government, Richard Crossman (who went on to become editor of the *New Statesman* and whose diaries were an important source for *Yes Minister*).

Despite my enormous breakfast I'm getting hungry again, and could do with a rest. It begins to dawn on me that there is nowhere to sit in the suburbs. Here is just for living, or for leaving. I suppose I could sit on the ground, but all is concrete. The only grass is private property. Eventually I see a bus stop and sit on one of the carefully angled seats – precisely designed to negate the comfort that the homeless might seek. I put my pack and walking stick on the ground beside me and eat a Mars bar. I'm getting strange looks.

Up ahead, on Cooks Lane, are two groups of kids – the first group in T-shirts and trainers, the second in black blazers and striped ties.

'Are you a tourist?' shouts a boy from the first group as we wait at a zebra crossing on opposite sides of a narrow road. And, by way of explanation: 'You've got a map.'

I decide not to bore him with my earlier deliberations on this very subject. Besides, his logic is hard to fault.

'Yes,' I say.

'Where are you from?'

'London,' I say.

'London!' he exclaims with glee. Then he looks at my walking stick with bafflement. 'Well you don't need sticks like that round here!'

The lights change and the first group sidles past me, laughing. The group in uniform passes by in silence.

This morning I feel even more attuned than usual to human ridiculousness – or rather, to my own ridiculousness. Being mocked by children doesn't help. But they're not the only ones: a builder laughs good-naturedly as I stop to take a photo of a preposterous Modernist church – Our Lady Help of Christians Catholic Church on East Meadway. It turns out to have been designed by Richard Gilbert Scott, son of Giles and great-grandson of Sir George Gilbert Scott, the architect behind St Pancras station. The church was built in 1966 and is immediately striking for the curved, copper-faced trusses which form its incredible roof. Gavin Stamp of the Twentieth Century Society describes the roof as 'a dramatic, theatrical treatment which suggests both a delight in expressive, sculptural forms and a desire to continue with the modern Gothic spirit which the architect's father had done so much to sustain'.

Inside, tall, narrow stained-glass windows by John Chrestien take the eye upwards, and suddenly the roof's outlandish shape begins to make sense. The effect is like standing in a dry dock between the bows of two great ships.

Outside, a woman with a Zimmer frame makes a slow, precise manoeuvre around a discarded pizza box. An elderly man wears crisp new gardening gloves to survey his front garden. It's all brick!

I cross over the train line, which heads north into Birmingham centre via nearby Lea Hall station. The station was opened in 1937 and refurbished with strange, space-themed public art in 1998. The line itself, now operated by London Midland, was conceived and engineered by Robert Stephenson, best known for designing the famous Rocket steam train, along with his father George. According to William Dargue, a Birmingham primary school teacher and local history blogger, the construction of the line involved the physical labour of 20,000 men and took almost five years. Dargue also notes the train's immediate impact: 'A horse-drawn stage coach on the 100-mile journey to London took some twenty hours plus two overnight stops to reach its destination. The journey by train took just five hours – it was now possible to get to London and back in the same day.'

After the station a sign informs me that I'm entering an alcohol-restricted zone. 'Police have powers to restrict drinking in public in this area,' it says. I pass a fenced-off estate just before a crossroads with Queen's Road and continue trudging along this apparently never-ending road: the B4128. Cooks Lane, East Meadway, Meadway, Bordesley Green East, Bordesley Green, Coventry Road. By the time I get to the A4040, I'm running much later than planned.

As in London, city walking proves to be considerably slower and more exhausting than I'd anticipated. I've arranged to meet with Jonathan Watkins, director of Ikon gallery of contemporary art, in Birmingham city centre, in order to discuss how HS2 will affect business in Birmingham. Our meeting is not scheduled until 4 p.m. but I'd been hoping to explore some of the centre first and have some lunch. Not for the first time, I decide upon a change in strategy. Not for the first time, I decide to cheat. I hail a bus and climb aboard.

'Shouldn't you be walking?' laughs the driver as I pay for a ticket. The bus is full and my rucksack takes up too much space. Two women in yashmaks eye me with irritation or suspicion. Walking sticks are not popular in the city.

As the bus progresses, suburbia transitions into inner city. The demographics change fast. The bus driver is right: I should be walking this, I think to myself with both regret and relief. Signs rush by: 'Shannon's pub – hot and cold food on match days' or 'Baguette Heaven – Halal'. We pass a broken-up billiard hall; The Garrison, a long-closed pub; the blackened bricks of a Victorian boys' school; the white dome of the Muslim Association building; and Birmingham Metal Company, clinging on under the arches. Each is evidence of the city's past, signs perhaps of its future.

Economists and historians have long praised the diversity of Birmingham's trades and industries. Mining collapsed in the early twentieth century when all the surrounding materials had been exhausted and the mines began to flood. But then the motor industry emerged. Iron fell and steel rose. Heavy industries left for the coast and Birmingham focused on finished products. Tipton stopped making iron and started producing sausages. But while such diversity has ensured the continuing prosperity of the city as a whole, it has hardly helped many of the individuals within it. G. C. Allen argues, for example, that in the nineteenth century it was extremely difficult for workers to move from one industry to another. While capital remained mobile, the fates of people were intimately tied to a single industry.

There is a bigger point to be made here about industrialisation, and about who gets left out when we talk about 'progress' and 'growth' in terms of metrics, and even places. For Marxist historians such as A. L. Morton, industrialisation is a necessary evil. Such writers may be quick to note the horror of conditions for the urban working classes – the noise, dirt, back-breaking labour and exploitative nature of a system under which the few create great profits for themselves at the expense of the many. In *Capital*, Marx noted that Birmingham's industries employed 30,000 children and young persons. But Marx also saw the advantages of industrialised labour. By bringing multitudes of workers together, capitalism enabled the group to work more productively than would the same number of workers working individually. 'Concentration of large masses of the means of production in the hands of individual capitalists,' he writes in *Capital*, 'is a material condition for the co-operation of wage-labourers.' For Marx, therefore, as well as for subsequent followers such as Morton, industrial capitalism is necessary in order to bring workers together and foster the conditions for the better society, for communism.

The process of urbanisation serves to place the working classes not only in proximity to the means of production, but also in close contact with each other. Meanwhile, industrialisation brings the inherent conflict between the owning classes and the working classes into acute focus. The opposition between the two becomes clear: revolution is unavoidable. Such is the traditional leftist reading of industrialisation – as a necessary step on the road to working class revolution, and the ultimate goal of equality. United together, the workers become, in Marx's phrase, 'the weapons that bring death' and capitalism thereby engenders the possibility of its own destruction. As Terry Eagleton has put it: 'The fact that people are massed anonymously together may be in one sense an alienation, but in another sense it is a condition of their emancipation.'

But in many industrialised countries, the revolution failed to appear. The emancipation espoused by Eagleton never arrived. In others it ended in disaster. Today, there is a view gaining increasing traction that traces many of the problems we find ourselves facing now back to industrialisation itself. Perhaps, after all, industrialisation was not part of the solution, but part of the problem. This is one reason why Marxism is often disparaged by today's green thinkers. It is undeniable, for example, that the state of the environment was vastly different in pre-industrial societies. Birmingham is a case in point. The effects of industrialisation on the surrounding environment have been devastating. Coal mining led to widespread flooding; the Forest of Arden has been systematically destroyed. As early as 1929, Allen wrote: 'Over the greater part of Birmingham and the Black Country, the original surface features have been so entirely destroyed by industrial activity and urban development that little attention need be paid to topography.' Even those woodlands which escaped destruction were heavily polluted. In the 1950s, when biologist Bernard Kettlewell was looking for highly polluted woods in which to carry out his now seminal experiments on peppered moths, it was to Birmingham that he came.

Perhaps that is simply the price of social and economic progress. We have more things than ever before, we live longer. We measure our 'quality of life' and we find that it is improving. According to the Office for National Statistics, between 1912 and 2012 our life expectancy has increased by nearly three years per decade. For males, life expectancy at birth increased from fifty-one years in 1910-1912 to seventy-nine years in 2010-12, while for females it increased from fifty-five to eighty-three years. Their research argues that much of this increase is due to improvements in infant and child mortality in the first half of the twentieth century, while gains in life expectancy at older ages have mainly occurred in the last fifty years. But life expectancy is just one factor. *The Economist* magazine's quality-of-life index includes nine criteria that are assessed and measured. These are: material wellbeing (calculated as GDP per person); health (life expectancy); political stability and security; family life (effectively the divorce rate); community life (based, weirdly, on church attendance or trade-union membership); climate and geography (nice weather); job security; political freedom; and gender equality (based on parity of earnings alone).

This reductionism should not surprise us: it is called *The Economist* after all. Sadly, such surveys are taken as evidence for the reality of capitalism's promise of ever-expanding prosperity for all. But it is a serious error. The creation of vast wealth for a tiny minority, for example, is sufficient to skew GDP, without having the slightest impact on the everyday lives of the majority. This is then averaged per person so that it appears our 'material wellbeing' is improving. Furthermore, the reduction of quality of life simply to length of life ignores issues such as mental health, self-worth and self-expression, strong relationships, love, freedom, happiness, meaning and purpose. Of course, such things cannot be reduced to mere metrics. In a world that can only value the measurable, they are therefore often overlooked. Furthermore, even if such surveys were accurate representations of our quality of life, and could therefore be used in support of industrialisation, we should also be asking who is this 'we' to whom we refer? As Birmingham, like much of the UK, shifts from industrial production to the 'knowledge economy' (culture, finance, services, tourism), manufacturing has been outsourced to less 'developed' countries. Our iron ore now comes from China; so too our cars.

Will industrialisation eventually bring 'quality of life'

to these countries too? Among politicians and many in the public sphere there is a line of thought that has become known as tech-optimism. This is the belief that, while science and technology may have contributed to the social inequalities and environmental disasters that we now find ourselves facing, it is better technology and more science that will eventually provide solutions, without us having to change our lifestyles. For many, technology and progress are inextricably linked. It is technology that has set humans apart from other species and allowed us to shape the world as we see it today. In their 1961 book, *A Short History of Technology*, T. K. Derry and Trevor I. Williams stated their belief that 'technology comprises all that bewilderingly varied body of knowledge and devices by which man progressively masters his natural environment'. Knowledge leads to mastery. Mastery leads to progress. Progress is good, therefore technology is good.

But in light of more recent understanding about humanity's true impact upon the natural environment, such opinions are increasingly under fire. In *Prosperity Without Growth*, economist Tim Jackson attacks the naivety of those who believe that technology will somehow provide all the answers:

we are desperate to believe in miracles. Technology will

save us. Capitalism is good at technology. So let's just keep the show on the road and hope for the best. This delusional strategy has reached its limits.

This is the line of thinking that champions first nuclear energy then wind turbines, new types of chemical fertiliser then genetically engineered crops. Jackson points out that capitalism – at least in its current form – is reliant upon an exploitative attitude to the environment that simply cannot be sustained. 'Those who hope that growth will lead to a materialistic Utopia are destined for disappointment,' he writes. 'We simply don't have the ecological capacity to fulfil this dream.'

As is being pointed out with increasing frequency, the technocratic arguments that Jackson criticises have their basis in the outdated arguments of the early Enlightenment. It is what has become known as scientism. To place such faith in the redemptive power of science is to make the same mistakes that today's smug atheists delight in attributing to religion. We mine rare minerals for our new computers while instantly outdated technology goes to form vast mountains of e-waste. In 2015, the world's data centres used 416.2 terawatt hours of electricity – that's more than the UK's total consumption. The construction of many solar panels involves toxic heavy metals. In an interview with Paul

Kingsnorth in an early issue of the *Dark Mountain* books, Doug Tompkins, founder of outdoor clothing company The North Face, says of wind turbines: 'The way of thinking that could create those windmills is the same way of thinking that caused climate change in the first place.'

The facts tell a different story about capitalism's ability to disseminate wealth equally. Out of a global population of 6 billion in 2000, journalist Chris Harman has estimated some 2 billion can be categorised as 'working class'. The UN has estimated that around 33% of the urban population in the developing world live in slums. Eagleton describes such slum dwellers as the 'fastest growing social group on earth'. As Jacques Derrida has rightly written:

> no degree of progress allows one to ignore that never before, in absolute figures, never have so many men, women, and children been subjugated, starved, or exterminated on the earth.

The wealth of Birmingham was built on two different – but linked – bases. The first was the creation of – and the creation of demand for – a seemingly interminable array of ultimately useless goods. Birmingham manufactured springs, steel tubes and tinplate wares. It produced medals and silver cups; buttons made of metal or vegetable-ivory or covered in fabric. There were factories for fenders and fire irons; bedsteads and golf balls; crown glass, flint glass, sheet, plate and optical glass. Industrialisation created its own demand: new factories were constructed to create new tools for other factories. Birmingham conceived such industrial innovations as the Siemens process (for the chemical purification of silicon), Muntz's metal (three parts copper, two parts zinc), and John Roebuck's 'lead-chamber' process for producing sulphuric acid. 'In Birmingham alone 500 varieties of hammers are produced,' wrote Marx in 1867. What a world of rubbish we created.

Not only have we created all this rubbish, we have imbued it with meaning too. French theorist Jean Baudrillard has argued that objects no longer exist to serve a use but to position us within a network that governs our social status and even our personalities. In J. K. Rowling's Harry Potter books, the evil Voldemort stores parts of his soul in a series of mostly mundane objects: a diary, a ring, a locket and a trophy (as well as a diadem and a snake). In so doing he imbues these things with power and value. In some ways capitalism requires that we all do likewise. Numerous articles in *New Scientist* have argued that 'our urge to accumulate has deep roots', that 'possessions enrich our lives', and that 'it's human nature to own things'. But today's bloated materialism need not be seen as 'natural'. It is neither universal nor unchanging. It has a history and it can be changed.

In his literary history of the bourgeoisie, Franco Moretti observes the obsession with objects that characterised the writers of the nineteenth century. I would cite Charles Dickens, who incidentally was president of the Polytechnic Institution of Birmingham, as the clearest example. In *A Christmas Carol*, which Dickens first read in public at Birmingham Town Hall in 1853, Scrooge goes with one of the phantoms to 'an obscure part of town'. The subsequent scene – or rather, the objects within it – are described in great detail:

> Far in this den of infamous resort, there was a low-browed, beetling shop, below a pent-house roof, where iron, old rags, bottles, bones, and greasy offal, were bought. Upon the floor within, were piled up heaps of rusty keys, nails, chains, hinges, files, scales, weights, and refuse iron of all kinds. Secrets that few would like to scrutinise were bred and hidden in mountains of unseemly rags, masses of corrupted fat, and sepulchres of bones.

Here Dickens presents us not with a wealth of material possessions but with the detritus caused by industrialisation: iron objects rusted and now useless, replaced by new products in steel, and then stainless steel. But why does he feel the need to list them all? Moretti has argued that in seeking to account for everything, realist novelists from Daniel Defoe to George Eliot struggled to convey what actually mattered. In seeking to account for the world, they became accountants: adept at numbers and quantities, prices and lists, but rarely able to discern true value. For Moretti, this obsession with precision rarely enlightens us about what is really important; instead, we are left with 'many perspicuous details, adding up to a hazy whole'. But why? asks Moretti. 'What has made precision so much more important than meaning?' He is asking this question about the realist novel but, as we shall see, we might just as well ask the same question about contemporary politics, about economic policy, and about the process by which large-scale infrastructure projects such as HS2 are conceived and imposed.

In the logic of capitalism, meaning is bound up with a commitment to progress. In Birmingham, this can be seen in the evolution of the bicycle. In order to maintain levels of demand, new models were continually introduced. This involved both innovation and improvement: bicycles became cheaper, lighter and more comfortable. But we are now becoming aware of the waste that capitalism leaves behind. Such progress renders older models suddenly undesirable, or now in the case of more complex technology, completely redundant. As a direct consequence, by 1997, the UK was sending around 100 million tonnes of waste to landfill sites per year. Since new taxes were introduced, this figure has fallen to less than 39 million tonnes in 2013. That is still over half a tonne per person per year. In *A Geology of Media*, Jussi Parikka draws our attention to the vast wastefulness of contemporary technology. He argues that we should look at each newly hyped Apple product not as a shining example of human technological progress but as yet another addition to a list of 'zombie media future fossils'. As Ken Worpole put it so eloquently at the conclusion of *The New English Landscape*: 'We have been throwing things away for centuries, only recently realising that there is no such place as away. We all live downriver now.'

If the creation of demand for stuff is one key fact behind Birmingham's industrial growth, then the second is war. Time and again in the history of Birmingham's industries, it is clear how growth was maintained by Britain's bellicose foreign policy throughout the nineteenth century and into the twentieth. We've already seen the link between colonialism and the rail industries. Nowhere is the impact of war more obvious than in the effects felt after World War I. The effect of the war on manufacturing technique, as G. C. Allen points out, 'was almost everywhere beneficial'. Mechanisation, electrification, specialisation and standardisation were all rapidly introduced as part of the 'application of scientific methods to industry' in this new phase of industrial development. In 1913, the year before the war, Birmingham exported some 7,595 motor cars and 16,850 motorcycles. By 1924 these figures had risen to 12,754 and 37,607. Small, struggling trades such as needles, finished brass, jewellery and clocks continued to decline. Meanwhile, the big factories only grew. Capitalism specialises in economies of scale. Nearly four times as many people were involved in the motor and cycle trade in 1924 as in 1907. By 1927, one motor factory in Northfields employed 10,000 workers.

War may have underpinned Birmingham's industrial wealth in the nineteenth century, but in the twentieth century it was war by which the city was dramatically reshaped. Due to its strategic importance as an industrial and manufacturing city, and in particular, due to the importance of its arms industry, it is hardly surprising that Birmingham was one of Germany's key strategic targets during World War II. Birmingham was a target of war because it was a centre of war. Some 1,852 tonnes of bombs were dropped by the German Luftwaffe between 1940 and 1943. According to Gordon E. Cherry's 1994 study of the city, a total of 12,391 houses, 302 factories and 239 other buildings were destroyed, with many more damaged. 2,241 people were killed, and 3,010 seriously injured.

In Honor Gavin's *Midland*, the central character – known as 'the bab' – works within the office of Herbert Manzoni. Her responsibility is to record on a large-scale map of the city the location of each and every building destroyed during the Birmingham Blitz. Early on in the process, the bab spills tea on the tablecloth, and mistakes its pattern for the gridlines of the OS map. 'The brown spots of tea she takes for bombs.' It proves to be a precursor of what is to come.

As the bombs continue to fall, and reports of lost buildings flood in day after day, the process of recording all the information on a single map becomes harder and harder. The circles grow and blur together, and the map becomes increasingly illegible. That is why Ordnance Survey don't attempt to accurately map landfill sites. 'The more accurate information the bab attempts to incorporate into the map the more the map ridicules the notion of accuracy.' Eventually, the task of recording all the damage begins to become impossible. The map is dominated by damage – what has been destroyed overtakes that which is left. Soon it becomes completely unreadable:

The map's a mess. The things that should give it its meaning, these things no longer even *show* on it. The alleyways, churches, synagogues, ODEONs and swimming pools are sunk, censored, obscured.

And then a little later:

> The bab herself no longer knows. The more attentive she
> tried to be, the more chaotic the map became. The more
> thorough she was in making her markings, the more the
> map blurred. The map blurred so much that it began to
> look as if the suburbs had turned back into fields, fields
> that had been flooded with blood.

Maps that try to account for everything very quickly make
no sense. There must always be limits. It is noteworthy that
the effects upon individual people – their lives and deaths –
are of no relevance to the bab's increasingly absurd process
of mapping. It is possible that Gavin is making a criticism
of the ambitions of Modernist architects and planners,
who are frequently accused of overlooking the realities
of individual experience in favour of the grand structure.
It is also possible that Gavin is making a broader point
about maps themselves. As we saw from the history of
the Ordnance Survey maps, so often in our attempts to fix
geographical reality, we neglect those people who are most
directly affected. By giving voice to the city's oft-voiceless
inhabitants, Gavin suggests the importance of literature, as

a creative means of non-objective expression, in helping us better to understand the world and our places within it.

The novel is prefaced with two quotations. The first is from Herman Melville; the second from Manzoni himself. It's that famous line: 'I have never been very certain as to the value of tangible links with the past.'

In light of Manzoni's work on the city, it's a telling statement. It also seems to be one that could have been spoken by Birmingham itself at various times in the recent history of the city. Perhaps that's what Gavin was thinking: *Midland* features several strange passages narrated by the city itself.

Manzoni's statement also prompts some important questions: what in fact are the benefits of 'tangible links with the past'? One answer is that, despite the best efforts of certain architects and engineers, developers and planners, such links are unavoidable. They may be more or less tangible, more or less imaginary. But, if this walk has taught me anything, it is that traces of the past always linger on into the present. This may be in the form of old railway lines, slowly overgrown; fields, hedgerows, or ancient earthworks; administrative boundaries; private property; or even simply in the memory of the stories that have attached themselves to places that matter to us. Time does not exist in a single line: Manzoni's structures continue to affect the present. As Freud once wrote, '*Saxa loquitur*' – 'the stones speak'. However clean the slate is wiped, the past lives on into the present.

A more positive answer might be that we need the past in order to make sense of the present. Without 'tangible links' to our past, there can be no sense of identity – for places or for people. This is why it remains important to learn to read the landscapes of the countryside and the city. That is why radical redevelopments are often so vehemently opposed, for they engender a kind of cultural amnesia. Supermarkets and shopping malls, airports and train stations: these 'non-places' deliberately aim to exist outside of place and time in a never-ending immediate present of consumption.

As Alastair Bonnett wrote in his book *Off the Map*:

> As many cities are still learning, sweeping away the past deprives the world of more than just rare and beautiful landscapes. You also remove the memories, stories and connections that hold people together, socially as well as individually. Turning complex, diverse places into shallow, simple ones creates a more culturally vulnerable population, an unrooted mass whose only linking thread lies in the ideology that is fed to them from above.

There can be no identity without some access to the past

– be it shared or individual. This may explain the recent resurgence of psychogeography, of walking and writing and the digging up of hidden histories. When the status quo relies upon the constant upheaval of relentless novelty, there can then be something radical about conservatism – in the sense of looking backwards, of preserving a threatened past. The fascination with the past that marks much contemporary art and literature might then be seen as a direct response to a commercial world interested only in a permanent present tense. Bonnett continues: 'Without the binding presence of the past, places are emptied of a meaningful future.' No tangible links with the past means no sense of community; 'just spaces of temporary individual habitation'. With his obsession with roads and transport, speed and mobility, maybe that's what Manzoni wanted.

Today, Birmingham still produces cars, weapons, plastics and glass, but it no longer feels like a centre of production. Instead, like many other cities, it is now a temple to buying and selling. As Jonathan Meades puts it: 'Central Brum is like a vast, open-air airport lounge – a place that is passed through out of corporate necessity and commercial exigency rather than personal choice.'

My bus terminates and it's hard to escape the feeling that Meades may be correct. On Edgbaston Street stands the church of St Martin in the Bull Ring, where a thirteenth-century building was knocked down by 'improving' Victorians and replaced with this rock-faced edifice. Looming across it is the undulating bubonic surface of the Selfridges Building, completed in 2003 at a cost of £60 million. This is the work of Future Systems.

Revisiting the building for *Icon* magazine in 2015, architecture critic Owen Hatherley described it with a trace of disdain as 'futuristic, erotic and outlandish', then 'slinky, curved and clad in aluminium "sequins"'. The building was conceived, Hatherley argues, as a kind of artwork – unique and immediately identifiable. Such high-impact designs by the so-called 'starchitects' – globe-trotting architecture mega-stars like Renzo Piano or Frank Gehry – have become increasingly popular with cities attempting to place themselves on the global map. Gehry's Guggenheim in Bilbao is perhaps the example par excellence. The city's existing artist communities have been largely whitewashed from the ensuing narratives of regeneration. Instead of a major art gallery, Birmingham opted for this vast shopping mall, and to an extent it succeeded: 'It became,' writes Hatherley, 'one of the definitive symbols of "regeneration" in British architecture.'

Beneath the theatrics, however, lies the everyday reality of a bland, placeless shopping mall – it is the work of engineers Benoy, best known for their contributions to large-scale projects in Hong Kong, China and the UAE. With a distinctly male sneer, Hatherley describes Future Systems' work as 'the Paco Rabanne frock on a body eviscerated by the value engineers'. 'Future Systems,' he concludes, 'created the ultimate architectural advert, which is what Birmingham apparently wanted and needed. Benoy, and its ilk, always provide the small print.'

Birmingham gets what Birmingham wants. This idea is not new. Writing in 1975, journalist Tony Aldous said much the same about the old Bullring. While celebrated critic Ian Nairn praised the 1964 building, and many other critics savaged it, Aldous himself struggled to care. His interest was in the preservation of Georgian crescents or Victorian halls. The inner-city commerce of Birmingham's Bullring was rather beneath him: 'For myself, I cannot get too upset about this aspect of the new Birmingham. This is what Birmingham wanted.'

To some extent, both Hatherley and Aldous are correct. Locally born academic Chris Prendergast has written of the immediate success of the new shopping mall. In 'The Bullring Effect', an essay published by Influx Press as part of an e-book about Birmingham called *Build and Destroy*, Prendergast describes how in its first year the new mall saw 600,000–700,000 visitors per week. Fifty-eight per cent were from outside the city centre. Prendergast also likens the Bullring to Bilbao: 'The Bullring's development has been part of a similar post-industrial process which has embraced a movement towards the service sector.' The result, he argues, has been 'a fundamental change in the city's image'. This, after all, was the purpose of the building. To that end, it has been a success.

In a small public space around the back of the church are a Nando's, a Pizza Hut and a Wagamama. Two Japanese girls are taking photos of each other. At ankle height is a small sign: 'Public notice: Please refrain from walking on the landscaped garden.' Nearby, water flows down a piece of public art. It is the work of locally born poets Polarbear and Simon Turner. Written in the stone are sundry hectic words and phrases: 'Maps made of man' or 'Everything happens here and all at once'. I wonder if this is meant as a celebration of the vibrancy of urban life. After four days of solitary walking, it just feels bewildering.

Polarbear is otherwise known as Steven Camden. His essay, 'Kiss My Brum', is the companion piece to Prendergast's in *Build and Destroy*. Like the characters in David Lodge's novel *Nice Work*, Camden sees the identity of Birmingham's inhabitants as unavoidably tied to the idea of work. He describes his own employment history – and it echoes that of the city itself:

I earned a crust doing many jobs before I arrived at my profession. I knocked down walls on demolition sites, I bent metal floor panels in a foundry, I constructed patios on barn conversions, I painted, I decorated, I entered reams of faceless data whilst sat in a cold portacabin.

Destroy and build. Build and destroy. Prepare the way for shopping, tourism, finance and the 'culture industries'. On the day I'm here, New Street has been transformed into a building site. A plethora of signs insists it remains 'business as usual'. Keep eating. Keep buying. All is well. The whole world is here: women in sportswear and saris, pushing prams or pulling children. Men in suits or shorts; one in pale denim jeans with Blakeys in the soles of his black Oxfords. A transvestite all in gold – resplendent in the lunchtime sun. 'Everything happens here and all at once.'

I stop for lunch opposite the distinctive arch of the Piccadilly Arcade – built as a cinema in 1910 before being converted into shops in 1926. On the first floor, behind white-tiled walls, is a Cotswold Outdoor Centre. I sit eating a baguette in a chain sandwich store, trying to transcribe the local accent: 'Merndigh' is the best approximation I can make for 'Monday'.

*

Over the course of this walk a pattern has emerged. In London there is widespread ignorance of HS2. Apart from those directly affected, the vast majority of people simply don't seem to know or care. It is just another thing being built. Out beyond the M25, however, the antipathy grows. In a sense this is hardly surprising: to walk the route of HS2 is not to garner a representative sample of popular opinion. But that has never been the point. The point has been to find out the impact upon those people and places most directly affected, and to see what that might say about wider attitudes towards community and place, progress and the environment. Towards Birmingham, opinion gradually shifts from antipathy through ambivalence to genuine support for the project. Mostly, people's opinions are shaped by the immediate effects that they will feel – what they stand to gain or lose. But there has been great selflessness too – a desire to see a bigger picture. And again, this has been true on both sides – from Andrew Bodman's devotion to opposing the project to Adrian Aylward's espousal of the need to upgrade transport infrastructure, despite the likely impact on the Buckinghamshire Railway Centre where he works.

Nobody, however, has been such a consciously 'big picture' thinker as Jonathan Watkins, director of Ikon, one of Birmingham's leading contemporary art galleries. Watkins, who was born in the UK but studied in Australia, was director of the celebrated Chisenhale gallery in London from 1990 to 1995. He then worked at the Serpentine before being appointed to his current role here in Birmingham in 1999. I've met Jonathan once or twice at art fairs in London, but only briefly. I had a hunch he'd have interesting things to say about art, about Birmingham and about HS2. I'm not wrong.

Ikon was founded by local artists in the 1960s. Its first space was an octagonal glass-walled kiosk in the Bull Ring shopping centre. Since then, the gallery has occupied a number of locations across the centre of Birmingham: a former mortuary in the basement of Queens College on Swallow Street; the Birmingham Shopping Centre above New Street Station; then a former carpet shop next to the Alexandra Theatre. In 1997, with funding from the National Lottery, Ikon moved to its current site – the Grade II listed neo-Gothic red-brick pile that was once Oozells Street Board School. It is one of over forty such institutions set up across the city following the Elementary Education Act of 1870, which aimed to provide education free from the influence of the Anglican or Catholic Churches. The act was the result of campaigning by prominent Birmingham leaders of the National Education League – another example of the city's long history of nonconformism.

Ikon arrived at Oozells Street as part of a major redevelopment of the surrounding area: from former industrial site to 'mixed-use canal-side development'. This area is known as Brindleyplace – its development in the 1990s was the work of Argent, the same developers responsible for the recent work around King's Cross in London. According to Argent, Brindleyplace is 'widely seen as a model for successful urban regeneration'. It is Argent who are carrying out the current developments to the east of Centenary Square. Their humble title for the project? Paradise.

Outside Ikon, the surrounding square is clean and bland, lined by bland banks and office blocks. I'm sitting enjoying the sun outside the gallery's cafe as Watkins approaches. In circular, tortoiseshell glasses and white linen button-down, with his grey-blond curls neatly trimmed, he looks like a subtly prosperous, forward-thinking architect. In short, he looks the part.

Watkins is passionate about Birmingham. He has lived here for eighteen years and has clearly grown to love the city. 'Birmingham is the butt of all the jokes,' he says. 'But I like it *because* it has such a bad press – it feels like I'm enjoying a secret. It's greener and more comfortable than you think.'

This chimes with Jonathan Meades' assessment of the city in his 1998 film, *Heart By-Pass*: 'It's an ignored void at the heart of the country.'

But he is also surprisingly honest in his criticisms. He describes the local authority as a 'basket case' and laments the city's lack of cultural offerings. 'It's sad that Birmingham doesn't have enough cultural life – it's bigger than Manchester.' Watkins believes that part of the problem is the locals themselves: 'It's about what Birmingham feels it deserves. The people are working class and feel they shouldn't be too ambitious and reach for cultural advancement. It's endearing and unpretentious and I love it for that.'

Watkins is especially interesting on this side of Birmingham's character. I've often been dubious about the idea that the population of a city can have a shared character – especially a city with a population in excess of a million people. But Watkins disagrees: 'What I've noticed about Birmingham is that it's the least nostalgic place I've ever been in. They don't think twice about knocking things down. Birmingham marches on. Its motto is "forward".' Hence the title of that Influx Press e-book: *Build and Destroy*.

Above all, Watkins is passionate about the need for regeneration. Unsurprisingly, he is a keen advocate of HS2. 'I like the idea of HS2,' he says. 'I'm a supporter of it. We need to connect up. There are high-speed trains in China, and from Antwerp to Paris. Why should there be HS1 but not HS2? It's not just about Birmingham, but connecting up the whole country.' As director of Ikon, Watkins was involved in a scheme to establish a Museum Quarter around the Birmingham terminus of HS2 at Curzon Street. 'We know what regenerates a city,' he argues. 'Museums are key. China gets it, Barcelona gets it, London gets it. If there were no museums in New York, hardly anyone would go. Museums symbolise cultural wealth, and they give people things to do.'

According to a Curzon Square 'vision' document produced by Ikon with Glenn Howells Architects, the aims of the Museum Quarter were to boost 'graduate retention', attract businesses and tourism, and improve the standard of living for Birmingham's residents. 'Adjacent to the proposed HS2 rail terminal, Curzon Square will be a cultural oasis,' declares Watkins' introduction to the document. 'Its venues will be impressive architecture in a village-like critical mass of artistic attraction.'

The plan was to combine a second Ikon gallery with a new building to house a national art collection (such as the Arts Council's collection or the Government Art Collection) and a new museum of photography – to be housed in the surviving Grade I listed neoclassical entrance building of what was formerly Curzon Street station. The vision is almost painfully unthreatening: 'Curzon Square will be a safe, pleasant place for everyone,' it says. The focus is on 'peace', 'green space' and 'cultural diversity'. The accompanying illustrations are sunny and childlike.

But Watkins will have to wait, because the Museum Quarter vision will not be going ahead any time soon. 'There will be a museum quarter here one day,' he says, but he is unlikely to be involved. The station at Curzon Street will be too big, he laments, with too much space taken up by construction and cabins. 'The site would not become available until at least 2027,' he says, 'and, frankly, I can't wait that long.' Such vision documents are the wasted labours of today's service industries. Like the fenders and fire irons of Birmingham's industrial heyday, they too are destined for landfill.

Instead, the latest masterplan for Curzon Street is a much more obviously business-oriented offering. In Birmingham City Council's Masterplan for Growth document from July 2015, HS2 is portrayed as a 'once in a century opportunity to radically enhance the City's national rail connectivity and accelerate its economic growth potential'. Despite illustrations bearing a marked stylistic resemblance to those in the Ikon vision, here the emphasis is on retail, business and, most memorably, 'an integrated, holistic and deliverable movement strategy'. Like those realist novels, the document is packed full of precision. It is being claimed that the redevelopment of the Eastside and Digbeth areas will boost the Birmingham economy by £1.4 billion a year, create 36,000 jobs, 600,000 square metres of 'employment space' and an additional 4,000 homes. There is some mention of green space, but references to anything cultural only occur as part of lists of other, more important, factors. By contrast, the word 'growth' appears no less than 113 times. Progress, as ever, feels relentlessly persistent.

After leaving Jonathan, I head to Birmingham's new library, before going on to the station to take the train home at last. The library – a huge, multi-tiered gateau of a thing – looms high over the simple neoclassicism of Baskerville House on one side and the curving concrete of The Rep on the other. It was designed by Mecanoo architects with engineers Buro Happold and opened in 2013. It is said to be the largest public library in the UK. Mecanoo's distinctive design replaced a Brutalist inverted ziggurat by John Madin, which twice failed to gain listed status despite the efforts of English Heritage. Instead, Madin's controversial concrete edifice – which itself replaced a beautiful Victorian structure – was granted immunity from listing. Demolition finally began in November 2015.

In *Heart By-Pass*, Jonathan Meades described the centre of Birmingham as like an airport. That was in 1998. Much has changed since then, but the airport comparison remains apt. 'Like an airport,' Meades said, 'central Brum attempts to overcome its featurelessness with tokenistic works of symbolic intent.' Meades cites Antony Gormley's 1993 public sculpture *Iron Man* by way of example. It's arguable that the new library building is merely a grand extension of the same logic. Both make passing references to the city's industrial past: Gormley to the iron industry (and, for Meades, the city's love of heavy metal), while the library's external circle patterns apparently refer to industrial gasometers and the jewellery trade.

Like Selfridges, the Library of Birmingham has provided the city centre with a recognisable architectural icon. It has drummed up media coverage and brought in visitors: in 2014, no less than 2.4 million people visited the library, making it the tenth most popular visitor attraction in the UK. But there have been problems too. At £188 million, the cost of the library has been widely criticised, and the timing of its opening was certainly unfortunate – just as widespread cuts were announced to library services across the rest of the city. Within one year, the council announced that 100 of the library's 188 staff were to lose their jobs and opening hours would be cut from seventy-three per week to just forty.

Certainly, on the day I visit, it feels significantly understaffed. It also doesn't feel like a library. Instead, it is a vast futuristic structure of shiny black curves. Circular white lights adorn ceilings; escalators rise out of view, their edges trimmed with blue neon. One day, it seems to say, all libraries will be like this: it's a library for people who don't like libraries. It's library as day out. There is even a roof garden, with planted boxes of rosemary, sage and, oddly, nettles. Perhaps they're a sop to the psychogeographers. Perhaps the planting budget has been cut. Large groups of tourists ride the glitzy escalators up to the higher levels. They step outside, take photos of the view, and leave immediately.

I try to find a locker in which to leave my backpack, but I can't follow the directions given by the girl at reception. I head instead to the toilet, where every conceivable surface is sloping. I try to put my notebook down and only succeed in turning the taps on, then the hand-dryer. I'm quickly becoming irritated with modernity. On the fourth floor I finally find a locker, but I have no change. I ask a man in a lanyard standing nearby. 'Sorry,' he says. 'I'm from the catering company. You can ask at the info desk downstairs.'

Like the tourists, I'm not here for the books either. I'm here to gawp at this bizarre building. And I'm here to see an exhibition of work by one of my favourite contemporary artists – Sophy Rickett – which happens to coincide with my arrival in Birmingham. I finally find the library's gallery space, but it's locked. A friendly member of staff unlocks it for me – he is as baffled as I am as to why it was closed. On his waistcoat is the library slogan: 'Rewriting the Book'. I wonder whether this book will end up there one day. I wonder how long it will last – the library, that is, but also this book. The walk is over now. The time of writing is ahead.

In the white-walled gallery of the Library of Birmingham hangs a series of square black-and-white photographs of butterflies. The title is somehow ominous: *The Death of a Beautiful Subject*. I wonder what the subject is, what has died. I assume initially that these are species of butterflies that have become endangered or extinct; that the artist is commenting on the loss of natural beauty. In some works the butterflies have been whited-out. In others it's hard to see a butterfly at all. But Rickett's photographs are often borrowed or appropriated. Behind them are personal histories that may be hidden, at least initially, from the viewer. In this case, the images were originally taken by the artist's father. Rickett has revisited her own past to examine her father's interest in photography and, possibly, the origins of her own. What strikes me in particular is the power of showing such works in the Library of Birmingham. In a city so marked by its desire to erase the past, this appeal to memory and to family history has its own peculiar poignancy. Beneath the modern image of a modern city hides a myriad of possible pasts to be discovered or invented altogether.

Rickett has produced a small moss-green booklet of images and text to accompany the exhibition. I pick up a copy of the booklet and I leave the library. I walk to the train station. I wait for my train. I'm going home.

X

The Train Home

The rhythm of the train is quite different to the rhythm of the walk. The rhythm of thought changes too.

Sitting here on this train, I no longer need to walk, navigate, make decisions, question those decisions, stop, worry, turn back, retread my steps. Unsurprisingly, it feels relaxing. The immediate present is no longer of concern, so my thoughts begin to drift backwards, trying to make sense of the walk I have just completed. It is months now since I first set off, with no real idea of what I expected to find, who I might meet, or what I would learn. I drew a line through the map and I followed it, more or less.

In her fascinating and powerful history of walking, *Wanderlust*, Rebecca Solnit writes: 'For writers, the long-distance walk is an easy way to find narrative continuity. If a path is like a story ... then a continuous walk must make a coherent story, and a very long walk makes a full-length book.' Then, she adds: 'Or so goes the logic ...' There is, it seems to me, just a smidge of contempt about this last little aside – a suggestion that this kind of logic is too easy. But perhaps I'm just getting defensive. No one likes having their own thought processes skewered in writing – fourteen years before they've even had them.

One part of this narrative logic is that of continuity. A continuous walk makes a coherent story. But this walk, of course, has not been continuous. In Northamptonshire,

I experienced pains through my knee and hip, and was forced to cut short the journey. It was several months later that I was able to return and complete the walk. The sense of achievement that I had anticipated upon finishing has not materialised. Partly, I think, this is because the injury was not even serious. Not only had I failed to complete the undertaking I had set myself, but I had failed for such trivial reasons. If only I had known, I could simply have taken a few painkillers and just carried on.

In fact, it occurs to me now that it was not simply my knee that prevented me from completing the walk entirely on foot. Almost every day, I retreated in some way from the task I had initially set myself: I took the tube in Ruislip, boarded a bus in Birmingham. I stayed at my parents' house in Buckinghamshire twice, drove back and forth in the cars of anti-HS2 campaigners. I rang my wife to check on pubs or campsites. If the intention was ever to remain in some sense self-sufficient, then each day of the walk was its own small failure.

A second aspect of the narrative logic that Solnit identifies is that of character development. The external journey ought to be mirrored by an internal one. Our narrator ought to learn something, not only about the world, but about himself – or herself – too. Mostly, for reasons Solnit also explains, it's himself.

Sitting on the train, staring out of the window, I try to think back over the duration of the journey. Have I learnt something that would – in the time-honoured fashion – render this walk, and therefore this book, in some way significant? Or have I failed at that too?

For one thing, I have learnt that I am not a nature writer. I simply don't know enough to write about the natural world like W. G. Hoskins or J. A. Baker, like Robert Macfarlane or Helen Macdonald. And I don't think I ever will. I won't sleep happily atop a mountain like Macfarlane or experience searing intensities of feeling like Macdonald. If I'm honest, I was probably conscious of this before I set off, but it took the real, actual experience of walking through England's changing landscapes to be faced with the extent of my own ignorance, and to admit it – to myself and here, in writing. But, more importantly, the experience has taught me that perhaps it doesn't matter so much after all. Yes, I would like to learn more about the environment, to identify birds and understand formations in the landscape. I would like to read the signs of the world. But there is more than one way to respond to a place, and its people.

In *A Field Guide to Getting Lost*, Solnit again perfectly captures my own failures. Near the beginning of the book, she writes:

There's an art to attending to … the thousand things that make the world a text that can be read by the literate. The lost are often illiterate in this language that is the language of the earth itself, or don't stop to read it.

Over the course of this walk I have learnt very little of what Solnit calls 'the language of the earth itself'. Rather, I have learnt a great deal about the extent of my own ignorance, my own 'illiteracy'. It comes as some consolation that I am by no means the first to realise this. Even Richard Jefferies struggled sometimes. In an 1887 essay he describes a series of walks through a nearby wheat field. He describes the field as a 'flat and uninteresting surface' and admits that 'I can trace nothing on this surface'. This is not because there is nothing to be traced but because of his own human ignorance. Dogs, by contrast, can smell 'the invisible signs of the hare': 'The dull surface is all written over with hieroglyphics to the hound, he can read and translate to us in joyous tongue.' It is us humans who are unable to read the signs in the landscape. 'Nature is a language. Can't you read?' sang Morrissey in 1986. My answer, I've come to realise, must be no. That, perhaps, is a start.

In an attempt to begin to rectify this illiteracy I bought a book entitled *The Walker's Guide to Outdoor Clues and Signs* by author and 'natural navigator' Tristan Gooley. In it is all sorts of advice about how to glean knowledge of the world from what you can see around you. In the UK, more branches grow on the south side of trees than the north. Foxgloves, poppies and thistles love disturbed ground. Each layer of branches (or 'whorl') on a conifer signifies one year of growth.

Gooley explains that it is possible to ascertain so much about time and place thanks to the way in which patterns of behaviour are repeated – not only by animals or plants but by humans too. Gooley explains why most sheep shelter on the north-east side of a gorse bush, and how we can tell. He explains why shops on one side of the street do better than those on the other, and why the west ends of UK cities have historically been more prosperous than the east. 'We may have free will as individuals,' he writes, 'but not as a species.' What he means by this is that, although we can never entirely predict how an individual will respond to a given set of circumstances, we can nevertheless be relatively certain about predicting the response of the majority of people.

Gooley here seems to have hit upon a profound truth. For what he is saying applies to a whole wealth of disciplines outside of his chosen terrain. Writing about the strategies of the social sciences, for example, David Pepper has described the way in which, although free will might seem to present a difficulty to the construction of general theories of society, in fact, it is often incorporated simply by introducing scope for an element of chance. Pepper is not unaware of the problems of such an approach, and it's worth pointing out that these 'random' anomalies are not merely statistics – points on a graph or chemicals in a lab – which defy explanation and, which – in their individuality – can simply be ignored. When it comes to HS2, each 'anomaly' is a person, like John or Stephen or Jenny or Chris, each with their own life and loves, worries, joys, values and relationships to others and to the world. The requirement to attempt to take account of any exception is therefore not merely a philosophical nicety, but a political necessity. In some cases, people's lives are at stake.

What is important to note is that Gooley is only attempting to describe, not to prescribe. His generalisations aim to make sense of the world around us, not to change it. Unfortunately, it is exactly this prescriptive approach – based upon a comparable generalising tendency – that informs today's decision-makers: bureaucrats, scientists, politicians and business leaders. For what Gooley argues chimes surprisingly closely with a much earlier statement by none other than Edward Bernays. Bernays – the nephew of Sigmund Freud – was one of the most influential theorists on the role of propaganda in democratic societies. He believed that the views of the public were not to be relied upon and needed guidance from those in positions of authority. After World War I, when the very word 'propaganda' had acquired a bad name (ironically enough), Bernays is said to have championed the term 'public relations' instead. He has been quoted as saying, 'It is sometimes possible to change the attitudes of millions but impossible to change the attitude of one man.' It is this exact observation that closely informs what we think of today as democracy.

*

Outside the train the landscape retreats once more to the status of scenery. I am no longer in it, part of it. The world retreats once more to spectacle. Hedges and fields blur by. Suburban fringe. Industrial estates. Empty buildings. Ugly new houses. A sign for the Risborough Box – the UK's largest signal box, I later learn, currently being turned into a museum by a group of volunteers. The signals of one age become the signs of another. I see horses in a field, and I'm thankful for distance and this speed and this glass. The logo of Chiltern Railways partially obscures the view.

If walking is a way of being in the world, then sitting on a modern, air-conditioned train is just one of many ways that we can cut ourselves off from it. Or at least a certain conception of it. The world becomes divided: on this side of the glass are the noises and smells of our fellow travellers, the occasional shrill ring of a telephone, an opportunity to buy scalding hot tea, a tinny announcement, the dull grey pattern of the seat in front. On the other side is another world just passing by.

What the experience of the train does is to reinstate the division between inside and outside that walking had seemed to overcome, or at least conceal, or render irrelevant. Here, from my seat, this division takes the form of the finger-smudged glass of the train window. The window enacts this division and clarifies it, makes it clear – in a sense that is not only literal but metaphorical too. The window is a physical barrier that separates inside and outside. In that sense, it makes the division between the two clear, as in obvious, evident. There is a palpable, physical separation between the two. But in addition, and at the same time, the window is also clear – literally. I can see right through it. The window enacts a division but conceals it too. Is that clear?

It seems to me that this might be worth dwelling upon – for the convergence of literal and metaphorical here is no mere coincidence. In fact, the correlation between seeing and knowing has been with us perhaps since the very origins of knowledge. But it is one that is especially pronounced in English: verbs such as 'see', 'perceive', 'recognise', 'discern', 'detect' or 'examine' all reinforce the idea that to see is to know. In Latin, there were a dozen words for 'know', of which several (including *nosco, cognosco, intellego* and *percipio*) all have strong associations with sight. But a number of other verbs demonstrated a very different conception of knowledge: *teneo* meant to know only as a consequence of having, holding or possessing, while *scio* (from which we get the word science) meant to know in the sense of understanding how to do something (it was also sometimes used to mean to know, ahem, carnally). Similarly, *habeo* and *disco* also implied that knowledge was a thing to acquire through work, learning or ownership, rather than simply something gleaned on sight.

In French, there is a nice distinction between two ways of knowing: *savoir* and *connaître*. Savoir is in questions and it is followed by other verbs – in which case it means to know *how* to do something. It is also simply used on its own: *Tu sais que je veux dire? Oui, je sais. Connaître*, meanwhile, means to know in the sense of being personally familiar with something, or to have experienced it oneself. It is usually applied to people or places. At the risk of overplaying this distinction, it seems to me instructive. I might even be tempted to suggest that this walk has in some ways enacted an exploration of the relationship between the two. To read about a subject, an idea, a philosophy is to know it in the sense of *savoir*. To walk in the world for any length of time is to begin to know it in the sense of *connaître*. This is a similar point to that made by Bruce Chatwin when he contrasted the knowledge of lived experience with knowledge gleaned from 'other men's books'. To be back on the train, and see the landscape through the glass of this window, is to know it – if at all – only in the sense of *savoir*.

The point I'm making is that sight and knowledge are not the same, even though, linguistically and conceptually, they have long been very closely linked. But it was arguably not until the seventeenth century that such metaphors of sight came to dominate the way that we try to think about knowledge. The very word 'Enlightenment' demonstrates what was at stake: science would shine its unrelenting light upon a dark, mysterious world. Arguably, the philosophers of the Enlightenment were merely taking up the metaphors they'd found in Christianity. It was Jesus, after all, who said: 'I am the Light of the world; he who follows Me will not walk in the darkness, but will have the Light of life.' In Genesis, God's second act of creation is light. 'And God said, Let there be light: and there was light. And God saw the light, that it was good: and God divided the light from the darkness.'

In 1695, John Locke, one of the foremost philosophers of the Enlightenment, published *The Reasonableness of*

Christianity, in which he reads the Bible – and the New Testament in particular – as entirely consistent with the love of science and reason. He argues that, when it comes to the uneducated masses, it is better to *show* evidence of God than to go through the pains of rational explanation: people must 'see the demonstration'. Jesus, for example, came to show us the truth of God. His miracles (from the Latin verb *miror* – I wonder at) were precisely the demonstration (from *demonstro* – I show) that Locke advocates. He writes:

> And I ask, whether one coming from heaven in the power of God, in full and *clear evidence* and *demonstration* of *miracles*, giving *plain* and direct rules of morality and obedience, be not likelier to *enlighten* the bulk of mankind, and set them right in their duties, and bring them to do them, than by reasoning with them from general notions and principles of human reason? [my italics]

Here is Jesus not only as teacher but also as politician, as scientist. Before His light, the 'bulk of mankind' – those in darkness and ignorance – must surely stand in admiration and belief. Clear evidence, demonstration, miracles, plain rules, enlightenment: for Locke and for so many since, these are the criteria for religion and for science, for politics and for any attempt to understand, engage with, or convey the truth. From Locke and others, such metaphors soon spread to the humanities and beyond. Philosophers became concerned above all with clarity. It was in the cold light of reason that we ought to see the world. Later, the historians of the nineteenth century would also see themselves as shining a light upon the documents of history. In this conception, archives were viewed, according to German academic Stefan Berger, as 'dark places, which had to be illuminated by historians'. In many cases, this was probably literally true.

Today, it is in the domain of politics that this kind of language is most prominent. 'We want to be the most open and transparent government in the world,' announced David Cameron upon becoming Prime Minister in 2010. The following year, the Open Government Partnership was founded by a multinational group of politicians and bureaucrats 'to provide an international platform for domestic reformers committed to making their governments more open, accountable, and responsive to citizens'. On the website of the UK branch of this Open Government organisation, we're told that 'transparency and open government are ideas whose time has come'. This is why the revelations about the offshore finances of his father, subsequently revealed in the Panama Papers, were so damaging to Cameron. After initially insisting that it was a 'private matter', Cameron eventually admitted to profiting from the trust. 'I want to be clear,' he said. 'I want to be as clear as I can about the past, about the present, about the future, because frankly, I don't have anything to hide.'

Transparency has become an end in itself. But what does it mean to see through something? The logic of today's bureaucracy is that by seeing 'the workings of government' we can understand them, participate in them and influence them. We can hold our governments to account. Sight equals knowledge. Knowledge equals power.

Some months before setting off on the walk, I watched footage of a 2011 meeting of the parliamentary transport committee in which then-Transport Secretary Philip Hammond is asked a number of questions about HS2. It's worth mentioning straight away the very availability of such footage. The implication is that we are somehow given a view into the inside of the government machinery, that such video footage allows us to see what is going on. The process is transparent. Or at least it looks that way.

Of particular interest are two facets of Hammond's language. The first is the specialist terminology of the bureaucrat – full of 'benefit-cost ratios' and 'modal spreads'. The second is the Latinate vocabulary of vision: words like 'clarity', 'evidence', 'envisage', 'review' and 'speculate'. These two facets are in a sense contradictory, yet in their effect, they complement each other perfectly. We are given the illusion both of 'transparency' and of the knowledgeable expert, whose knowledge we – Locke's 'bulk of mankind' – do not share and ought only to admire. Viewable now on the screen, the committee functions not only as a tool for bureaucratic analysis but as persuasive public spectacle. In truth, Hammond's grasp of the sheer quantity of data involved in a project like HS2 is indeed admirable. The little miracle of the expert.

In an hour-long appearance, during which Hammond speaks for approximately half the time, he uses the words 'clear' and 'clearly' no less than seventeen times. 'There is clearly a need for increased capacity,' he says. 'We have a clear agenda'; 'we have made it clear'; 'it is very clear'; 'it is clear to me'; 'the devolution settlement is clear'; 'a path … is clearly achievable'; 'the government has made it clear'. All is quite clear in the mind of Philip Hammond and the system he represents.

It is interesting to note how, as a consequence, Hammond is able to dismiss an article in *The Economist* magazine that is critical of HS2 because, at least in part, the magazine's journalists do not use a byline. Such writing may employ the first type of vocabulary – as we saw in the previous chapter, publications like *The Economist* are rife with the language of cost-benefit ratios. But it neglects to mobilise the machinery of transparency. Unlike Hammond who, of course, is here and visible and fully accountable before the committee. This is the masterstroke of bureaucracy. But it is an illusion.

This is because what we are given to see here is one very limited – and not especially significant – aspect of the bureaucratic process. Yes, we can see Hammond before the committee. Yes, we can see how he answers certain questions, how he shuffles his papers and marshals his facts. But Hammond's position has already been decided. He is defending a project that he – or at least his government – approves of. What we cannot see is where this approval originated. What we cannot see is the true locus of the act of decision-making. The very origins of the HS2 project remain shrouded in mystery – for they are beyond the remit of the committee. The Conservatives have argued that HS2 is a Conservative project won in opposition. Peter Mandelson has claimed – somewhat disingenuously perhaps – that it was actually dreamt up under New Labour simply to give Gordon Brown something positive to announce.

'Whose idea was HS2 anyway?' asked left-wing blog *LabourList* in 2013. 'Lord Adonis commissioned research on the new rail project when he was Transport Secretary in 2009, and former Chancellor Alastair Darling gave it his backing in 2010.' But neither really answers the question. Writing for *The Spectator* in 2015, Sebastian Payne also cited

Adonis: 'Lord Adonis gave birth to the idea of HS2 prior to the 2010 election.' But Adonis himself is only quoted as having 'pioneered HS2 from the very beginning' not actually having conceived the idea itself. This is a common pattern: Adonis is recognised as a champion of the scheme, but in a bureaucratic system that shares responsibility across many committees and departments and processes, exact origins can rarely be traced with precision. The same argument could be made about Hinkley Point or London's Garden Bridge. Without origins, no blame, and no responsibility.

Adonis himself of course was never a democratically elected MP. He was a journalist at the *Financial Times*, then *The Observer*, before being appointed to Tony Blair's policy team in 1998. Blair made him a life peer in 2005 and he was then made Minister for Education, before becoming Minister for Transport under Brown in 2008. Neither the origins of HS2 nor those of the man who has so consistently championed it have anything to do with accountability, transparency or democracy. Instead, the project has emerged out of the darkness and somehow acquired its own almost unstoppable momentum. In *The Guardian*, Simon Jenkins described HS2 as 'the zombie train that refuses to die'. In fact, it is arguably the very unaccountability of the project which has contributed to this momentum: with nobody responsible, the project is not tied to the fate of an individual. It is in the system now. Our politicians seem not only unwilling but unable to stop it.

This happens because, even though countless committees are set up to question and scrutinise, convene meetings and write reports, their remits are routinely sufficiently narrow that the actual project itself – the basis for its very existence – is rarely questioned. Always that task is deferred elsewhere, out of view. This tendency is not new: in *The Roots of Modern Environmentalism*, David Pepper cites research carried out in the early 1970s by Israeli political theorist Yaron Ezrahi and American sociologist Dorothy Nelkin into the use of evidence provided by technical experts in political decision-making. Pepper writes: 'Evidence from this source [scientific experts] would aim to restrict discussion to questions of *how* to achieve aims like meeting an assumed increase in demand for electricity or for air travel. It should not encourage questioning of whether these aims *should* be achieved.' This is exactly what we see with Hammond before the Transport Committee in 2011 and it's exactly what happened with the select committee in 2015. The *how* is all that is up for discussion; the vital question – is this really necessary? – is left unasked by those that matter, and unanswered.

This is not simply to argue that decision-making happens in the dark – implying that all we need do is switch on the light. On the contrary, who can see influence? What does power even look like? This is what literary critic Franco Moretti, writing on the semi-legal actions of the bourgeois characters of Henrik Ibsen, describes as 'the grey area': 'That's how things begin,' he writes, 'in the grey area.' Moretti cites a line spoken by one of Ibsen's dubious middle-class characters: 'I can show my books to anyone.' This could be David Cameron speaking. Perhaps it should be Philip Hammond. Shortly after he was made Chancellor by new Prime Minister Theresa May, *Private Eye* published an article on Hammond's financial affairs. The article compared Hammond's use of various 'tax-efficient' methods to the arrangements between disgraced billionaire Philip Green and his wife Tina that sparked such public outrage after the collapse of BHS. The article detailed various arrangements by which some of Hammond's shares in construction and care home developer Castlemead were transferred to his wife. On becoming transport secretary, Hammond's remaining shares were transferred, appropriately enough, to what is known as a 'blind' trust, to which Hammond then loaned money – £1,734,000 in 2011. As the article notes, 'it is unclear how much of this loan still remains unpaid.' What should Hammond's response be? Cameron's 'it's a private matter' or Ibsen's 'I can show my books to anyone'? What difference would it make?

Arguably, it is the most opaque systems where the

machinations of power are most obvious. Autocratic governments rely on the pomp and ceremony of the spectacle to make the centre of power clear to everybody. They also rely on force. But in modern democracies, the supposed transparency of the government is inextricable from mechanisms of a much shadier kind: corporate lobbying, arms deals, secret police, propaganda. The more 'transparent' the government, the more invisible the mechanisms of power. American academic Darius Rejali has even argued that the type of regime affects the methods of torture employed. Autocracies use death and torture as a kind of public spectacle. Democracies, with their obsession with what can be seen, favour 'techniques that leave no visible trace'.

Such techniques form a part of what Edward Bernays has described as the 'invisible government'. What this phrase suggests is that, while we are looking in one direction, real power is being mobilised elsewhere. As he wrote in his 1928 book *Propaganda*: 'The conscious and intelligent manipulation of the organized habits and opinions of the masses is an important element in democratic society. Those who manipulate this unseen mechanism of society constitute an invisible government which is the true ruling power of our country.'

It should hopefully be obvious that I am not advocating

for some kind of shadowy repressive statism. We all know what Stalin did. Rather, the point is to unpick the metaphor of transparency and to think about its limitations. More transparency does not mean more accountability. More transparency does not mean greater democracy. In fact, it often means the opposite, as transparency is substituted for the desire for more – and more genuine – democratic participation. As academic Jonathan Fox has written: 'while critics call for accountability, powerful elites respond by offering some measure of transparency instead.' This was exactly Cameron's response to the Panama Papers. Fox continues, with precision: 'One person's transparency is another's surveillance. One person's accountability is another's persecution. Where one stands on these issues depends on where one sits.'

From my own seat on this train, it's hard to avoid the nagging sensation that my walk may conform to the very logic that I am questioning here. Franco Moretti cites American art historian Svetlana Alpers and her writing on the artists of the Dutch Golden Age in the seventeenth century. The desire of these artists was to 'describe the world seen', especially in the genres of landscape and still life. In Chapter IV, we saw the influence of these artists: how *landskip* became 'landscape', shaping not only our aesthetics but our land too. Then in Chapter IV, we saw how walks such as this rely on the principle of immersion – that to really understand something it is necessary to go out there and to see for oneself. It's not so different from what the parliamentary select committee did. Throughout the walk, I have taken photographs, and throughout this book I have sought to describe what I could see. But have these sights provided insights? And have these insights really provided any knowledge or power for change? Perhaps not.

However, in addition to what I could see, I have, I hope, attempted to attune myself to that which is not visible: technology, lines of communication, community, pain, worry. I have tried to look at what is out of sight, what has been lost and what has yet to come. What has been important to me about this walk are those moments which remain inexplicable in terms of sight alone. While the appearance of a bright white horse in the middle of the night in Perivale was certainly a moment whose visual impact has stayed with me, it was the non-visible context (of time and place and my own unexpectedly intense anxieties) which made it such powerful event – for me at least.

Those experiences of fear and worry and doubt – of being lost in a world whose signs I was failing to read – were completely unexpected. As somebody who writes primarily about art, I had anticipated more what the walk might look like than what it would feel like. The pain in my knee, my failure to complete the walk, my rapid mood-swings: each of these proved to me that the rich reality of lived experience cannot be reduced to the visual alone. Perhaps it's a mundane observation. But sometimes it's the mundane that is the hardest to see clearly.

Much more important than my own narrow experiences, however, have been the people I've met, whose lives continue beyond the brief moment of my encounter and its subsequent recollection in this book. What started as an attempt to explore different places, and the concept of place, has made me realise that one of the most important aspects of place – especially those places that this walk has taken me through – are the people who live and work there – who have done so in the past, and will do in the future. Yes, the world has existed without humans, and will do so again. But while we're here, we ought not to succumb to the misanthropy of those who welcome the eco-apocalypse.

As I realised in Chapter V, not a single person appears in any of my photographs. Now I think about it, perhaps this is hardly surprising: photographs function as an aid to memory; I'm unlikely to forget the people I've met. For it was these people who really made this walk meaningful. People cannot be reduced to graphs or visuals. Sight alone is not enough. Nor, indeed, are words. People like John and Pauline, full of bravery and fire; Stephen, fighting the fight of his forefathers; Jonathan, the modern visionary; or Andrew, using the tools of the bureaucrat against the bureaucracy. Each of them exceeds the limitations of my words.

*

There is one moment in Hammond's appearance before the committee that comes to mind as I sit on this train from Birmingham. It occurs when he is asked about who will actually use HS2. This element of his appearance was seized upon by anti-HS2 campaigners – in particular Hammond's use of the phrase 'rich man's toy'. In fact, the phrase was first used to describe HS2 by one of the MPs questioning Hammond. Hammond sought to counter the question by stating that all trains were, to some extent, 'a rich man's toy'. He cited statistics that the income of passengers on trains was above that of the national average. Strangely, this fact was employed not to argue, as you might expect, that train fares ought to be reduced across the network, but to argue instead that this was simply the status quo and could not be challenged – certainly not within the remit of this particular committee. Hammond's logic is that the ticket pricing of HS2 will merely be a continuation of a cold, hard fact. What he neglects to mention is that this fact was never inevitable; it had a historical cause – namely the policies of his government. StopHS2 campaigners argued that this approach shows 'his complete lack of empathy with commuters struggling to cope with *his* [i.e. Hammond's] eye-watering fare rises'.

What it also shows us is a critical facet of the way such committees work: the vital premises that ultimately underpin the subjects for discussion are always elsewhere. The logic of the committee is the logic of deferral. We may think we see what is happening but meaningful 'accountability' is always diffused across a network. This means that we can watch as many committee meetings as we like: true power will always lurk just a little out of sight. The actual moment of the decision is always somewhere in the past or in the future.

Hammond elaborates on who he expects to use HS2:

If you're working in a factory in Manchester you might never get on HS2, but you will certainly be benefitting from it if the sales director of your company is routinely hopping on it to go and meet customers, to jet round the world from Heathrow in a way that brings in orders that keep you employed.

Again, this was seized upon by campaigners. But in a strange sort of way it's hard to fault Hammond's logic. Once again, it is the premises that are open to question. Or rather, it is these premises that – in the context of a parliamentary committee – are precisely *not* open to question. Namely, that a system in which some people work in a factory and others jet around the world is the system that we ought all to embrace. These are the natural laws which we must simply accept. Certainly, we're not going to be challenging them here in this committee meeting. It is neither the time nor the place. But when is the time? Where is the place?

What strikes me is the way in which so many of these different issues come together in a project like HS2. To see the workings of a bureaucracy is not to be able to influence it. To see the world pass by through the window is not to really know it – its past and its future, its people and their lives. But for our rulers, from where they sit, to see is to know. To sit on HS2 as it speeds from city to city will only reinforce their perceptions of the world. If Hammond – and anti-HS2 campaigners – are right, then the train's passengers will be largely limited to those select few for whom sight really does mean power: politicians, civil servants, business leaders and the like.

It has been proposed that the train will travel at speeds of up to 250mph, although the feasibility and even safety of such speeds has been questioned in documents produced by HS2 Ltd itself. Nonetheless, such an apparent need for speed explains why the line must be so straight. There is no time for picturesque meanderings around natural obstacles. Instead, the line carves through the countryside in tunnels and cuttings or tree-lined embankments. 'Slow days are gone days / These days.'

One aim is to conceal the train lines from the world. This is understandable, but it also provides another example of our obsession with visibility. It explains the before and after photographs in my copy of HS2 Ltd's Draft Environmental Statement. From a distance, these renders suggest, it will be quite hard to tell what's there. The implication is that what cannot be seen cannot really be objected to, and therefore should not be opposed. This is the same logic as that of bureaucratic transparency: the insistence that we can somehow see through to the mechanisms of government means that what cannot be seen cannot be fought. That is how power works.

But a secondary effect is that, once on board HS2, there will be nothing for these passengers to see – no sense of time or distance or of the places they pass through. Instead, they will sit and talk, or think, dream up new schemes, prepare for meetings, respond to emails. The world will further be reduced to the visible, the knowledge only of *savoir* – the files and the documents, the graphs, the data-sets, the cost-benefit ratios and modal spreads. Travelling one way in the body, they will travel another in the mind. Neither has any relation to where they actually are in the world. The ghosts of the past – of memory, of landscape – are easily brushed aside.

*

Months have passed now since I first drew that line of orange highlighter through nine outspread Ordnance Survey maps. The maps remain largely the same – a little weathered perhaps, a little crumpled. But the world, it seems, has changed. The news is full of terrorism. The UK has voted to leave the European Union. The far right rises.

At the start of this book, I was convinced that HS2 was a vitally important project to question and analyse – on account of its scale and the number of people affected and what it might say about the country we live in. What subsequent events have suggested is that, on the global scale, HS2 and its impacts aren't so important after all. However, what remain significant are the implications that the process behind a project like HS2 suggests: the illusion of transparency, the obsession with profit, with value only of an economic kind, the wilful ignoring of those exceptions that do not fit the model, and the inability to take into account real people and their lives as anything other than obstacles to be overcome or bought off. When the system encounters the individual, the individual, like the ghost, is simply invisible.

And yet, it occurs to me that such acts of exclusion are ultimately inevitable. As Polarbear suggests and the bab's map of bombed-out Birmingham proves, we cannot hope to account for everything, 'and all at once'. There is no way we can even begin to think about the world without reducing, limiting, simplifying: from the functioning of human eyesight (focusing on movement, filling in the gaps) to the operation of our memories; from the decisions over what paths to take and why, when to stop, where, and when to set off again. Even – or especially – in the process of selection without which no narrative could ever be created. Storytelling is as much about what is left out as what is included – and this as is true of philosophical theories as it is of contemporary news media or history or science or economic policy or a little book such as this one. Always something is being left out. Sometimes we don't even know what it is – and it is precisely then that it becomes most important to try to find out, and to find out why.

I look again at that orange line. Just as acts of exclusion must be inevitable, so too is the drawing of lines. Lines of best fit, lines of poetry, lines to connect A to B (the past to the present, the present to the future), or to divide X from Y. Lines between the wild or the natural, the known or the unknown. Lines around a country or a community. Lines to separate people from animals, or from each other.

In the case of HS2, of course, such lines are irreducibly literal. Their exact locations are the subject of ongoing and costly debate between bureaucrats and businesses, politicians, experts, lawyers and local residents. 'Where do you actually draw the line? Is there a line to be drawn?' asked Labour MP Mark Hendrick, a member of the HS2 select committee, on the subject of noise. 'Wherever you draw the line, it will be regarded by somebody as inappropriate,' observed property consultant Colin Smith on the subject of compensation. 'Really, what I want to argue for is a rather more flexible and sensible drawing of the lines,' said Conservative MP Jeremy Wright.

In the end, perhaps Labour MP Kelvin Hopkins has come closest to my own line of thought. As he put it in a House of Commons debate in 2014: 'It seems that, in the first instance, the route was created by non-engineers drawing lines on maps.' Hopkins continued:

As a small child, my son used to take Ordnance Survey maps, and used a felt-tip pen to draw railway lines across them. It ruined the maps, but the method used to determine the route of HS2 was not far from that.

Like a small child, I also drew a line across my Ordnance Survey maps. Like a small child too are the whims of sovereignty. Accountability, as we have seen, has its limits. No quantity of committees or enquiries or cost-benefit analysis can conceal the fact that, in the end, the moment of the decision occurs in the place that is hidden. The decision, by definition, is an arbitrary event. In the exact moment of the decision, sovereignty answers to no one – even here in this democracy. A judgement must be free; otherwise it is not a judgement. Such freedom hides instinctively from the light.

There is now a line on the map – a line that I failed to follow. Neither performance artist, nor ghost. It denotes a line through life and a line through the world. But it remains to be decided exactly where it will run, who will be connected, what will be divided. It is, still, a line on the map. Perhaps, too, a line in the sand.

Without lines, no knowledge, no narrative, no meaning. But the line must be followed; not simply drawn. To follow the line is to form a narrative through events, an attempt, however meandering, to connect a beginning with an end in a way that means something. A narrative is a journey, a walk, this walk. And now, as we reach the end of the line, the light here seems to shine a little differently, if perhaps no more clearly than before.

Select Bibliography

Peter Ackroyd, *Thames: Sacred River*

Tony Aldous, *Goodbye Britain?*

G. C. Allen, *The Industrial Development of Birmingham*

J. A. Baker, *The Peregrine*

Alastair Bonnett, *Off the Map*

Steven Camden and Chris Prendergast, *Build and Destroy*

Ben Campkin, *Remaking London*

Colin Cartwright, *Burning to Get the Vote*

Bruce Chatwin, *The Songlines*

Matthew Clegg, *The Navigators*

Alan Corkish (ed.), *In the Company of Ghosts: Poetics of the Motorway*

Jason Cowley (ed.), *The New Nature Writing*

Gillian Darley, *Villages of Vision*

Roger Deakin, *Wildwood*

Jacques Derrida, 'The Animal That Therefore I Am'

Jacques Derrida, *The Beast and the Sovereign*

Jacques Derrida, *Specters of Marx*

T. K. Derry and Trevor I. Williams, *A Short History of Technology*

Charles Dickens, *A Christmas Carol*

Terry Eagleton, *Why Marx Was Right*

Roy Fisher, *Standard Midland*

Clive Foxell, *The Metropolitan Line*

Honor Gavin, *Midland*

Tristan Gooley, *The Walker's Guide to Outdoor Clues and Signs*

David Graeber, *The Utopia of Rules*

Nick Groom, 'Review: Map of a Nation'

John Guest (ed.), *The Best of Betjeman*

W. G. Hoskins, *The Making of the English Landscape*

Richard Hillyer, *A Country Boy*

Tim Ingold, 'Earth, Sky, Wind, and Weather'

Tim Ingold, 'The Temporality of Landscape'

Tim Jackson, *Prosperity without Growth*

Richard Jefferies, *Landscape with Figures: Selected Prose Writings*

Paul Kingsnorth et al (eds.), *Dark Mountain*, issues 1-8

Brian Lewis (ed.), *The Footing*

John Locke, *The Reasonableness of Christianity*

David Lodge, *Nice Work*

Helen Macdonald, *H is for Hawk*

Robert Macfarlane, *The Old Ways*

Sara Maitland, *Gossip from the Forest*

Karl Marx, *Capital*

Jonathan Meades, *Heart By-Pass*

Mary Midgley, *Science as Salvation*

George Monbiot, *Feral*

Franco Moretti, *The Bourgeois*

A. L. Morton, *A People's History of England*

Laura Oldfield Ford, *Savage Messiah*

Leslie Oppitz , *Lost Railways of the Chilterns*

Jussi Parikka, *A Geology of Media*

David Pepper, *The Roots of Modern Environmentalism*

Oliver Rackham, *Ancient Woodland, its History, Vegetation and Uses in England*

Oliver Rackham, 'Ancient Woodland, Modern Threats'

Oliver Rackham, 'Landscape and the Conservation of Meaning'

Mark Rowlands, *The Philosopher and the Wolf*

Mark Rowlands, *Running with the Pack*

Saki, *Collected Short Stories*

Phil Smith, 'The Contemporary Dérive'

Rebecca Solnit, *A Field Guide to Getting Lost*

Rebecca Solnit, *Wanderlust*

Colin Tudge, *The Day Before Yesterday*

Hugh Warwick, 'Plant Migrations'

Denis Wood, *The Power of Maps*

Michael Wood, *In Search of the Dark Ages*

Esther Woolfson, *Corvus: A Life with Birds*

Ken Worpole, *The New English Landscape*

Acknowledgements

My thanks go firstly to those who helped this book escape the confines of my computer: Gary Budden and Kit Caless, for taking a chance and devoting their time and effort into its editing and publishing. I'm delighted to be working with such an independent-minded publisher. I'm also extremely grateful to Dan Coxon for his keen-eyed proofreading and copy-editing and Maxim Peter Griffin for his wonderful cover art and chapter maps.

I'd like to thank all those who gave their time to speak to me during the walk from London to Birmingham: Adrian Aylward, Stephen Fletcher, Chris Langton, Dan Mitchell, Stewart Pomeroy, Roger and Jenny Waller, Jonathan Watkins, and the many others whose names I never asked. I'm especially grateful to Andrew Bodman and to Pauline and John Hughes for their kindness and generosity during the walk and for their continued communication and support afterwards.

Lots of other people have also helped along the way, whether they know it or not. I'm indebted to Camilla Nelson for her ideas on nature and landscape, to Anaïs Tondeur for her thoughts on art and walking, and to Alasdair Glennie for the vital loan of a tent and sleeping bag. I'm immeasurably grateful to my parents for their support over the last thirty or so years. I'd especially like to thank my father for instilling in me a love of walking and reading and for indulging my childhood interest in art. His 'StopHS2' sweatshirt is where this all began.

Above all I'd like to thank my wife, Dr Crystal Bennes. It was writing an article for her magazine, *Pages Of*, in 2014 that made me think I might be able to contribute something to the burgeoning literature on place and landscape. It was out of our subsequent discussions that the idea for this book began to emerge. That article forms the basis for chapter III.

Thereafter, it was Crystal's enthusiasm that encouraged me to undertake the London-Birmingham walk in 2014. It was Crystal who picked me up in the car in Amersham and dropped me at Aylesbury. She answered my phone calls every day, located pubs online when I'd forgot to check, and booked a campsite when I couldn't face any more 'wild' camping. She then read through numerous drafts of the book's early chapters, appraising every word with her uniquely undiplomatic editorial style. This book would be much the poorer were it not for Crystal; in fact it probably would not exist.

– Tom Jeffreys, 2016

About the author

Tom Jeffreys is a writer, editor and occasional curator with a particular interest in contemporary art that crosses over into the sciences or explores our relationship with the environment. His work has been published in, among others, *Monocle, Apollo, Frieze, The Independent, The Daily Telegraph, New Scientist, Cricinfo,* and *World of Interiors*. Previous curatorial projects have included poet-led urban nature walks and exhibitions dedicated to the beauty of the mundane and the role of archives in our understanding of the natural world. Tom is also editor of *The Learned Pig,* an online magazine with four areas of interest: art, thinking, nature, writing.

About the author

Influx Press is an independent publisher based in London, committed to publishing innovative and challenging fiction, poetry and creative non-fiction from across the UK and beyond. Formed in 2012, we have published titles ranging from award-nominated debuts and site-specific anthologies to squatting memoirs and radical poetry.

www.influxpress.com

@Influxpress